RAY JONES

Lifelong Huntsville resident, businessman, farmer and author of personal history.

"A wonderful story of a very humble man who, even though he was highly successful in business, maintained his affection for his family, community and friends. Bill Propst is and has been one of Huntsville's most outstanding and generous citizens."

ED BUCKBEE

Author, space advocate, founder of the United States Space Camp.

"In the midst of the race to the moon, Bill Propst applied his retail skills and pharmaceutical training to achieve success in the Rocket City. From his friends, you will emerge with a deeper understanding of the man, his zeal, his achievements and his desire to enhance education, research and entertainment in the fastest growing city in the South."

HARVILEE PHILLIPS HARBARGER

Lifelong Huntsville resident, homemaker, businesswoman, landscape architect, and co-founder of the Huntsville Botanical Gardens.

"Authentic in its style of storytelling, this book is an honest look into the life of a truly wonderful and hardworking man, a truly brilliant businessman and a truly giving man. The stories told within, by Bill Propst's family and friends, about his life and how eagerly he has shared his blessings with Huntsville are proof of the man's generous nature."

PENNY BILLINGS

Market President, BancorpSouth - Huntsville

"The story of Bill Propst is told throughout our city by names on buildings and accomplishments. But this book tells the story of the person – through friends, family and business associates – a very personal insight to a great man. A true gift."

CHAD EMERSON

President and Chief Executive Officer, Downtown Huntsville, Inc.

"What a fascinating start to the Iconic & Unforgettable project. The generosity and civic-mindedness that Mr. Propst and his family have embraced has been a great blessing for all of Huntsville. This is truly an individual who has given back to his community."

© 2018 Vanguard Narratives Perfect Bound First Edition

All rights reserved under International and Pan-American Copyright Conventions. Published in the United States by Vanguard Narratives, Huntsville, Alabama.

The Vanguard Narratives' colophon and Iconic & Unforgettable are trademarks of Vanguard Narratives.

A Special Adtran Edition of this work was printed and published by Vanguard Narratives.

The Philosophical Reflections of William Self Propst, Sr.
Iconic & Unforgettable
p. cm.

978-1-7321587-0-2

First Edition

Metadata 1. William (Bill) Self Propst, Sr., 2. Vanguard Business Leaders – United States – Biography. 3. Propst Drugs, Kmart Pharmacy, Qualitest, Vintage Pharmaceuticals, Propst Properties 4. Pharmaceuticals, Generics, Manufacturing, – United States – History I. Title 5. Philanthropy

FRONT ENDPAPER: Self Family Farm House.
COVER PHOTO, Page ii: William Self Propst, Sr., Print of pastel portrait, ca. 1995.
TITLE PAGE: Young William Self Trippi celebrating his first birthday, 1938.
BACK ENDPAPER: William Self Trippi, age 5, with brother, Michael Trippi, age 9.

Printed in the United States of America
www.vanguardnarratives.com

Exterior Book Design by Adriane Van Kirk
Interior Book Design by Erica Parker

ICONIC & UNFORGETTABLE

THE PHILOSOPHICAL REFLECTIONS OF

William Self Propst, Sr.

VANGUARD NARRATIVES

PAPERBACKS / HUNTSVILLE, ALABAMA

THE ICONIC & UNFORGETTABLE MEMORIAL PROJECT
ABSTRACT

The "Iconic & Unforgettable" collection is a memorial effort honoring vanguard business leaders - visionary business leaders of significance whose bodies of work were instrumental in creating their community's economic culture and, consequently, affording its citizenry a secure base within which it has continued to work and build. The objective of each collection is to educate and inspire today's business leaders as well as the business leaders of future generations.

Personal narratives have been obtained via personal interviews. Limited genealogy and other historical research have been conducted to supplement the memories and reflections gathered during the discovery process of this project. As is typical, personal reflections leave room for variances from the details of events as they might have otherwise been captured in real-time from live video or audio recordings.

The purpose of the books in The Iconic & Unforgettable Memorial Project is to share philosophies and personal reflections so that the essence of the vanguard is evident to the reader. To this end, two approaches were taken in the writing of this book. One, the personal narratives are only lightly edited versions of the verbatim transcriptions of each interview. Less-than-perfect grammar is a common attribute of the casual conversation. Additionally, it is the nature of a narrator to switch tenses back-and-forth between the past, the present and the future when telling stories. These tendencies, and others, have been retained to reveal the idiolect of each person's natural speaking voice. Two, the historian has captured and shared within the pages of each book the motivating morals, values and ethics that inspired and directed the vanguard's daily decision-making processes.

Business pursuits, community philanthropy, unique investments of personal time, efforts spent supporting the fabric of family life, friendships, partnerships, recreational diversions - these are the cornerstones of life. These are the essence of a vanguard. Examples of such are what the reader will find in the books within The Iconic & Unforgettable Memorial Project.

DEDICATION

This book, and the others within the series of The Iconic & Unforgettable Memorial Project, is dedicated to mentorship and the intentional daily creation of responsible and impactful legacies.

An Acknowledgement
by Tom Young

We, along with so many others in our community, are grateful to Bill Propst for creating a generous legacy. Bill was destined to be successful in business and life. From a young age, he was a hard worker and a strong thinker.

Bill was instrumental in creating the concept of housing pharmaceutical stores in big box stores like Kmart. He had a vision for providing pharmaceuticals to all Americans in an affordable and timely fashion. This passion led Bill to start Qualitest Pharmaceuticals and Vintage Pharmaceuticals. With the support of his sons Bill Propst, Jr. and Trey Propst, and his son-in-law, Mike Reiney, he built Qualitest/Vintage Pharmaceuticals into the 5th largest generic drug manufacturer in the nation. Bill and his company were known throughout the industry for providing quality products at affordable prices.

Since the sale of Qualitest in 2007, Bill has strengthened his involvement in the Huntsville community as a leader and philanthropist. His kind-hearted and generous spirit has influenced and helped grow our public spaces, our institutions and individuals. Allen and I feel privileged to know Bill and his close-knit family and are proud to support this book celebrating some of his accomplishments.

Tom and Allen Young
Kord Technologies

An Acknowledgment
by Deke Damson

In their youth, happenstance acquainted our founder, Jerry Damson, with Bill Propst, Sr. As the two men matured into their twenties, they each saw in our city the potential for a future, but not one just for themselves and their families. Jerry and Bill saw a future for Huntsville and they set out to be a part of its creation. Both men and the legacies they've created are defined by their grit and the strengths of their characters. From that commonality, a seven-decade friendship was cemented.

Through the years we, the Damson family, have respected the well-lived life of our friend, Bill Propst, Sr. His drive to create something worthwhile motivated and inspired. His passion for the community resonated with our own. His caring nature and acts of generosity humbled us as his friendship delighted us.

Thus, it is with great honor that the Jerry Damson Automotive Group acknowledges our friend, William Self Propst, Sr., a man whose only mode of operation is to work, as described by Jerry, "from can to can't," as one of Huntsville's Iconic & Unforgettable Vanguard Business Leaders.

Deke Damson
Jerry Damson Automotive Group

About the Personal Historian
DAWN RENAE CARSON

In January 1984, Dawn transferred to the University of Alabama in Huntsville from Snead State Junior College where she had attended night school throughout her last three years of high school. At that time in her life, she would often say that she loved to learn and wished she could get paid to go to school. This passion and respect for education were transferred into her life as a parent. Homeschooling both of her children before beginning her professional pursuits in 1997 was a very special season in Dawn's life, one that was driven by a desire to pass along a legacy that left her children feeling capable and empowered.

Established by an atypical path in her upbringing and a series of losses of loved ones at an early age, the concept that everyone's legacy impacts the next generation is a value system deeply rooted within Dawn. It has been a powerful compass in her life, guiding and directing her much as a mentor would.

Once in the workforce, the blessings of having many real-life mentors, exposure to entrepreneurs, businessmen and women in a variety of industries and a plethora of opportunities to serve the community fostered a unique combination within Dawn that has fueled her passion for Huntsville, Alabama, the community she considers her hometown. By saving and sharing the life stories of the businessmen and women in her hometown who have worked to significantly better the lives of others, she hopes the legacies of these vanguard business leaders will continue to resonate in the generations to come and empower the members of each generation to strive daily for responsible stewardship of their own impactful legacies. To this end, Dawn Renae Carson became a personal historian and The Iconic & Unforgettable Memorial Project was born.

Prologue

Starting with the very first interview, Mr. Propst left me in a state of awe. "What kind of man is this," was my prevailing thought. I clearly had not ever met anyone like him. He didn't fit any of my existing definitions for personality types. Yet, somehow, there was something about him that was familiar.

This giant of a man whose life story I was charged with recording has lived an epic life. That was quickly obvious. He was a man with a strong sense of right and wrong. He was a man who thought before he spoke and he expected you to do the same. He was a man who cleverly handled conflict, often with actions far more poignant than words could ever be. Indeed, he was a man who wasn't known for mincing words. The ones he shared with you, you could take to the bank. The more I learned about Mr. Propst, the more insufficient I found my vocabulary. I had a challenge on my hands.

It wasn't until my interview with Bill Propst, Jr., Mr. Propst's youngest son, that the words to describe this somehow familiar, giant of a man and his epic life came to me. In our interview, Bill, Jr., as he's proudly known, told me that his father is known for saying, "John Wayne really should make a few more movies." Upon hearing that, my problem was solved. Instantly, I understood why Mr. Propst had seemed so familiar while also bigger than life. From that moment forward, for me, Mr. Propst was 'a modern-day John Wayne in a suit.'

John Wayne might have had the Wild West to tame of its bad guys and their bullets, but Mr. Propst's challenges played out on the much larger stage of the pharmaceutical industry against bad guys from Big Pharma, the DEA and the FDA. This set of bad guys wielded bullets of another type. Their arsenal consisted of federal regulations, lawsuits and bureaucracy.

Not unlike the intricacies of John Wayne's conflicts, Mr. Propst's path was riddled with the typical demonstrations of conflicting personalities, grudges, thievery, deceit, sabotage, carelessness, pride and other difficult egos. Any one of these would persuade the majority of us to find an easier path. Not Mr. Propst. He was always creating something, building a better future for his family. None of the aforementioned hurdles, nor a major heart attack resulting in quintuple cardiac bypass surgery, diabetes, rickets, scarlet fever or any of his other health issues, were stumbling blocks for the man who, for all intents and purposes, seemed destined to live a life the rest of us are only accustomed to seeing play out on the big screen.

I am very proud to have helped Mr. William S. Propst, Sr., one of Huntsville/Madison County's vanguard business leaders, take his place in history as part of the inaugural class of The Iconic & Unforgettable Memorial Project. There's no doubt in my mind that if John Wayne were able to read this book, he would close the back cover wishing for yet a few more chapters.

Dawn Rena Carson

TABLE OF CONTENTS

INTRODUCING WILLIAM SELF (BILL) PROPST, SR.
Career Highlights XIV
The Birth Story: Setting The Stage For Greatness 1
Introductory Narratives of Lifelong Friends
    Jerry Damson 7
    W. F. Sanders 13

FAMILY & FRIENDS
The Self Family 27
Entrepreneurial Heritage 33
The Early Years 37
1954-1955 43
1955-1956 47
Family Members
    Eloise McDonald Propst 55
    Mary Lynne Wright 59
    Bonnie McDonald Wilson 63
1964 67
The Children
    Emily Propst Reiney 73
    Trey Propst 77
    Mike Propst 83
    Bill Propst, Jr. 89
Personal Friends
    Rebecca Taylor Larrowe 99
    Benny Nelson 101
    Dr. Charlie Warren 103

PROFESSIONAL PURSUITS
Preface 115

TABLE OF CONTENTS

PROFESSIONAL PURSUITS cont.
Lambert & Propst Steel Company 121
Propst Drug & Propst Drug K 137
Kmart & The Formation of Qualitest 163
Qualitest Pharmaceuticals & Vintage Pharmaceuticals ... 183
Propst Properties 207
Professional Friends
    Paul Higdon 215
    John Schultz 221
    Chris Byrom 233
    John Hughey 239

COMMUNITY INVOLVEMENT
The Community He Calls Home 257
Community Leaders
    Steve Maples 267
    Paula Steigerwald 271
    Jim Hudson 276
What's On The Horizon 286
Legacy Letter 291
A Narrative From Bill Propst, Sr.'s Alma Mater
    President Westmoreland, Samford Univ. 293
City Representative
    Loretta Spencer, Former Mayor of Huntsville, Ala... 299

Afterword 305
Epilogue 307
Acknowledgements 311
Photo Credits 312

XIII

Timeline: Bill Propst, Sr. — Industry / History

1897 Sebastian Spering (S.S.) Kresge founded his first company
1901 Walgreens founded (Chicago, IL)
1902 Target founded as Goodfellow Dry Goods (Minneapolis, MN)
1912 S. S. Kresge incorporated S.S. Kresge Corporation
1916 Kmart incorporated (Troy, MI)

1937 William S. Propst, Sr. born (February 15 | Walker Chapel)
1944 Margaret Self Trippi married Paul Propst (October 15)
1945 Sam Walton purchased a branch of Ben Franklin stores
1946 Paul Propst appointed to the small Methodist Church in Hazel Green (October)
1952 Met Jerry Damson Columbia Military Academy (Columbia, TN)
1954 Graduated from Columbia Military Academy
1954 Florence State Teachers College
1958 Sold interest in Lambert & Propst Steel Company
Son, Trey Propst was born (September 21)
1960s Huntsville's Industrial Development Board was founded
1961 Graduated Samford University School of Pharmacy (Birmingham, AL)
1962 First Target store opened (Roseville, MN)
S. S. Kresge Corporation opened the first Kmart store (March 1)
1962 Son, Mike Propst was born (August 3)
1963 First Propst Drugs #1 opened in Dunnavant's Mall (October 31 | Huntsville, AL)
1964 Opened Propst Drugs #2 Pearsall Shopping Center, North Parkway (Huntsville, AL)
1965 Opened Propst Drugs #3 Whitesburg Drive and Airport Road (April | Huntsville, AL)
Opened Propst Drugs #4 Oakwood and Andrew Jackson Way (Huntsville, AL)
Met and became friends with Dr. Warren
1966 Daughter, Emily was born (March 16)
Opened Propst Drugs #5 Five Points, Pratt Avenue (Huntsville, AL)
1968 Dr. Martin Luther King, Jr. assassinated (April 4)
1968 Opened Propst Drugs K Stores (Florence, AL | Birmingham, AL | Chattanooga, TN)
Kmart requested Propst Drugs K open 98 more pharmacy departments (Fall)
1969 Son, Bill, Jr. was born (March 16)
Opened 6 more Propst Drugs K in 6 other states in the southeast U.S (Spring)
1970 Propst Drugs K sold to Kmart. Family moved to Michigan
First official day with Kmart, pharmacy division (February 1)
1975 Jimmy Hoffa disappeared (July 30)

Industry / History — Timeline: Bill Propst, Sr.

1976, 1979, 1980
Invited to join advisory boards: E. R. Squibb, Marion Laboratories & Hoffman La Roche

1982
Started Qualitest: A Kmart business partnered with Tennessee Wholesale

1984
The Drug Price Competition and Patent Term Restoration Act (Hatch-Waxman Act) standardized procedures for recognition of generic drugs

1986
Retired from Kmart
In partnership with Kmart moved Qualitest from Nashville, TN to Huntsville, AL (June 16)
Paul Higdon started working at Qualitest (November 1)
Bill Jr. started working at Qualitest (December 1)

1987
Set new price list for Qualitest (January 23)
Sold the Michigan house, Eloise joined Bill in Huntsville

1989
Bought Tennessee Wholesale and Kmart interest in Qualitest

1990s
Established 401K for employees

1992
Invited to join the Board of Directors of First Commercial Bank
Bought Vintage manufacturing company in Charlotte, NC (April)
John Schultz came on board with Vintage as product development manager (April)
Bill Propst, Sr. has a heart attack and undergoes heart surgery (August)
Dedication of Michael Andrea Propst Pharmaceutical Laboratory (November 6 | Samford University)

1996
Paul Higdon started in Purchasing Department
Awarded Samford University Alumnus of the Year

1998
John Schultz moved to Huntsville to manage Vintage's liquid plant

2002
Established the Margaret Self Propst Teacher of the Year award

2007
FDA launched the Generic Initiative for Value and Efficiency: which modernized and streamlined the generic drug approval process, increasing the number and variety of available generic products

2007
Sold Qualitest & Vintage Pharmaceuticals to Apax out of London, now Endo Pharmaceuticals (October)

2008
John Hughey came on board to help start Propst Properties (February)

2009
Samford University's Science Center named William Self Propst Hall (March 10)
Awarded American Heart Association's Philanthropist of the Year Award

2010
Inducted into the Alabama Healthcare Hall of Fame

2011
Samford University established the Margaret Propst Professor of Natural Sciences (December 7)

2012-2013
Endowed the Margaret Propst Professor of Natural Sciences, effective with the 2012-13 academic year

2015
Awarded Huntsville-Madison County Hospitality Association Pineapple Award

The Personal Highlights of
William (Bill) Self Propst, Sr.

Education

Lewisburg Grammar School	Lewisburg, Ala.
Southside Grammar School	Birmingham, Ala.
Hazel Green Grammar School	Hazel Green, Ala.
Brilliant Junior High School	Brilliant, Ala.
Arab High School	Arab, Ala.
Coffee High School	Florence, Ala.
Columbia Military Academy	Columbia, Tenn.
Florence State Teachers College (Now University of North Alabama)	Florence, Ala.
Auburn University	Auburn, Ala.
Howard College (Now Samford University)	Homewood, Ala.

The Entrepreneurial Highlights of
William (Bill) Self Propst, Sr.

Businesses Owned

Lambert & Propst Steel	Huntsville, Ala.
Service Steel Company	Huntsville, Ala.
Propst Drugs Store #1	Dunnavant's Mall – Huntsville, Ala.
Propst Drugs Store #2	Pearsall Shopping Center Huntsville, Ala.
Propst Drugs Store #3	Airport Rd. Huntsville, Ala.
Propst Drugs Store #4	Five Points, Pratt Ave. Huntsville, Ala.
Propst Drugs Store #5	Oakwood Ave. Huntsville, Ala.

THE ENTREPRENEURIAL HIGHLIGHTS OF
William (Bill) Self Propst, Sr.

BUSINESSES OWNED cont.

Propst Drugs-K					Florence, Ala.
						Birmingham, Ala.
						Chattanooga, Tenn.
						Rocky Mount, N.C.
						Florence, S.C.
						Lafayette, La.
						Daytona Beach, Fla.
						Overland Park, Kans.

WAEY Radio Station				Bluefiled, W. Va.

Qualitest Pharmaceuticals			Huntsville, Ala.

Echelle Cosmetics				Grant, Ala.

Vintage Pharmaceuticals			Charlotte, N.C.

Propst Properties				Huntsville, Ala.

MYCO						Bradenton, Fla.

The Professional & Personal Highlights of
William (Bill) Self Propst, Sr.

Honors, Accolades & Awards

1976 E. R. Squibb Advisory Board

1979 Marion Laboratories Advisory Board

1980 Hoffman La Roche Advisory Board

First Commercial Bank Board of Directors (1992 – 2003)

1996 Samford University Alumnus of the Year

2009 American Heart Association's Philanthropist of the Year

2010 Alabama Healthcare Hall of Fame

2015 Huntsville – Madison County Hospitality Association Pineapple Award

THE CHARITABLE HIGHLIGHTS OF
William (Bill) Self Propst, Sr.

Michael Andrea Propst Pharmaceutical Laboratory
        Samford University, Homewood, Ala.

Margaret Self Propst Teacher of the Year Award
Endowment Fund
        Samford University, Homewood, Ala.

William Self Propst Hall
(Samford University's Science Center)
        Samford University, Homewood, Ala.

Propst Arena   Von Braun Center, Huntsville, Ala.

Paul Propst Center for Precision Medicine
        HudsonAlpha, Huntsville, Ala.

Eloise McDonald Propst Welcome Center
        Huntsville Botanical Garden
        Huntsville, Ala.

The charitable givings listed within the pages of this book represent only a fraction of William (Bill) Self Propst, Sr.'s charitable generosity.

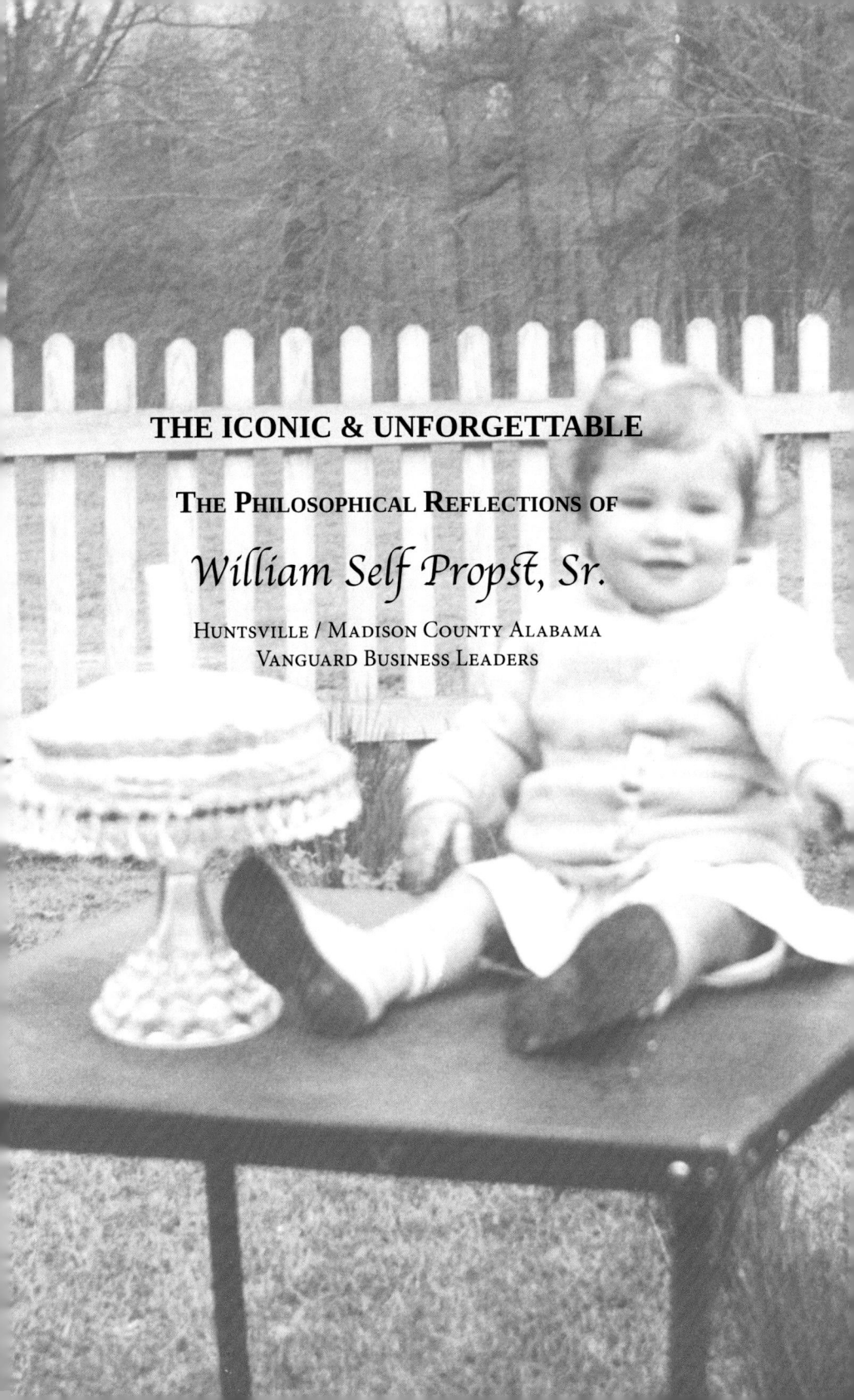

THE ICONIC & UNFORGETTABLE

The Philosophical Reflections of

William Self Propst, Sr.

Huntsville / Madison County Alabama
Vanguard Business Leaders

William Self Trippi, 1942.

Setting The Stage For Greatness:

The Birth Story of the Iconic & Unforgettable

William (Bill) Self Propst, Sr.

Huntsville / Madison County's Vanguard Business Leader

The winter of 1937 was a humble and simple time in Alabama, particularly for its rural residents. Sparsely populated communities offered only the basics of necessities. Families of this era carved out their lives one long day at a time, filling them with hard labor. Relying heavily on the fruits of their own land, hard work was directly proportional to the level of difficulty of their struggle to survive. Seeing this relationship from the very start of their lives, their children never questioned the need for hard work from dawn to dusk. They knew what it took to survive and that even their contributions to the many daily chores filled a valuable role in their families.

Families of such small settlements didn't want for much else than what they found or grew on their own land. The few things they did need were often found at their small wood framed country store. Walker Chapel was such a place as this. Located nine miles north of Birmingham, Alabama, and just one mile west of the coal mining community of Lewisburg, Walker Chapel was home to a people well-rooted in their faith, devoted to their families and committed to honoring their elders.

At the epicenter of Walker Chapel's social life was the local Methodist church. True to its small outwardly appearance, once inside, the community's church-goers found only a small number of hard, wood pews. Although limited in its ability to host the worshippers of Walker Chapel, which was likely a full headcount - excluding only those physically unable to grace the doors of the church - its offerings were quite adequate for the residents of this small, dirt-road settlement.

In fact, the population of the area was, and is still, too small to be included in an official census, so we don't know the exact number of individuals who called this area home during the winter of 1937. But we do know, however, that on the night of Valentine's Day, the Self family, in anticipation of adding one more to the population, summoned the services of young Doctor Mitchell to their home.

Virgil Leonidas Self, known simply as V.L. or Judge, and his wife, Annie, were the expectant grandparents of the soon-to-be born baby. Their youngest daughter, Margaret, and her husband, Michael Andrea Trippi, were expecting their second child in a home birth as was the standard in 1937, particularly in rural areas such as Walker Chapel.

As the stories go, it was a beautiful night. Although cold and crisp, the bright moonlight made for safe travels for the young doctor. A nighttime medical excursion was a common occurrence for this patient and very caring man. Although he was a learned man, diligently staying abreast of the treatments, equipment and medicine available at the time, reading medical journals at every opportunity, Dr. Mitchell was a man who knew how to stay out of the way as much as he knew when to intervene.

Waiting patiently in the kitchen of the Self's uninsulated farmhouse for the proper time to deliver Margaret's second baby, Dr. Mitchell prepared himself for the duration of her labor. The first order of business, shake off the cold of the night. His travels to the farm had left him with a chill. He warmed himself by the wood-burning cook stove on which pans of well water were being kept warm to be used as needed. He sat down, took his shoes off, lowered the door to the stove, put his sock feet on the opened door, leaned back in one of the Self's straight-backed kitchen chairs and read a medical publication by the light of a coal oil lamp. Time spent in deep thought seemed to be the norm for this tall and frail man. Even when talking to you, he would push his glasses high up on his forehead, close his eyes and tilt his head back toward the ceiling, leaving it clear to anyone watching that much personal reflection was going into his replies. Dr. Mitchell, now comfortable and as warm as he'd ever get in a drafty farmhouse in the dead of winter, settled into his evening of research. Margaret, laboring nearby with her mother and sister in attendance, was never a distant thought.

As it turned out, this particular home birth provided the good doctor plenty of time to read the medical journals and other publications which he'd habitually brought with him...all night in fact. The doctor's self study program came to an end at 4:05 the next morning, February 15, as Margaret and Mike Trippi joyfully welcomed their newest baby boy into their family. Weighing nine pounds and 13 ounces, their youngest son was named William Self Trippi.

Also rejoicing about William's birth was V.L. and Annie (Papa and Mama) and Margaret's sister Pearl. Unfortunately, this bond of family unity was soon to suffer a severing blow. William's parents separated only six months later. Their divorce quickly followed, leaving William, his brother, Michael, and their mother to live their next eight years on the Self family farm with Papa and Mama, V.L. and Annie.

Since William never got to know his biological father, the hardworking V.L. was the dominant male figure responsible for grooming the young boy through the formative first eight years of childhood. Embraced in a guided environment of love and attention from all the members of the close-knit Self family, both boys gained a strong sense of confidence. This foundation of confidence coupled with the character-shaping values strongly modeled by V.L., well prepared William Self Propst to shape his life into one that is Iconic and Unforgettable.

What were the guiding principles taught to young William by his grandfather? They were simple truths. Simple truths which became the keys to success for Bill Propst, Sr., as he is now widely known.

Get a good education.
Work hard.
Plan ahead.
Maintain high ethical standards.
Make sure your word is your bond.

Clearly, the first eight years of William's life provided the vitally important humble beginnings which, once applied throughout his many ventures, would make Bill, Sr. a man who retrospectively appears to have been predestined to an impactful life of significance. As his eldest son, Trey, references in his personal narrative (found in the family section of this book), people like to say he was lucky. But those who know him know better. They know that luck had nothing to do with it, unless by luck one means, get a good education, plan ahead, work hard and be an ethical man of your word.

HOW WILLIAM (BILL) SELF PROPST, SR. CREATED HIS *LUCK*

In the pages that follow, the reader is provided with personal illustrations from William (Bill) Self Propst, Sr., himself, family members, close personal friends and business associates detailing from their unique perspectives how William (Bill) Self Propst, Sr. created his 'luck' and fashioned his life into one which unmistakably merits being honored by The Iconic & Unforgettable Memorial Project as one of Huntsville's Vanguard Business Leaders.

A Personal Narrative Introduction of William (Bill) Self Propst, Sr.

Jerry Damson

Lifelong Friend

Butch, my wife, and I went down to see Bill and Eloise the week of his 80th birthday. They weren't there. We left him two birthday cards. I wanted him to be there because I was going to tell him, "Bill, I can't understand it; you didn't invite Butch and me to go on your beach trip with you. I even went and bought a new bathing suit - a Speedo - and I bought Butch a string bikini."

That's how Jerry Damson starts his interview. Obviously, he's a man with a sense of humor. He carries on:

I had never flown in a private jet until Bill bought one. We've traveled to see some football games. That was nice, I have to say. There's something I don't like about Bill, and I've known him since 1953. He's always been this way. You can't pay for anything. He will not let anybody pay for anything. All these games we went to, we had a suite, a box suite. Have you ever been to the Dallas stadium? It is unbelievable. Five stars is not enough to describe it. Of course, he got a box. It had a buffet in there with food as good as you could get anywhere. It wasn't home cooking, but it was very good. There were two bathrooms. The best thing about a suite is the bathroom; you don't have to go stand in line. In Tuscaloosa, it's nice, but nothing like Dallas. You're so high up that you can't really follow the football game so they have those two screens for you to watch that cost $42 million. We'd sit and watch the game on the screen.

We flew to all these games in his jet. We went to Tuscaloosa one time and it took us 22 minutes to get there. Coming back, it took 21 minutes. As we were flying, you could see people lined up to get to 65 North. They were lined up further than you could see. I told whoever I was sitting with, 'we will be home at Signature Aviation before the last car here gets on the interstate.' We probably were.

That's the quietest airplane I've ever flown in. I can stand up straight in it. It carried nine people that day, but it will carry ten. He's got a full-time pilot and co-pilot who work for him full time, whether he's flying or not flying.

Anyway, he did all that and wouldn't let us pay for anything. I think Bill is having as much fun, if not more fun, giving money back to the community than he had making his money. He has given many millions that a whole lot of people don't have any earthly idea about.

A FRIENDSHIP TAKES ROOT

I met Bill at Columbia Military Academy in Columbia, Tennessee. I got sentenced up there in the 8th grade. It's the best thing that ever happened to me. I stayed five years 'til I graduated from high school. I was the only boy in the history of the school, at the time, to go five years and graduate a Private, same thing I was when I started. I would get ranked, but then I would get busted for doing something wrong.

Bill came in 1952, after Christmas, walking on crutches. I remember that, the crutches. I knew him during all that time. He graduated two years before I did, so I lost touch with him while he was at Samford getting a pharmacy degree. When he graduated from Samford, he came back to Huntsville and went to work for Walgreen's downtown. Bill Hutchens owned it.

I'd gone in the Army while Bill was getting smart. By the time he opened his first drugstore, I was already in the used car business. Neither one of us had two quarters to rub together, so he borrowed from a man named Luther Latham in Arab - $7,000 - to open his first drugstore.

After he got up and running, he called me one time and said, "I need the cheapest car you've got for delivery." They delivered drugs back then.

A few weeks later he called me and told me, "I've already spent more damn money on that car than you sold it to me for."

"I sold you just exactly what you asked for - the cheapest car I had."

"Well, I need another one but I don't want a straight shift. These kids that deliver these prescriptions tear the clutch out. Every time I get it fixed, they tear it out again."

NO TIME TO PLAY

We'd go out to eat sometimes. I remember we used to go to Gibson's on North Parkway. They had great catfish. Bill and I used to eat there a good bit. We'd go to some of the clubs, not a whole lot, because we were both working day and night. Next thing I know, he's got six or seven stores. He was working from can to can't. He opened and closed every day.

IN THE MIDDLE OF THE NIGHT

In 1968, on the 4th of July, we went to Betsy and Peter Lowe's place on Elk River, just like we always did. Deke was four and Susan was five or six weeks old. Susan got to coughing and so forth. We finally left Deke there and drove to the emergency room in Huntsville. They couldn't determine what was wrong with her, which was understandable because she had whooping cough. They had never seen whooping cough. She almost died. They gave us prescriptions and sent us home. Now it's probably midnight. There weren't any drugstores open at night back then, so I called Bill. He was working primarily at the Five Points store then. He said, "I'll meet you at the drugstore in 15 minutes." I met him. By then I'd already taken Butch and Susan home. He gave me what I needed, I start thanking him and then I said, "I've got to get this home to Butch and get back to Elk River before Deke wakes up. If he wakes up and Butch and I aren't there, he's going to go ballistic." He said, "Well, let's go."

"What do you mean, let's go?"

"I don't want you driving over there by yourself. I don't want you to go to sleep."

"Hell, how much have you slept?" Couldn't have been more than two or three hours.

I took the medicine back home to Butch, then Bill and I drove to Rogersville to get Deke. We turned right around to come back home. As I recall, it was probably five o'clock in the morning by the time we got back. He had to get right back to the store, to open and close. Now that's a friend. That's exactly right. That's a friend.

That drugstore, at one time, probably filled more prescriptions than any drugstore in Huntsville. I wouldn't be surprised if Star Pharmacy which Darden Heritage owns, along with Propst Drugs across the street, doesn't do the same, fill more prescriptions than anybody in Huntsville.

A PREMONITION

Back in 1964, Butch and I were walking out of the Madison County Fair with Deke. Back then they had it on Airport Road. Bill and Eloise were walking in as we were walking out. Eloise's boys were with them. They were little too, like Deke. We stopped and talked a few minutes. They went in as we went out. I told Butch on the way to the car, "They're going to get married."

She said, "What makes you think that?" I said, "I guarantee you they will get married." I believe it was less than 60 days before they proved me right. They're a great couple. I've known Eloise forever, too.

Anytime Bill came home from Michigan, you could find him and Eloise at Boot's Restaurant and Lounge. He'd be there all the time. He'd be drinking unsweetened iced tea. Still does. He drinks more damn ice water, too, than anybody I've ever seen. He blames Butch for all his community giving, but the man has given here, there and yonder. My wife has asked him for a lot of it, so he likes to kid her. He calls her Little Red Riding Hood and he calls me Wild Man. Has forever. I was wild before, in military school and everywhere, until I ran into little Butch.

TWO ACCORDS MAKE A RIGHT

Maybe three years ago, I'm not good anymore keeping up with time, he called me and said, "I need two new Honda Accords."

"What are you going to do with them?"

"I'm going to give one of them to my housekeeper and one of them to my yard man."

He said he wanted two black ones. I said, "Bill, don't get black ones. I know you and Eloise both drive black Mercedes, but in an area that is so damn hot, you don't want a black car." But, he insisted. He wanted at least one black and I talked him into buying maroon, or something red, for the other one.

The day he wanted to give them, we took them over there to his house. We were standing out front with Eloise, maybe Bill, Jr., too. I don't remember. Bill says to his yard man, Leon Sr., "Leon, bring that car over there."

"Where do you want me to put it?"

"It's for you."

"Where you want me to put it?"

Leon Sr. is like me, he can't hear thunder. But, he finally understood what was going on. By that time, Bill is tearing up, Eloise is tearing up, and I'm tearing up. That's just not something people do, even people with a lot of money. But that is the kind of person Bill Propst is.

DESCRIPTIVE REFLECTIONS

He's a Christian and a family man. He's just a damn good man. Bill has 1,100 or 1,200 acres of farmland out at Owens Crossroads. I don't think he has gone lately, but he used to get out there on a tractor or combine and bale hay. He loved it. He doesn't get around like he used to, so I don't think he goes anymore. He sure used to love it. People don't know that side of him.

I think that Bill is probably as good of a friend I've ever had. He's the kind of friend you want and the kind you want to keep. I'd do anything in the world for him.

A Personal Narrative Introduction of William (Bill) Self Propst, Sr.

W.F. Sanders

Longtime Friend

I just resigned as chairman [of the Industrial Development Board] less than a year ago. I'd been on it awhile. I was in my 29th year. I've been involved in the community in a broad number of ways, which I've loved every minute of, in addition to running my own business here. I grew up in Huntsville and I have a great love for Bill Propst. I've known him for a long time. Or, as I've always called him, Mr. Chairman. I first met Bill, if my memory is correct, it was in 1955. We were both in school at a small college in Florence called Florence State Teachers College. That school ultimately evolved into the University of North Alabama.

We were not particularly close friends. He was, to me, always kind of quiet and studious. I might say I was a little bit different from that. We separated ways at the end of 1955 or 1956. He went to Auburn and I went to University of Alabama. Basically, we lost contact for the next 50 years, maybe longer. We were on different tracks. But then, when he moved one of his companies [Qualitest] back here to Huntsville, we reassociated with each other. As a result of that, a very strong friendship has developed. As I said, I always saw him as a studious, serious type person, which he may refute. I was a little bit on the other side. I had a big time and enjoyed school.

How close am I to him? He knows if I call him and he doesn't take my call, I'm not going to be upset about it. He says, "Call me anytime you want to." I never call him at home, although I think sometimes he would appreciate it. Just hearing from somebody he knows that he can talk to a few minutes, you know. I can go to his office anytime I want. But, I never go without calling him first and asking permission to come over because I just value his time; and yet, you've got people that do take advantage of him. I don't think I'm in his real inner circle, but I'm not far out of it. We're having lunches every Friday. That's pretty good stuff.

There are a lot of great things about the man. I've just been privileged [to know him]. I'm so delighted we reconnected. I think it's 20-25 years now that we've been reconnected. It was right after he got back to Huntsville. In all fairness, I know we connected early on, but we've really grown close over the last 15 years. We sat down one night and had dinner and that's really when it began to unfold. I knew long before that that I'd like to be closer to him. I didn't realize it would develop into the relationship that it has. Of course, he's been so ultra, ultra successful. I mean, there are three people in this community that are ultra-wealthy and he's one of them. Mark Smith is one. Nobody really knows how much Olin King was worth, but it was substantial. But, again, no one knows.

I get tickled …I can't remember…there's this man called the Yellowhammer; he sells wood in this state. They claim he's the wealthiest man in the state. So, I asked somebody one time if they had any idea [how much he was worth], and they said he's worth about a half billion dollars. I said, "I don't believe he's the wealthiest man in this state."

"What are you talking about?"

"I just think there are some others." There are a couple people in Birmingham wealthier than that, you know. Of course, I have no earthly idea what Mr. Propst's actual worth is.

I see two different things about Mr. Propst that have struck me and stayed with me. He's a humble person and he's a very giving person. There are people in this town, and this is true of anybody that is successful, that just don't like him. They think he's greedy and, you know, out for himself only. That is the furthest thing from the truth about the man. But unless you know him, you would not know the many philanthropic things he does.

Now, some things he's done are public. We're sitting here right now looking at the Propst Arena over there [at the Von Braun Center]. He did that because of the need to have a more modern facility in this community to attract concerts, ballgames, hockey games and these type of things. He didn't do it [for notoriety]. In fact, I'm sure he didn't realize they were going to put his name up there. He may not have done it had he realized that. But then I look at what's going on out at the Botanical Gardens and this fabulous new facility they are building. I have no idea how much money Mr. Propst gave, but I'm sure it's substantial. That is one of the most wonderful botanical gardens in the country. It's constantly bringing tourists into town. You haven't seen a lot of publicity about that. You haven't seen any publicity about any of these things he's done. That's the high side of Mr. Propst.

What people don't know is what he does for the underprivileged and people in need. I [get to] see that in him. I happen to serve on a foundation; it was the first major private foundation of any size [here], and he knows that I'm on that foundation. From that one, there have been four or five other major foundations established in this community.

The one I serve on is the Lowe Foundation - the Jane K. Lowe Foundation. There's also the Alpha Foundation and Mr. Propst has his foundation now. These are not small foundations. The Lowe Foundation started with $40 million. It is about $35 million now, but we've distributed right at $25 million over the last 12 to 14 years.

From time to time, Mr. Propst will just drop a hint, "Is there somebody you think we ought to look at that's needy. Some of these smaller institutions that deliver a lot of giving to people?" There's the 305 8th Street out in west Huntsville that takes care of elderly, disabled people. There's the Boys and Girls Club, there's another boys club and there's a Lincoln Foundation out there now, near the old Lincoln School. So, I'll drop hints to him. I never know if he gives to them.

HONORING A DEBT OF KINDNESS

We were swapping some stories here a month or so ago and we were talking about things we regretted in our lives. I was telling him about this story I had when we were both over at Florence State Teachers College. We didn't have any money back in those days. I'd get $5 a week to do my laundry and buy any excess food, movies or anything else. That doesn't sound like much, but that's back when $5 was a lot of money.

I'll never forget one weekend it was homecoming weekend and this little girl I was dating wanted to come and I invited her. It became Thursday night and I didn't have any money. So, I went up and down the hall trying to borrow $5 to $10. This guy that I'd known since I'd been there, Moultrie, let me have $10, and man, I was in business. I could get the tickets to the game and we could go eat. But somehow I forgot about that until two or three years later when it popped back in my mind. I spent the next several years trying to find Moultrie, and I couldn't find him. I wanted to pay him back the $10, and I was going to give him the appropriate interest rate.

I was sad as I was telling that story, and Mr. Propst didn't say anything for a few minutes. He just looked down at the floor. I thought, oh, I guess I've just hurt myself here. In a few minutes, he opened his drawer and started digging around and pulled out this envelope and handed it to me. I opened it and it was a $20 bill in there. And, there was this precious letter written to him by this young girl. She was probably 15 or 16 or 17 years old. She had been in his drugstore, Propst Drugs, out at Five Points and she had stolen several articles because she didn't have any money. But she put $20 in this envelope and said, "I wanted you to have this back." That was such a touching moment [for us] because he had the very same thing going on that I did. He's been trying to find that lady and he can't find her. It's like my situation. I've even gone to the school. I'm afraid my friend must have passed away because he was such a popular guy that you would think he would be easy to find.

HIS PHONE RINGS ALL DAY LONG

So, there are literally hundreds and hundreds of stories about Mr. Propst's giving. He's a very giving type person. Because of that, his phone rings all day long. Some people just want to say hello to him, like myself. And then there's people calling him wanting money.

One time a dear friend of his was quite ill and he flew him to one of the premier cancer institutes in this country in his own plane, you know, paid for it. [Tearing up] You'll have to forgive me. I'm very devoted to him, and he just has so many friends and loves on them all.

At Christmas, they'll prepare a package of $50 to $100 worth of things for a needy child, and then there's a group that chooses a family that it goes to, and he just instructs them to take it out. It can be 30, 40, or 50 children at Christmas time.

Here's one of the things about Bill that fascinates me. One day (it was Thanksgiving week) the doorbell rang, I opened the door, and there he stood. He had a ham. No, I think it was a turkey and the ham came at Christmas. Every year since then he's done it. It's been 15 or 20 years now that I get a ham and a turkey from him. One day, he slipped and said, I had a hard time getting my 80 turkeys delivered. So, he's doing this for 80 families in this community! The interesting thing is there's only maybe four to six people in my status of friendship that get them. Most of those turkeys go to people that used to work for him, people with whom he stayed in touch and has great respect.

He's never really explained this to me but I know that he helped some of the folks who worked for him…during the building of his [drug] company. There were a lot of people to whom he actually gave ownership. Quite a few people came away very well-off because he decided he wanted to share. He's still got some people working for him that have been working for him for years.

FROM THE BACK PEW QUIETLY COMES A BLESSING

One day, and this has been about six years ago, we were just chatting and at that time I may have been trustee of the church or something. He said, "What's going on with the church?" I told him they were wrestling with [a funding issue]… "They need a new steeple, they need new gutters and everything." I told him, "They raised a lot of money, but we're not able to complete the deal." I didn't ask him for the money. Well, about two weeks later I'm sitting there…I sit about two rows down and he sits in the back further down… and I had this tap on the shoulder. I said, "Hey, Mr. Chairman, how ya doing?"

"I'm doing fine."

"Do me a favor - would you see that the proper people get this envelope." It had "W.F." on it.

"Well, I ain't the proper people." (laughs)

So, I got home and I opened it up and I'll never forget. It was a check for exactly the amount of money we needed to finish that project. I'm not sure how he got the number; he didn't get it from me. So I delivered it to the proper people. Of course, they just bugged me to death to know who it was. Somebody leaked the name. I don't know how many people finally knew it [was from him]. I don't know if he knows that. He would care, because he doesn't want that.

I CALL HIM MR. CHAIRMAN

I call him Mr. Chairman because he's owned a lot of businesses. I just see him as the kind of person that if I were running a company he would be my chairman. I don't know that he ever assigned those kinds of names to the people in his company. He might be irritated that I call him that. But, if he is he's never said anything. It's just pure respect for him.

We usually lunch on Fridays, and that is a wonderful experience. He has the most uncanny wit and…He can remember stories, but I'm sure like all of us, he embellishes them a little bit. Which we all do, you know. I wish I had his kind of memory.

We'll sit down to eat lunch and sometimes we can't eat because so many people come over to visit with him. He's very approachable. You know people just come over and he stops and shakes their hand and talks to them. He apologizes [to me] because he got interrupted. It doesn't happen every day but it happens frequently. Sometimes he'll say to them, "Sit down and have lunch with us. We've got an extra chair."

We eat everywhere. One of our favorite places before they closed was Ruth's Chris which was right across the street over here. They're down the street now, but they're not open for lunch, and I don't think they're going to be. We still go occasionally to the Embassy Suites restaurant. There is a place called G's. It's truly southern cooking. He'll order and I'll fuss at him. I don't fuss at him much, but he doesn't follow his doctors orders. He'll order a plate that has two fried pork chops, and he might have pinto beans and slaw and he might have some macaroni and cheese. Whichever one of us didn't order meat, it's usually me, I usually order a bowl of pinto beans, tomatoes and sometimes cucumbers, which I hate - but I love...he'll throw me one of the pork chops... (laughs) We also go out to a place called Mama Annie's occasionally, which is right off of [Alabama] A&M's campus.

Then there's a place called the Furniture Factory. I'm not part of the afternoon group that goes there with him. We go there for lunch rather frequently. He eats breakfast a lot at Blue Plate and he eats down at Ted's sometimes. Gibson's, he eats there a lot. But there are not a lot of fine dining places open for lunch. We've gone many times, but not any more, to Cotton Row. When it's lunch, we just like simple foods, you know. Ruth's Chris had that kind of menu for us and we loved it. We met there for a long time. We've been out to Grille29 but that's such a long trip. He'll always say, "Just choose where you want to go." Sometimes we'll go around in circles. But it's places like that. It's usually just soul food.

If I go to lunch by myself, you know, thirty minutes and I'm through. We're usually an hour and a half, minimum, sometimes two hours, because on Friday afternoon we just sit back and relax and enjoy each other.

DESCRIPTIVE REFLECTIONS

He has a brilliant business acumen. He has a heart larger than life. A quick wit. Not only is he able to remember, but he has the ability to size a person up quickly. He can really do that in a hurry. He can tell if that person is sincere or somebody trying to pull the wool over his eyes. He's remarkable in that avenue.

I've used his wisdom in my own operation. I would have to say that a lot of the people that work for him, he would have had to mentor them in order for them to keep up with him. He would have had to cause them to grow to stay in the same league that he's in as he moves through. I would have loved to have been one of his children. It really would have been nice to be raised with that wisdom.

Something else. He's very political. He keeps up with politics very closely. When he spots somebody that he really likes, that he thinks would be good for this community, he'll open his pocketbook to them. He's just an ideal individual to me. I'm just delighted that we were able to connect with each other.

One more tender story that comes to my mind about his giving. Do you ever watch these ads from St. Jude's hospital? Those things just tear my heart out. I walked into his office one day not long ago, maybe six or eight weeks ago. I was standing there waiting to get in to see him. There's a table to the left as I walk in and there were three plaques on that table. Each was for a home that was built in Nashville, Tennessee. They were all built and given to St. Jude's. They all sold for well over a million. So, somewhere in his organization he built those homes and gave them to them. Then they sold them and gave him those plaques.

That's just another small picture of what the man is and what he does. The man on the street doesn't have a clue about this.

I'm not trying to glorify him. I'm just telling you the truth. I'm close enough to him to see what the general public doesn't see.

William Self Trippi, age 5, with brother, Michael Trippi, age 9, 1942.

William S. Propst, 1954, Columbia Military Academy in Columbia, Tenn.

ICONIC & UNFORGETTABLE

Family & Friends

William (Bill) Self Propst, Sr.

"Most of the time we didn't have a bat or a ball, but Michael would get an old broom, cut off the handle for me to use as a bat, and pitch a Pet Milk can as a ball for me to hit."

William (Bill) Self Propst, Sr.

EXCERPTS FROM THE MEMOIRS OF

William (Bill) Self Propst, Sr.

THE SELF FAMILY

Virgil Leonidas Self (Papa), my grandfather, was about six feet tall, slim, muscular, with broad shoulders, weighing about 200 pounds. That was just a great physique for an aging man who most folks called "Judge Self." Papa could be gruff in the mornings, especially if Mama got him up before breakfast was on the table and his coffee was poured. After Papa finished breakfast, he was tolerant, hardworking, and most assuredly a very stern man. He was absolutely not a man to be pushed around.

Annie Beasley Self (Mama), my grandmother, was a stocky, Irish, hardworking, and very religious woman who was the mother of eight children, four boys: Otis, Hobart, Geddes and Aurel, and four girls: Pearl, Velma, Grace and Margaret, my mother. Mama was the real glue in the family, a great motivator, patient teacher, hard worker and strict disciplinarian.

We lived in Walker Chapel, Alabama, a small dirt road settlement located about one mile west of the coal mining community known as Lewisburg, about nine miles north of Birmingham. The community was sparsely populated with only a few houses, several farms, an old-timey country store, and a very small but beautiful white Methodist church blessed with a tall steeple and belfry. The church adjoined a very small poorly maintained cemetery located on the gravel road leading to Lewisburg and the two-lane paved highway to Birmingham.

On the night of February 14, 1937, Papa and Mama were waiting on my birth with Aunt Pearl, my father, Mike Trippi, and of course, Mother. Dr. Mitchell, a young country doctor practicing medicine in this sparsely populated area, had been called to help with the delivery. He arrived just after dark. Water was drawn from the well and kept warm in pans on the kitchen stove so it would be ready when needed. At 4:05 a.m. the following morning, February 15, I was born, weighing 9 pounds 13 ounces, and I was named William Self Trippi.

There was already trouble in my parents' marriage. About six months after I was born, my parents separated and Mother filed for a divorce. Michael, Mother, and I continued to live on the farm with Papa and Mama for about eight years. Papa was therefore the dominant male figure in my life since I never got to know my biological father.

Michael and I were not born into a life of luxury, but we were fortunate. We had the basics in food, clothes, a roof over our heads, and a family that cared for us. While we didn't have a lot of material things, we really didn't know it because we lived with Papa, and because, after the depression, very few other people had as much as we did. The most important gifts we received from Mother, Mama, Papa, aunts and uncles, was a lot of attention, affection and guidance. Special emphasis was always placed on values and the assurance we could do well if we got a good education, worked hard, planned ahead, maintained high ethical standards, and last but not least, made sure our word was our bond.

As it turns out I believe I was the luckier of the two of us boys since Michael, my brother, had lived with, knew, and missed his daddy. Michael was really resentful of his daddy's failure to visit and support us. I say that due to some of the things Michael said many years later. In any event, I believe overall we were happy kids.

After the divorce, Mother went back to school. She attended the Draughon Business School. After graduating, Mother went to work for A.J. Rieb, the Traffic Manager for L & N Railroad, whose office was in the Woodward Building on 20th Street in downtown Birmingham. Mother did an outstanding job of supporting us, even though she only made between $25 and $30 per week.

I am told that each day for lunch Mother would go down to Leggett Drug Store located in the Woodward Building, eat lunch - normally a hot dog - and drink a Coke for a total cost of 15 cents. The balance of her check each week went for her ride back and forth to work with Mr. Leonard, one of our neighbors, and our support. Mother occasionally accumulated enough money to buy a war bond for Michael's and my education. Sometimes when working late or there were problems with Mr. Leonard's schedule, she would walk the six blocks to the Ridgley Apartments and spend the night with her sister, Grace Self. Only years later did I fully realize the very difficult economic times mother endured to support us.

Since Mother was working, Mama kept me every day and treated me as if she was my mother. Mama was a very good teacher and taught us how to work, negotiate, and to respect others as she tried to equip us for the future.

The roads in the Walker Chapel and Lewisburg area were either dirt or gravel except the paved two-lane highway that passed through Lewisburg leading to the city of Birmingham. The primary mode of transportation for the majority of the people at that time was the two national public bus companies, Greyhound and Trailways and a local bus company, Blueline. All of the bus companies ran on a regular schedule as advertised. I must say each of them was pretty prompt, dependable, and charged fares that were affordable even for those who were less fortunate.

The little country store in Walker Chapel was more like the convenience store of today, but with a much more limited number of items in stock. Some of the items sold were a few canned goods, candies, bread, fried pies, fresh eggs, pickled eggs, pickled pigs feet, hoop cheese, soft drinks, tobacco products, fresh vegetables in season, a few smoked and salted meats, cans of motor oil, gasoline and kerosene.

Soft drinks were delivered to the store in wood cases with wood dividers that created 24 slots. The popular soft drink brands at that time were Coca Cola, Pepsi, Double Cola, Orange Crush, Dr. Pepper and Grapico. It was not uncommon to see someone, usually a man, purchase a soft drink and a pack of peanuts, drink a little of the liquid, pour the peanuts in the bottle, shake well, and then drink and eat the mixture.

MY BROTHER

Michael was four years older than me but he always took care of me! He was patient, kind, protective, attentive and a good teacher. I guess he taught me about everything that a young boy should know, what to do, and what not to do, especially a young boy living on a farm in the country. He taught me how to ride a bike, patch a tire tube, put a chain on a sprocket and tighten it, plait a bracelet, dig worms, bait a hook, catch and clean fish, hit, catch, and throw a baseball, kick, catch, and throw a football, play basketball, make a kite using newspaper, sticks, string, and glue made with flour and water, how to make a tail for a kite out of rags, how long the tail should be, and why it was needed, how to make and use a slingshot, and many other things a young country boy should know.

When I was just a very little boy, Michael would pull me around in the Red Flyer wagon and take me almost everywhere he went. I remember one particular incident when he had tied the tongue of the Red Flyer wagon to the frame of his 20-inch bicycle and he was trying to pull me down the road on our way to the creek. Michael had tied the tongue of the wagon to the frame of the seat since it could not be tied straight behind the bicycle without rubbing or denting the fender. When it came loose Michael stopped and was trying to retie the tongue so it would not come loose, rub or dent the fender. Some boys came by on their bikes, also on their way to the creek, and told Michael to come on, go with them, and leave me. He told them to go on and after several stops to retie, we eventually got to the creek!

Most of the time we didn't have a bat or a ball, but Michael would get an old broom, cut off the handle for me to use as a bat, and pitch a Pet Milk can as a ball for me to hit. Occasionally we would get lucky and get a rubber ball and, even more rarely, a tennis ball. Sometimes Michael would make a ball by wrapping a marble or like object with string to what would appear to be the size of a store-bought ball, then tape the ball with black tape to cover and hold the ball together. That type of ball was always heavy and when it was hit with a bat the sound would just be a thud and it would not have any spring to it at all. Michael taught me how to step forward and shift my weight as I hit the ball. This movement with the resulting flexing of the muscle and body weight would make the ball go much further than just swinging with your arms. These lessons proved to be very valuable to me years later in organized sports.

Some nights Michael and I would lay out on the lawn and look at the stars. Michael would point out things to me like the Big Dipper, Little Dipper, evening star, and even the ever-changing number of stars in the circle around the moon which some say represents the number of days it will be before it will rain.

These were the days of William Propst's youth. They were simple times, but they were a family that loved each other and didn't want for anything more than that.

"I knew from the start it was a long shot. It takes more than harmony to be successful in show business."

William (Bill) Self Propst, Sr.

A SUMMARY NARRATIVE COMPILED FROM
EXCERPTS FROM THE MEMOIRS OF

William (Bill) Self Propst, Sr.

THE ENTREPRENEURIAL HERITAGE

Pharmacy is a family affair for the Selfs. Bill's uncle, Otis Self, the oldest of the four self brothers, owned and operated a number of drug stores and pharmacies in downtown Birmingham, Alabama and the surrounding area. Hobart Self, the second oldest brother, was also a pharmacist, owning several pharmacies in downtown Birmingham plus Kelly Drug in nearby Bessemer.

THE ENTREPRENEURIAL SPIRIT PERSEVERES

It isn't just pharmacy that was in Bill's blood; entrepreneurship was too. Uncle Otis also ran a dairy farm, Vitality Dairies, while running his many brick-and-mortar pharmacy ventures. Uncle Hobart raised and showed Tennessee Walking Horses. With her husband, Aunt Velma, one of the four sisters and an educator herself, ran a hardware store in Altoona, Alabama, maintained several pieces of rental property, a large pimiento peppers farm and, later in life, built a combination restaurant and Dairy Queen in Oneonta, Alabama. All the sisters were educators except for Bill's mother, Margaret. After her divorce from Bill's biological father, she attended and graduated from Draughon Business College and then went to work for A.J. Reib, the Traffic Manager for L & N Railroad.

The paternal bloodline was quite the resourceful bunch as well. As a fresh-off-the-boat, Italian immigrant, Bill's grandfather, Andrea Henry Trippi, quickly learned enough English to peddle fruit on the streets of Manhattan from a wood cart he made from castaway apple boxes.

The Trippis were business minded from the beginning. They moved from New York to Chicago for a brief period and then landed in Birmingham. Birmingham was a city submersed yet in its own humble beginnings. It was a city where commerce was kept alive on the backs of oxen which, in turn, kept the city's streets muddy by pulling wagons full of goods brought to town for trade.

Upon arriving, the Trippi's entrepreneurial spirit quickly went into action. They built a grocery store with an apartment on the second floor. With the money they saved from the grocery business, they bought property along 20th Street, the main street in Birmingham, and built many small rental houses in the 22nd Street area. Each week, tenants would come into the grocery store, pay their rent, pay for last week's groceries and buy more groceries on credit. The Trippi's enterprises proved to serve the family well. Later they were able to send their son, Bill's biological father, Michael Andrea Trippi, to the University of Alabama School of Law in style.

Mike Trippi arrived on campus in a new Packard Coupe and with 26 suits. Although Mike played as hard in school as he studied, he did well for himself. He made good grades and upon graduating, became a partner in one of the largest law firms in Birmingham.

The value of a higher education was also shared by the Self family. Although the youngest of the four Self brothers enjoyed only a short life, dying of an infected tooth at the age of six, all seven of the other children, including Bill's mother, were college graduates. Bill's own college career would have a false start, but the lessons he learned being raised in his grandparents' home for the first eight years of his life never left him. It was his mother's wish that Bill would get a college education, so he promised her he would.

In 1959, the time came when Bill decided it was time to honor his promise to his mother. At only 22 years of age, Bill was already a seasoned entrepreneur. Not only had he already started his first enterprise, the Lambert & Propst Steel Company, he had already sold out his interest in it. What's a young man to do with his whole life in front of him but to give show business a try? Soon after selling his interest in the steel company, Bill attempted that very thing. He and his first wife, Beverly, moved to Nashville in January 1959. There, Bill joined a group known as the "Keynotes." Show business proved to be an unsuccessful and short-lived venture. By spring of the same year, the Propsts had moved back to Huntsville. Bill was very disappointed but not surprised, saying "I knew from the start it was a long shot. It takes more than harmony to be successful in show business."

Back in Huntsville, while working at the same steel company of which he had just been a co-owner a few months prior, Bill began to think about some of the things his older brother, Michael Propst, had told him the summer before while the two toiled in the hot sun unloading, by hand, a trailer truckload of steel. At the time, Michael was already in pharmacy school at Howard College, now Samford University, in Birmingham. After unloading that truck of its steel in 100-degree weather, Michael told Bill that he could not wait for school to start back, become a pharmacist, work in an air-conditioned building and not have to pick up anything heavier than a gallon jug.

Although Bill was in a transition season in his life - and his brother's words, as well as his promise to his mother - weighed heavily on him, he was a young man who wasn't prone to making decisions carelessly. Going to school as a married man would put further strain on his marriage, and he knew it wouldn't be just a financial strain. This didn't make for a quick decision, but once made, Bill never looked back. As he said, "It wasn't the easy thing to do, but it was the right thing to do. Little did I know at the time, that the old saying, 'When poverty walks in the front door, love walks out the back' would apply to my life."

SUBJECT	DATE

Norm,

I thought you may enjoy this.

John

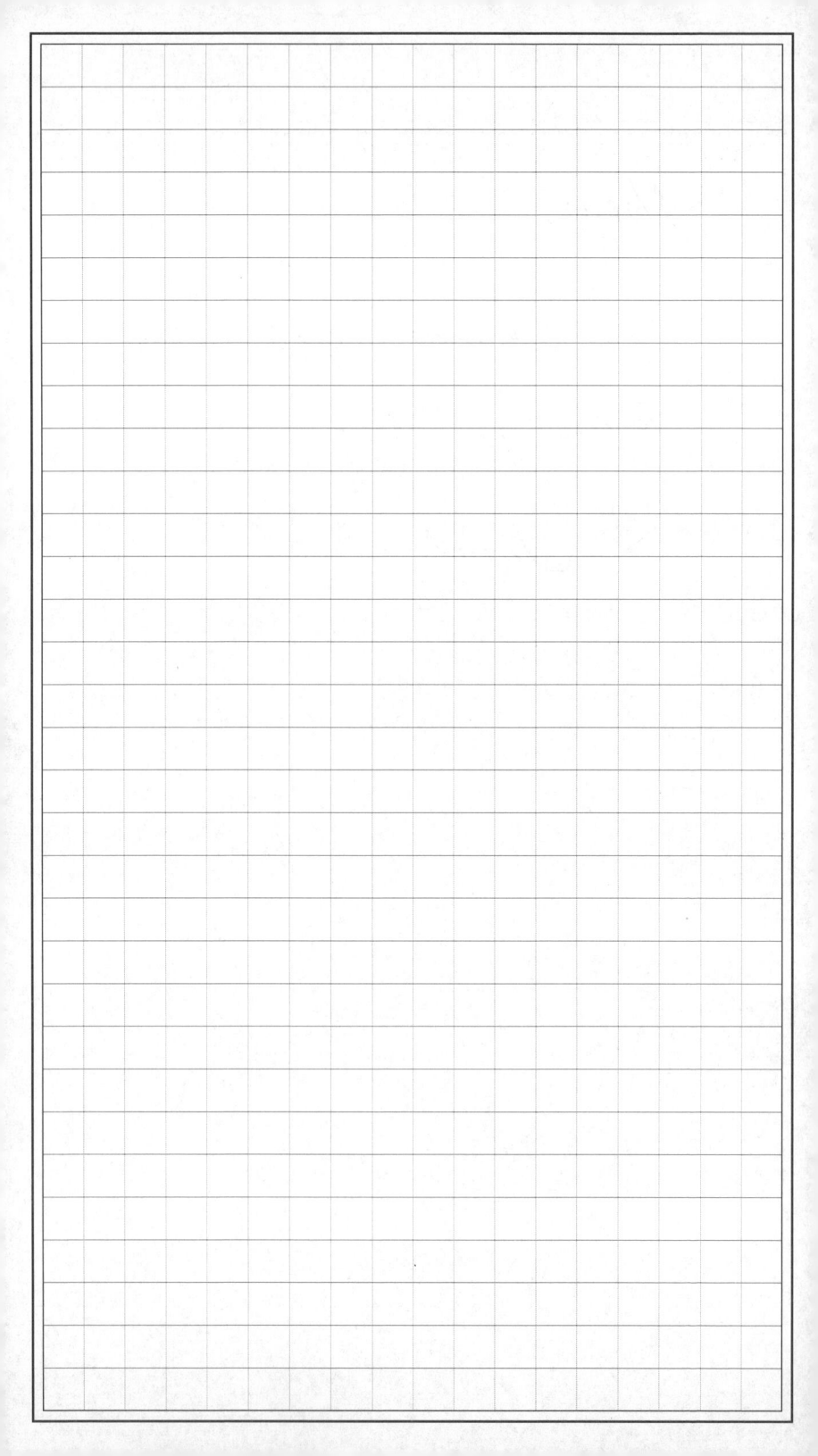

"When I get big I'm not going to take any more cod liver oil, I'm not going to eat any more eggs and I'm not going to drink any more milk."

William (Bill) Self Propst, Sr.

THE PERSONAL NARRATIVE OF
William (Bill) Self Propst, Sr.
AN INTERVIEW DISCUSSION ABOUT HIS YOUTH & HOW HE BECAME AN ITALIAN WITH A GERMAN LAST NAME

When I was two years old and spring came, Mama took me out of long pants and overalls and put me in short pants. That's when she discovered my knees knocked. I had rickets, so they put me in braces. I stayed in braces for five years. I had to wear them 24-hours-a day for two or three months and then they let me take them off at night. Once I tried to bury them in the yard.

Part of the regimen was to serve me soft scrambled, almost runny eggs, milk the goat and make me drink a glass of warm goat's milk, and take a teaspoonful of cod liver oil. I told mother one day, when I get big, I'm not going to drink any more milk, eat eggs or take any more cod liver oil. To this day I don't, unless I have an egg beater omelet with a lot of onions and peppers and Tabasco. I'm just not going to eat them. Papa would go out and milk the goat, come in and strain it and serve it. But let me tell you, warm goat's milk tastes like the goat smells. If you put it in the refrigerator, there's not that much difference between it and the cow's milk, but, boy, up until then....

When I was in college and we were living in Florence, I came downstairs one day and there was an egg, toast and a glass of milk. I buttered the toast and I got me some strawberry preserves. Mother saw I wasn't drinking any of the milk or eating the egg. She said, "Young man, you drink that milk and eat that egg."

I said, "Mother, you remember what I told you years ago? I said when I get big, I'm not going to eat any more eggs, drink any more milk or take any more cod liver oil."

Well, she got up and pulled my hair. (laughs) Oh, she was furious with me, never said anything else about it after that. Now, my favorite breakfast is country ham but I can't eat it or grits anymore due to health problems.

SOME THINGS ABOUT PAPA

Papa was a judge. I don't know if he was an actual judge or what he was, but everybody called him "Judge Self." I can remember him having court in the living room of our house. He could have been a justice of the peace, or whatever, I don't really know. I don't know anything about the background of my ancestors.

If I wanted to drive the truck when I was 10 years old, he would let me drive the truck. Michael and I worked - not anything that was only for adults - the things that we were capable of doing. We brought in stove wood and water, slopped the hogs and learned how to milk a cow.

The thing I remember most about Papa was he had a dairy and, before I started going to school, would take the milk to Foremost Dairies in Birmingham. I'd ride with him and on the way back, he'd often stop at the Blue and Gray Cafe on Highway 231 and sometimes get a beer. Sometimes he'd make me drink a Grapico, but sometimes he'd let me drink a beer. When we'd get home, Mama would just get bent out. But that didn't bother him since he ruled the roost. He loved to play dominos. We'd sit for hours and play. He was my daddy, my buddy, my friend.

His biggest impact on me was that you have to work, think, and be honest. He and Mama always told us that a man hadn't made any money until he collects.

As I said, we worked but we didn't have much. We had a lamp, not an expensive Aladdin lamp - just a regular lamp. One of my aunts had one though, and it would really cast the light. We had a wood cook stove, but we didn't have running water, and the house wasn't insulated. However, none of that mattered because we didn't need much. We had what we needed so we had a good time.

We went to church every Sunday and were normally the first at church. Mama would always invite someone to eat dinner with us. If she was going to have fried chicken, which we normally had on Sunday, she'd come in and cut that chicken's head off and cook it. It was good. There was nothing fancy about how we lived.

Mother worked for the Traffic Manager for L&N Railroad. She worked there for many years and was pretty good at what she did. She was a tenacious lady and when she had her mind made up, you might as well surrender. (laughs) I don't know that I inherited that, but I inherited a little temper. I'm normally pretty tolerant, up to a point. But, I don't like for anybody to try to run over me, if you know what I mean.

Not only was Mother a good provider, she was a disciplinarian, as was my grandmother. Mother always did everything she could for us. She'd take money and put it in the bank. When Michael and I got ready to go to college, there was money for us. But she was clear: if I didn't go to college, she wasn't going to give the money to me. It was for one particular purpose and that was it.

I think Mother and Mike Trippi just got married too young. She was 16 and he was 20, for one. And two, Mother... well, you'd have to know her, she was going to be in control. She had a strong personality and their two personalities clashed. Also, Mike was accustomed to living in town. But Papa lived out in the country, and the two of them lived there with him and Mama the whole time they were married.

Again, Mother was tenacious. If she made up her mind that she was going to play an organ, she'd play an organ. She'd practice until she got it down. And she did. She got really good at it. Everything she did was that way. Mother, my grandmother, my granddaddy, all of them, I couldn't differentiate between them when it came to being tenacious.

I got my business sense from Mama. Before I started school I'd go around the farm with the farm hands and I'd pick up scrap iron. If we went somewhere and I saw some scrap, I'd get it. I had a pile of scrap iron out next to the lot where they kept the cows before they milked them. One day a fella came by and wanted to know if we had any scrap we wanted to sell. I told him, "yep." We went out to the pile and Mama stood up on the driveway where she could hear everything that was said. He said, "I'll give you two dollars." I looked up at Mama and she said, "It isn't mine." So, I just looked back at him and he said, "I'll give you four dollars." I said, "Okay." Mama quickly said, "You're a fool." (laughs)

She was a good negotiator. We went down to Birmingham

together when Papa needed a new suit. She didn't go on 20th Street to Pizitz and Loveman's, or the big department stores, Blacks, and so forth. She went two or three streets over, to a little men's clothing shop. She went in, felt the cloth and so forth, picked out what she liked and asked how much it was. I think he said it was $28. She acted like she'd been shot. She started out the door and he told her to come back and they began to bargain back and forth. I think she paid either $18 or $20 for it. She taught me to negotiate and she used to tell me, "If you don't ask, you don't receive."

MEETING PAUL PROPST

Paul Propst had a seven-point circuit out around Paint Rock, Alabama, and moved to Woodville when he graduated from the seminary. His wife died from cancer while he was living there. He then was appointed to a five-point circuit, which included Walker Chapel where we lived. So every fifth Sunday, he'd be at our church and Mama invited him over, as she would every minister and many friends, to eat lunch on Sunday. It wasn't long before he and Mother started to go out socially. They ended up getting married on October 15, 1944, and we moved to the southside of Birmingham. I was in the third grade. Paul's daddy and mother gave them a house on 16th Avenue and 15th Street for a wedding present. They paid $8,000 for it.

The first couple of years after Mother and Daddy were married, Michael and I got to where we dreaded to see October come when The North Alabama Methodist Conference met. We would be thrilled when Daddy was reappointed to the church and town in which we were currently living. If we heard on Sunday night the new appointment would require us to physically move to another city or town we would pack on Monday and Tuesday and move on either Wednesday or Thursday. We always dreaded saying goodbye to our friends, but in retrospect we really didn't have much time to say goodbye to everyone due to packing and cleaning the house. We never knew what the next parsonage or church would look like and we had to scrub some houses. Some were small, others were dilapidated and some were filthy.

Of course after we moved we had to unpack, enroll in the new school, start trying to make new friends, establish our position with the coaches and future teammates, get through the inevitable confrontation with the bullies, and the resulting problem with overcoming a ruffian reputation due to our "hit the bully first election," but it all had to be done.

October 1946 Daddy was appointed to the small Methodist church in Hazel Green, Alabama. Hazel Green is a small community about 14 miles north of Huntsville and about four miles south of the Alabama-Tennessee state line. It was a beautiful farming community with rich red clay soil and a gently rolling terrain.

"In October of that year, I was diagnosed with Scarlet Fever and our house was quarantined."

William Self Propst, Sr.

AN EXCERPT FROM THE MEMOIRS OF

William (Bill) Self Propst, Sr.
1954-1955

When you leave a school where you are in the middle of everything that goes on, and then go to a new school that you feel puts you down, it makes all the difference in the world to a young person. While no faculty member intends to put a child down, the perception by the child can really become a problem to an immature 10th grader or a person in that age group. That's what it was like for me when we moved to Florence.

Florence was a nice town, but totally different from the rural communities to which I had become accustomed. In other cities and towns, there was always ample opportunity for a young person to work especially in the farming communities, but not in Florence with its Florence State College, TVA, Reynolds Aluminum, and the dominant union philosophy.

I went out for basketball but only made the "B" team. I had made All County the year before, in Marshall County, so it was hard to be put on the bench. I only got to play in one game. I quickly scored seven points and was taken out of the game and told I was hot dogging it. As it turned out, it really didn't matter because I had hurt my knee and had to have a knee operation and therefore would not have been able to play anyway. The knee got a staph infection and I was in the hospital for 30 days and then I walked on crutches and a cane for almost two years.

Due to my dissatisfaction at school, poor attitude, long hospital stay, and resulting absence from school, Mother and Daddy decided to send me to Columbia Military Academy in Columbia, Tennessee. It turned out to be one of the best things that could have happened to me at that time. I thoroughly enjoyed the faculty, structure, discipline and curriculum.

Since I could not play ball due to my knee problem, I decided to take additional classes, go to summer school, and graduate early. I graduated from Columbia Military Academy in 1954. In retrospect, this was a mistake for me at 17 because I was far too young and immature.

While I was considerably behind my age group in maturity I always seemed to be ahead of the group when it came to finances, recognizing business needs, business opportunities, scheduling, operational efficiencies, confidence, and disdain for certain inhibiting groups. I was always willing to work as long as it took to attain certain near-term goals, especially those that could lead to long-term success.

In the fall of 1954, I enrolled in Florence State Teachers College, now known as The University of North Alabama, commonly called UNA. The college was located in north Florence about five miles from our house. In October of that year, I was diagnosed with scarlet fever and our house was quarantined. Again, I missed a lot of school and ended up with grades that were nothing great, but at least they were passing.

In the spring of 1955, I met Carl Lambert, a structural engineer from Nashville, Tennessee, in the Lion's Den at UNA. The Lion's Den was a decent size room in the basement of the girl's dorm that contained a jukebox where the students would socialize and dance. After we had talked for some time, Carl asked several of us if we would like to drive over to Sheffield and get a drink. I had not had a drink of alcohol since I was a little boy and lived with Papa.

The Saturday night before, I had gone to a dance and one of the chaperones told Mother and Daddy that I was drinking at the dance. I tried without success to get them to believe me that I didn't drink. When Carl asked me to go get a drink, I said ok because I had decided if I was going to be accused of drinking, I might as well do it. So, off we went. Believe me, bourbon and Coke tastes awful, so I only took a few sips.

Carl had a small apartment very close to the school and had recently taken a job with the N.S. Hatcher Company and Tri-Cities Construction Company with offices in Sheffield, a short distance from the school. Mr. Hatcher hired Carl, an engineer from Englert Engineering Company in Nashville, to open and operate a steel fabrication company in the fast-growing city of Huntsville, Alabama. Huntsville was growing at a rapid rate due to the space program led by Wernher von Braun and his group of German scientists who had come to Redstone Arsenal after World War II. The area was booming with construction of houses, office buildings and shops. Scientists, engineers and other highly paid personnel were coming to Huntsville from all over the world. Hotels, motels, boarding houses, and restaurants were full. Houses and lots were sold as quick as a sign was put in the dirt.

Mr. Hatcher gave me a summer job working in Huntsville. Mother was not in favor, even if only for the summer. I had $25. Carl loaned me $30 and we drove to Huntsville. Upon arrival in Huntsville, we began to search for a place to stay and finally rented a room sharing the bath with eleven other men.

That job is how I met Eloise. Eloise's daddy had a construction business. Carl and I just didn't know anybody in town, but we began to meet a few people here and there. We were building a building where Shelby Contractors is now located on Church Street. I needed some fill dirt so I called and got S.O. (Shelby Odell) McDonald, to haul the fill dirt for us. The short of it is, I got a date with Beverly Lanza and we soon got married. Beverly and I divorced shortly after a year of marriage. I'd been divorced six years when I found out Eloise had gotten a divorce, too. Eloise and I ended up dating the very night I found out she was single again. Of course, she had two children by then, boys, Trey and Michael. We've been married 54 years this November [2018]. I guess that speaks volumes for my luck in landing such a fine woman.

"I called it my technicolor car since the motor burned oil."

William (Bill) Self Propst, Sr.

AN EXCERPT FROM THE MEMOIRS OF
William (Bill) Self Propst, Sr.
1955-1956

At Huntsville Steel Company, we soon had the roof and siding installed, doors hung, concrete floors poured and equipment set. Mr. Wells, an electrician who wanted to open his own business, called on us and requested us to permit him to give us a quotation on wiring the fabrication building. His price was low and his references were very good, so we gave him the contract.

Carl hired several people with fabrication experience. As it turned out, we were very lucky with the group of new hires since we became good friends with some of them and they introduced us to members of their families who were well-known and respected business people in the community. Those acquaintances later helped us tremendously through introductions and recommendations.

The company's first job was to fabricate some very heavy trusses for a skating rink owned by Rossi Smith located at Governors Drive and the soon-to-be-opened Memorial Parkway. When the job was completed, it just happened to coincide with the start of the fall quarter at Auburn University.

I had saved enough money to buy my first car, a 1951 Ford

convertible, for only $185. I called it my technicolor car since the motor burned oil. When the car was first started the smoke would rise up through the floorboard, and as it caught the sun's rays, you could see different colors like a rainbow. In any event, I had a car, and that was more than the majority of Auburn students had at that time.

Things didn't go very well for me at Auburn for a number of reasons. I was too immature to handle my new freedom and my primary interest was in having a good time. When you put both of those factors together and accentuate it with a number of exceptionally good-looking girls, you can understand my plight. The situation was not helped by the serious shortage of funds. It didn't take long for me to spend the small amount of money I had left after I paid for the car. Mother and Daddy were giving me an allowance of $2 a week, which at that time was not enough money to buy even an occasional hamburger and a Coke, much less to be able to take a date to the movies. Due to the shortage of funds, I spent most of my weekends driving to Huntsville on Friday nights to work for Huntsville Steel Company. When they had work for me, I'd work both Saturday and Sunday. With the money earned on the weekends, I was able to squeak by.

Late one Friday night, I was driving to Huntsville in my Ford convertible when there came a torrential rain that was blowing straight into my windshield. Water began to pour into the car and onto my lap from the loose connection and seal between the windshield and the convertible top. I made up my mind right then and there that I would trade that car the next day, if I could. I quickly came to the realization that if I traded cars, it would be necessary for me to quit school and go to work full time.

The following morning, I was driving down Holmes Street when I saw this beautiful 1954 maroon Super 88 Oldsmobile convertible with a white top and red and white leather upholstery. I didn't have any idea I would ever be able to trade for that car. I just wanted to look at it. About an hour later, Mr. Joyce, the salesman who had sold me my first car, and the father of one of my good friends, made the financing arrangements for me. We completed the trade and I drove off in a real classy car.

A couple of weeks later during final exams I received a call that Nina, my grandmother, had died so I drove to Birmingham to the funeral. That night I was at the funeral home sitting close to the door when a man and a boy came in and were greeted by a number of his old friends and family members. The man had his back to me, but all at once, he turned, stuck out his hand and said, "Hello William." That was the first time I had seen my biological father, Mike Trippi, since I was five or six years old.

The next day, after the funeral, some members of the family were invited to Uncle Mimi's house. I was getting ready to leave when Mike asked, "Can I see you for just a minute?" We went into one of the bedrooms and talked for just a few minutes. He told me he was sorry things had been as they had in the past. He then reached into his pocket and pulled out a large roll of money and began to peel off several large bills. He handed them to me saying he knew how it was when you are going to college, and he just wanted to help. I looked at the money for a few seconds as many things ran through my mind: how much I needed the money, reflection of the past, Mother and Daddy's efforts, and their feelings. I handed the money back to Mike and told him to take that money and do something for his other four children that he hadn't done for me. I then turned, went back into the living room, said goodbye to everyone and drove back to Auburn.

Some of my instructors did not believe my grandmother had died even though I showed them the obituary, because the article was for Trippi and not Propst. The ROTC instructor was more to the point, "You weren't here for the exam so you fail." I guess it didn't matter to me because I knew I wasn't going back to Auburn anyway.

The following Monday, I became a full-time employee of Huntsville Steel Company. Carl and I had our work cut out for us. Most of the local contractors had learned that the N.S. Hatcher Company and Tri-cities Construction Company - competitors of theirs - owned Huntsville Steel Company, and therefore they were reluctant to purchase anything from us.

During the time I had been away at Auburn, there had been a turnover in the shop personnel at Huntsville Steel. While the majority of this new group were extremely well-qualified as far as the quality of their finished work, welding, and fabricating, but they were seriously lacking in work ethic and an understanding of the necessity of completing a job on schedule as promised. Most had worked in a much more relaxed atmosphere and they just could not grasp the fact that a commitment to a contractor for delivery on a certain day must be kept.

Contractors normally base the work schedule of their employees, and other subcontractors, on their expectations of the promised delivery of materials and the completion of erection of the steel. Changes in the shop personnel were an absolute necessity. I was given the job of shop foreman, even with my limited experience and welding skills. I terminated the entire group over the next few weeks and hired a completely new crew.

A CHANCE TO MENTOR

In January 1956, a fellow by the name of Leo Brown came in the office and asked for a job. The secretary handed him an application, but he couldn't fill it out. He couldn't read or write but he did put his "X" on the form for his signature. We didn't hire him at that time or the next two or three times he applied. One morning he came in and for some reason the receptionist was not in the office at that time, so I spoke to him. He asked me for a job and once again, I turned him down. He then looked at me and really begged by saying, "Mister, I really need a job so I can feed my wife and daughter. I'll work for a dollar an hour." I felt sorry for him thinking anyone who would try as hard to get a job as he had, was as persistent as he was, and was willing to work for $1 an hour should at least be given a conditional opportunity. As it turned out, it was one of the best decisions I ever made in my young management life. Leo came to work and became one of the most, if not the most, dependable and productive employees who ever worked for us. We hired two other employees and we began to get out more fabricated steel each day than the eight men previously employed. Each day Leo and I would have a little school time. It wasn't long before Leo could write his name, read a little, and of all things, read a tape measure. After some time and a lot of studying, he could read and write pretty well.

JEFFERSON 6-1395

HUNTSVILLE STEEL COMPANY

Fabricators and Erectors of Structural Steel
Miscellaneous Steel   Ornamental Iron

BILL PROPST
SALES ENGINEER

800 CONCEPTION ST
HUNTSVILLE, ALABAMA

First job and office building, 1955.

Eloise McDonald Propst, 1955, Senior Portrait.

"Just leave my pantry alone."

Eloise McDonald Propst

The Personal Narrative of
Eloise McDonald Propst

I grew up here, went to Butler [High School] and then I went to Auburn for just a few months. When I came home, I went to North Alabama College of Commerce. It was a business school. That was it, high school and a degree at the College of Commerce. After that, I worked for the government for 10 years in sales as a buyer's assistant.

After I quit work, I helped Bill in the drugstore for a while. I never liked it, but I did it. I'd work in the post office or on the floor. I did that for a while at the store on the corner of Whitesburg and Airport.

THINGS WE LIKE TO DO

I went to the farm with Emily [our daughter] just yesterday. I had just gotten home the day before, but Emily says, "You need to get out of the house." So, we went. We rode out there and had a good time. But, I came home and went right to the grocery store. I cooked some pork chops for us and corn on the cob and some Brussels sprouts and a salad. That's how we all spend time together, eating dinner. We'll eat here or at one of the kids' houses.

Bill and I like to go to the beach. Although Bill isn't a beach person, we still have fun. He reads and watches TV. I go out on the beach to read and lay under an umbrella. Our little trips like that are special to us. Bill used to like to cook some on the grill. When we go to the beach, for no reason, he'll make a pot of spaghetti sauce. He never cooks here anymore. But he used to when we lived in Michigan. He'd come home at 5 o' clock and cook on the grill. I'd say, "What are you doing that for?" "I'm just going to make it and put it in the freezer then we'll have it for whoever comes." He likes to do that.

When we moved to Michigan, I didn't like it because I had never lived away. It was so different, so busy. When we first moved up there, we lived in Bloomfield Hills, the Troy area. Bill's office was downtown, probably 30 or 40 minutes from where we lived. I just never went downtown, because I never adjusted to the traffic.

Otherwise, I adjusted just fine, as long as the kids were home and they had activities. Bill traveled all the time, leaving on Sundays and coming home on Fridays, but I was fine at home with the kids. Once they started graduating high school and leaving, I was ready to come home, and Bill was too. It was kind of a mistake, as far as we're both concerned, moving to Detroit knowing we were going to move back to Huntsville. Our families were here, so this was always home. It was not the right attitude to have about moving and it wasn't fair to Michigan. We made the decision to move and it turned out to be a good move for us. It made us depend on each other; it made us closer, the kids closer. It wasn't all bad.

When we first moved, we lived in a really nice neighborhood, Bloomfield Hills, but the kids there were not well-disciplined. That's what made Bill say, "Let's move out to the country." So we did. We moved to one house just to get to the country, but we didn't like it so much. Eventually, we found a place on a piece of land that had once been a nursery.

The house wasn't finished when we had to move into it. The house where we were staying temporarily was sold causing us to move out of it and into the new house before it was even ready.

Bill moved us in on a Sunday, working late to get us all moved in, and flew out that night and was gone for two weeks, leaving the piano right where he left it, in the kitchen. And there was no covering on the floors yet either. Now, I can look back and I can laugh about it, but then it wasn't funny. We've done some crazy things, but we lived through them.

Once we moved out to the country, things improved. We had a garden and I worked in the yard a lot, but not like I did here once we came back. The winters there were so long.

When Bill first went to Kmart and started opening the stores, you talking about work – he worked. I can't remember how many he opened, but to open as many as he did and to do it as quickly as he did, he was on the go, from one place to another.

Besides being a hard worker, he's the most caring and giving person I've ever known. I've never known somebody that is so generous. When we go out to eat and he sees somebody we know, he's just got to buy their dinner. He loves doing that.

Bill just isn't happy unless he's creating something. I think it has been tough on him since he sold Qualitest and Vintage. But I tell him, "Honey, you don't need to go back into a big business. You just turned 81."

I'm glad he has Propst Properties though. If he didn't go to the office, if he just stayed home, he would be miserable. He just couldn't do it. Besides that, the reason I'm glad he has an office to go to, he'd be organizing things in my kitchen if he was home. When we had a drugstore, he was so used to things being perfect. I mean, the soup cans had to be in the pantry in alphabetical order. The big sizes had to be here and the little ones there - like how he had to do things at the store. And I finally said, "Just leave my pantry alone." It's funny.

Looking back, sure, the kids had their problems, fights and whatever, but they were always fairly close. We never had any big problems between them. We always tried to instill family and love.

Bill and I had a great life. We had our ups and downs, nothing bad, but every couple has ups and downs. It was hard on me, with him traveling so much, and I know it was hard on him as he was always so glad to get home and to see the kids. Bill was never selfish. Never. What he did, he was doing for us.

The Personal Narrative of
Mary Lynne Wright
Niece

My mother was Doris McDonald Baker and her sister is Eloise McDonald Propst. I call her Aunt Pete though, someone nicknamed her that growing up. I'm a native of Huntsville, born at Huntsville Hospital. I went off to nursing school at Samford University, finished, came back and started my career with Huntsville Hospital at just 19 years of age. I've been there ever since. This June completes my 41st year. The last seven has been as president of Madison Hospital. Uncle Bill likes to kid me that I just work part-time. Don't tell him but I like it when he kids me.

Aunt Pete is the only aunt I have left from my mom's side, so she and Uncle Bill have become my family "glue." This sounds really bizarre, but when your parents both die, you feel like an orphan, regardless of your age. For me, because I have Aunt Pete and Uncle Bill I don't quite feel that way. I know they're there for me. I could call them about anything and they would be there for me. When my dad got sick with cancer, I just walked in the house and said, "I need to talk." That's just the relationship we have. It's pretty special.

Aunt Pete is so strong and passionate. She has a heart that just amazes me. It's a heart for people and for life. She's been in pain since her cancer surgery but she handles it with such dignity and grace. She has always been one of those people I've looked at with admiration.

I spent time with them when she came home from her surgery. One night, Uncle Bill and I stayed up and watched westerns together. John Wayne westerns, "The Virginian" and "The High Chaparral." That's my Uncle Bill, the uncle that most people don't know, the one I get to spend time with. I cherish every moment with them. I don't like to go for more than a week without seeing them. When I come to Huntsville during the week on Tuesdays, I'll ask Aunt Pete, "Are you home? Can I come by? Can I come get a hug?" It's harder for me to see Uncle Bill because he also works during the day, so I'll text him. He's notorious for not texting back, so I'll get his attention with, "This is your favorite niece," and he's like, "What do you want?" [laughing] He is just this remarkable human being. I have a tremendous amount of love and respect for both of them.

Back when Uncle Bill had part of his business in North Carolina, he would call my dad and say, "Will you go with me? We need to go do something on the line." I would get so tickled at him because they would drive to Birmingham to get better fares. Once there, my dad told us they never stopped; they would start working from the minute they hit the ground. That was his work ethic. That was the way he set examples for people, that it's not all handed to you. Another example of that, I asked him once what he was doing driving a Honda. He said, "It gets really good gas mileage." I thought, okay, that's why he is where he is.

When they lived in Michigan, my dad would fly up to help them trim the Christmas trees on their farm. It would be just the two of them and Bill, Jr. trimming trees in the heat of the summer, with the snakes and whatever. He didn't hire someone to do it; he did it himself. That's just who he is. Nobody handed him anything. He literally created it all on his own. That's his legacy, really. When you work hard, you're ethical, you have morals, you believe in doing the right things for the right reasons, that's how you become successful and that's how you raise four really great kids.

I remember when we were just kids, on Christmas day and Thanksgiving day, Uncle Bill would go to the drugstore. But, he always made time for his family too. He would come home, eat lunch, visit or whatever and then he would go back to the store. That's how you become successful; that's how your customers know you care about them, and that's how you get loyalty from them and your workers.

One of the funniest things I remember was when I was 8 or 9 years old. They had just gotten married. We'd go over to their house and he would grill steaks for us. Well, I happened to like ketchup, so Uncle Bill explained that you don't eat ketchup on a t-bone steak. It was so funny. He did it in this mannerism that would make you think, "Oh, my gosh." So, never again to this day have I had ketchup on a steak. I was like, "Okay, Uncle Bill, I promise. I'll never do that again." [laughing]

He's been out of the pharmaceutical business for a while, but he is still so concerned with our country and what is happening. To sit and listen to him talk about the acquisitions and mergers of major companies, what each is going to do to us in the future and how we will respond to that when it comes to healthcare costs…. It's just so fascinating to listen to him because he thinks about things so differently.

I have watched him work really hard and do great things for our community. But one of the things I remember most is the love he had for my grandmother. Mother Mac is what we called her. Mary McDonald was her name, I'm named after her. At one point, he lived with her for a while. I remember him being so respectful of her and so kind, generous and loving. Same thing with my Aunt Ann. When she got breast cancer, they lived in Bay Springs, Mississippi. Uncle Bill basically brought her here to make sure she got the best healthcare. She lived with them for a while here in their house and they just took incredibly good care of her. At her funeral, Uncle Bill was going to give her eulogy. He got up to do it, but he couldn't because he was so emotional. I remember how bad he felt about that but I was sitting there thinking about how much he cared and that he was so compassionate. That is the kind of man he is. He is real. There's not a fake bone in that man's body.

The Personal Narrative of
Bonnie McDonald Wilson
Sister-in-law

I've been part of the family since I was 18 years old when I married Eloise's brother, Jimmy. It's kind of hard to know where to start. I first met Bill when he was working at Walgreens in Parkway City Mall. I went to get medicine for Michael, Eloise's youngest at the time. Jimmy and I lived next door to Eloise when we first married, so we helped her out when we could. I remember rocking Trey, her oldest, while he rubbed my ear to go to sleep. That was all before she ever married Bill, maybe 1963. Eloise never dated anyone after she got a divorce, other than Bill. She had little kids, so she worked and then went home, out on Winchester Road. She didn't have a decent car, so we would pick her up and take her to work. Jimmy and I were just kids then, nineteen. We had a good time together.

Later on, we all went to Florida a lot. We would stay at the Casa Loma Fiesta in Panama City and pile everybody in one room with a kitchenette. Bill was always digging in his pockets, getting money for the kids and stuff. It finally got to be a joke. He didn't have any money back then, but he always wanted to pay for everything. So we started saying, "Let Bill pay for it." We were trying to break him, but it never worked.

When Bill first moved back to Huntsville to start Qualitest, I was going there and entering drug orders for him after I'd get off work, from 5:30 to 10:30 or 11 p.m. I would enter the orders that he had gotten during the day. There was just him, one other guy that pulled the drugs to ship, Paul Higdon, and a bookkeeper in the very beginning. I was just there to help him get started because Eloise was still in Michigan with Bill, Jr. who was still in high school. I probably did it six or eight months, or maybe a year. It was just a little building out there off of Jordan Road... a little metal building. It's still there.

When Jimmy was diagnosed with ALS, Bill found a position for my son-in-law, Paul Harper, and moved him and my daughter here so she could be with her daddy. He's been very good to all of us, especially Eloise's mother, my mother-in-law. He was real good to her, too. He took very good care of her, and he took good care of me while Jimmy was sick. Jimmy couldn't handle the smell of food being cooked once he was on a respirator. It was suffocating to him, so I didn't cook. Bill was concerned I was getting too skinny so he brought me food every Sunday for the remainder of Jimmy's life.

One of the most special things, I think the most welcomed I ever felt in my life, was when they would all get so excited when we would come to visit. When they lived on the Christmas tree farm, they lived way down this dirt road. When we got into town we headed straight there. Just as we're turning onto their road we found them all right there sitting at the end of that road, waiting on us. The whole family was just sitting out there waiting on us. I can't tell you what that meant to Jimmy and me. They're all very special to me.

Two months, with Grandmother Self.

With Nona, the Maid

With Grandmother Self and brother, Michael

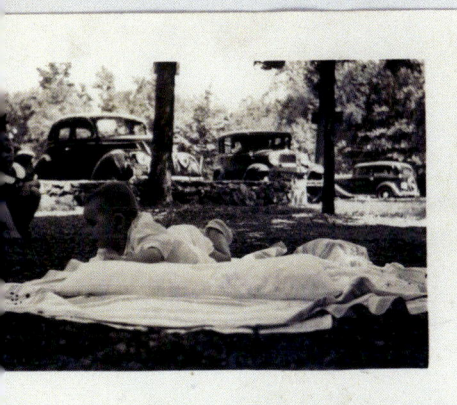

Four months (Brother, Michael, in background)

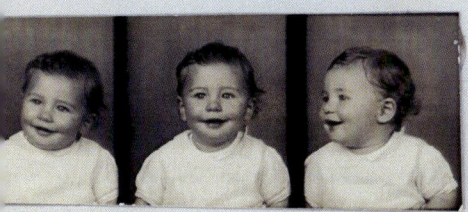

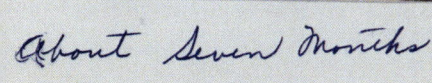

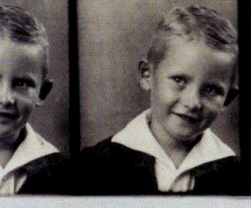

Four Months

About Seven Months

Brother Michael, 4 yrs., William five months

Bill Propst, Brilliant Junior High School.

"I turned in my notice."

Eloise McDonald Lanza (Propst)

AN EXCERPT FROM THE MEMOIRS OF

William (Bill) Self Propst, Sr.
1964

One Sunday afternoon, Luther Latham, my partner in the first Propst Drugs store called and asked if I would get a date and go to dinner that night with him and his wife, Joanne. I started calling the ladies I knew trying to get a date, but every one I called either had a date, had other plans, or was out of town. I was on the phone when Martha Jo Steele, Beverly's cousin, came in the store to get a prescription filled. Since I was on the phone, I asked her if she could wait just a minute. When I hung up, I apologized for keeping her waiting and I explained my plight. She told me that Eloise had just gotten a divorce and suggested I call her. I told her I didn't think Eloise would go out with me, but Martha Jo was sure she would.

I called Eloise and she said she would love to go, so the four of us went to the Mount Charron Country Club for dinner. The first time I went to Eloise's house, while I was waiting for her, Michael, who was just 18 months old, came into the den, climbed up in my lap and put one foot on either side of me. He just sat and looked at me. Both of her boys were very smart and well-mannered, and they grew up to be fine men.

During that evening, Luther asked us to go to a party with them the next night. We both agreed. That second night, someone else invited us to another party the following night. From that night on, things began to get serious. A few weeks later, we were at the house of Eloise's sister, Ann, when Ann asked me when we were going to get married. I simply answered, "When she quits work." We left Ann's and were driving down Governors Drive on the way back to Eloise's car when she asked me what I meant by the statement I had made. I simply said, "Just what I said."

The next day around eleven o'clock Eloise came into the store, walked in to the prescription department and said, "Guess what I did today?" I replied, "I don't have a clue." She said, "I turned in my notice." I knew from the onset if Eloise and I got married, I would not only be getting a wife but also two young children, Charles (Trey) who was five years old and Michael who was 18 months old.

I called Mother and Daddy and told them Eloise and I had decided to get married. Mother, of course, objected strenuously. Part of Mother's concerns was our former relationships and the possible difficulties we could face in the future because of them. I'm sure part of her concerns was the obligations being assumed with two children. Daddy didn't have much to say that night. The next day, he went to see the Bishop regarding him conducting the ceremony. That afternoon, Daddy called and told me he would be there to perform the ceremony. A couple of weeks later on November 19, 1964, we were married at the home of Ann and her husband, Jerome.

Jerome owned WNDA, a radio station in Huntsville. He gave us round-trip tickets on Southern Airways to New Orleans. Jerome had previously scheduled a meeting for the very next day at the Southern Airways office in New Orleans.

The last flight he could take from Huntsville after the wedding, and still get there on time, required him to travel on our same flight. So, Jerome and I had an agreement that after we boarded, from that point on we didn't know him and he didn't know us.

Shortly after takeoff, the stewardess announced over the P.A. system that it was Southern Airways' custom to welcome, congratulate and toast newly married couples and this afternoon they would like to recognize Bill and Eloise Propst. Needless to say, Jerome also rode from the airport to the city with us.

The next night, we decided to go to the French Quarter. Guess who was the first person we saw? None other than Jerome. We had a very good time visiting all of the joints and a coffee house. The next day Eloise and I went shopping at Maison Blanche, one of the major department stores in the country. I don't know why we went because we only had $160 when we left Huntsville. In any event, as we came back through the lobby of the hotel, I saw a poster advertising Joey E. Bishop, a comedian. I asked Eloise if she would like to go see him. Naturally, the answer was yes.

As we approached the maitre d', he greeted us with a French accent saying, "rezer-vay-cee-ooon?" I said, "No, just two." He knew then that "country" had come to town. He seated us next to the kitchen, even though the restaurant never got busy and there were quite a few tables that were never occupied. Every time the waiters went in and out of the kitchen, the swinging doors would almost hit the back of my chair.

We ordered a drink and then the waiter wanted to know if we were ready to place our order. Eloise ordered a steak and then the waiter asked, "Potato? Butter? Sour cream? Chives? Bacon? Salad? Roquefort?" She said yes, and I ordered the same thing. What I didn't know was that everything was a' la carte. Neither of us had ever seen an a' la carte menu before. While I had enough to pay the check, it was much more than I was accustomed to paying back home.

The next morning, I called the office to see how things were going. When I asked my bookkeeper, Vi, to read the reports she began to tell me not to worry, just have a good time. Finally I said, "Vi, read the damn report." Everything was fine at the Pearsall store but at the Dunnavant's Mall store, a bicycle had been received from our toy supplier, removed from the store, but no charge ticket written. The next item was the $300 shortage at the register in the prescription department.

I called the airport and we flew home. When I arrived at the store and asked Jack, the pharmacist, about the two items, he simply said, "I was going to quit anyway," and walked out the door. Now here I am, just married and having to open and close a store working from 8 a.m. to 10 p.m. Monday through Saturday and 1 p.m. to 6 p.m. on Sunday.

Bill Propst with mother, Margaret, and George Harold.

Margaret Propst, age 35, 1950.

The Personal Narrative of
Emily Reiney
The only daughter of
William (Bill) Self Propst, Sr.

Equestrian & Culinary Artist

My dad is a traditional man, a very timely person. He's always early, never a minute late. He's always starched and pretty formal. I love that about my dad. My dad's pants could stand up in the corner. His shoes are always polished. Even on Saturdays, he'll have on starched khakis and a button down shirt. It seems weird to see him when he's not wearing a suit. Occasionally, in the heat of the summer, he'll wear starched shorts. Then on Sundays, for church, he's back in a suit. That's just the way he is.

Sometimes it makes us all laugh. We went on a family trip to Turks and Caicos a couple of years ago. We took all the kids. We told dad before we left that he needed a white shirt and khaki shorts because we're going to have pictures taken on the beach. We get there and he didn't bring anything to wear. So we sent the concierge guy out on a mission to buy my dad a shirt. He comes back with this linen shirt with these gold swirls all over it. It looked Middle Eastern; nothing my dad would ever wear in his life. But he did. We get down to the beach and he's got on his gold shirt and his black dress shoes. We all tell him, "Dad, everybody is bare foot. You need to take off your shoes." He would not take off his shoes. He just wasn't going to do it. So, we take the pictures.

And, there he is. We're all barefoot and tan and he's stark white with a gold shirt and black dress shoes. [laughing] We photo shopped Bill, Jr.'s feet and put them on my dad. It helped him to fit in to the picture.

As formal as he can be, he's always been very nurturing. When we were kids, he'd crawl in bed with us and snuggle; he's always been loving. In Michigan, we lived about 45 minutes to an hour from where he worked and where I went to high school. We drove in every morning together. Some days we had to get there as early as 5:30 a.m. Typically, we'd have to leave at 5 or 6 o'clock in the morning. At the end of the day, I would wait for him to get off work at 5, 6 or 7 o'clock at night and we would drive home. So we got lots of car-talk time through high school. Of course, there were some arguments in the car. But most of the time, we made the most of our trips. We'd stop and get hot bagels on the way home. We'd eat bagels and talk. He always enjoyed being with us kids, always.

For sure, my dad has mellowed a lot. He used to be a bit of a hot head, real determined. And he has always been a dreamer. Always. It wasn't that he was striving to be somebody. It wasn't about money. It was about building something. He and I are a lot alike. For me, it's showing horses and my love to cook. For him, he liked having something that he could step away from and see progress. He thinks a line running pharmaceutical products is a beautiful thing - because it's progress. He loves that. It drives him.

Of course, there were times our family wasn't in the best financial situation. Like I said, my dad was always that dreamer. He always wanted to have his own business, and you know, financially, there were lots of hard times that came with that. My parents were just trying to make it. I can remember going to the grocery store with my dad. My dad was the grocery shopper of the family. He was so good at it. It was like his little drugstore. Because we lived in Michigan, if it snowed real bad, you had to keep lots of food in the house. So he would take inventory of what he had in the pantry before going to the store. We were a family of six so we'd usually end up with four carts of groceries. We were just a normal family trying to get by. I know there are some people that can't make a meal at home because they don't have anything. I'm not saying we were in that kind of situation. We were definitely fortunate. We were always able to throw something together and eat as a family. And, that we did, every night. It didn't matter if somebody had baseball practice, or whatever. We waited to eat as a family. Even if it was 9 o'clock at night, we waited 'til everyone got home and sat down. Except for rare occasions, we ate together, all six of us. That was our family time.

DAD MADE US WORK

Just like any normal family, Dad made us work. We chopped wood and cut the grass. We all had chores. I had to empty the dishwasher and set the table. Dad has always had an incredible work ethic so that's one of his biggest worries about his grandkids. They have to have a work ethic. There's no silver spoon here. They have to work. They have to earn a living, you know? Thankfully, all of our kids are on a good path, educated and not on drugs.

DAD'S ONE BIG SPLURGE

Dad has never splurged on anything except his plane. That has been the biggest gift to my family these past five or six years. It has allowed our parents to keep going and doing. He's also donated it for friends who have needed to travel to the Mayo Clinic. It's been a wonderful thing. Now, he's on 'GO' all the time. I think it would have aged them far more quickly had they not had it these past few years. We don't use it just because we want to. You know what I mean? It's not like that. It is his plane, so we don't go anywhere on it unless he's on it. He reminds you quite frequently how much jet fuel costs. It's a well-controlled splurge that's been a real gift to the family.

MENTORING HIS GRANDCHILDREN

Dad mentors my children, my son in particular. They talk all the time. My son calls him at least once a week. He's had all the boys up here to learn the real estate business with John (Hughey) and other things like that. My dad just takes a real interest in all the kids. Even if it's just texting, "What did you have for dinner the other night?" "What kind of classes are you taking?" My son sends him his papers and my dad reads them and kind of grades them and sends them back to him. He's a good egg. I'm very lucky. Sometimes I ask God, how did I get so lucky? I won the lottery with who God chose as my parents. When the time comes, I don't know what I'll ever do without him.

DESCRIPTIVE REFLECTIONS

Dad is strong. He's driven, generous, loving and caring about others. He really is all that, and I respect that a lot. He shares what he feels has been a gift to him.

THE PERSONAL NARRATIVE OF

(Charles Vincent) Trey Propst

THE OLDEST OF
WILLIAM (BILL) SELF PROPST, SR.'S CHILDREN

PHARMACIST & FORMER VICE PRESIDENT OF COMMERCIAL

QUALITEST & VINTAGE PHARMACEUTICALS

One of the first memories I have that I can really truly remember was the wedding at my aunt's house, my mom's sister, Anne Hughey. I remember being at the wedding and I think I may have met Dad's parents, my grandparents, for the first time. He's the only father I've ever known. Most people know that Dad is the only father I've ever known and that I consider him to be my father.

Shortly after they got married, we moved to Piedmont from Winchester Road. He had his drugstore over on Airport Road and Whitesburg Drive called Propst Drug. I remember going to the drugstore with my mother. He had a soda fountain, so we would eat lunch or ice cream or cherry sodas. He pretty much worked from 9 a.m. to 9 p.m. A lot of the times, the reason we went to the store, my mother was taking him the dinner that she had cooked. That was one of the main reasons we went down there. He worked a lot. I don't remember, as a kid, seeing him a lot. He was working retail, literally, open to close. That's just part of working retail. I mean, I did the same thing for years. When you have your own business, you have to work hard. It's part of it and Dad was definitely not afraid of hard work. I'd say in fact he's probably the hardest working person I've ever known. Some might say he's been lucky but, the truth of it is just as he's always said, the harder you work the luckier you get. I'm a pharmacist also, so I've worked retail too. I've owned my own store and done sort of the same thing.

THE HISTORY OF THE RETAIL SIDE OF THE PHARMACY BUSINESS

Well, I was pretty young when Dad started discounting at his stores, so I'm going based on what I've heard since. At that point in time, from what I've learned since I got out of pharmacy school and started practicing and seeing other independent pharmacies, Dad bucked the trend of how most independent pharmacists did business. He was very innovative and started discounting. And that developed his business and his philosophies.

Back in the old days, just like now, the pharmacists wanted to be paid for their services and all the education they had. Even when I started practicing and bought my store and began spending time with the older pharmacists, they didn't really want to concentrate on the drugstore and capitalize on the potential of the front end merchandise or the over-the-counter products, you know, the merchandising of the store. They wanted to fill prescriptions, and they wanted to make their money on the prescriptions. Dad saw the value in what he could do with the entirety of the store.

A lot of them had small apothecaries, in the old days, where they would fill 100 to 200 prescriptions a day, but their profit margins were pretty good. You could make a living and put your kids through school with a small apothecary filling 100 prescriptions a day because of the margins. They didn't discount prescriptions; they made good money on them. They didn't necessarily concentrate on the rest of the front end, so they would mark it up fairly high. They wouldn't even try to be competitive and discounting was not even heard of.

But in the old days, when Dad first started, you didn't really have the big discounters like Kmart. At that time, Kmart was much bigger than Walmart, but they weren't even in the south yet, just the north. Kmart was just starting to come to the south. There were various discounters, but they didn't discount pharmacy or health and beauty aids.

All you really had were independents. You had, say, Walgreens, or Super X and some of the old, old chains - a lot of the old-time pharmacies. They didn't really merchandise the front end. They didn't really concentrate on that. They would carry it, but they really weren't worried about having to be [priced] lower than Walmart. These days it's sort of the opposite. If you own a pharmacy, you better be able to merchandise properly and be able to compete with the Walgreens and the Walmarts.

Back in the old days, a lot of the pharmacists were content with having people come in to just get their prescriptions filled. Then they would go down the street to Walgreens or Walmart or Kmart and buy their Tylenol and their Listerine and their Crest toothpaste because the big-box stores and chains would sell those at a discount just to get people in the door. Basically, the discounters would create an image of a low price shop by having discount prices on certain items. However, as a rule, in the old days most of the pharmacies wouldn't do that. The independent drug stores didn't discount merchandise.

When Dad got in business, I think he saw that if he discounted, he could still make money. He saw that you didn't have to gouge or charge higher prices to make money. He had the vision that by creating a discount image, you get [more] people in the door and you do more overall business.

When he started discounting, I think there was a lot of resentment because it put so much pressure on the other pharmacies which had been able to enjoy a much higher profit margin. Some of the pharmacists complained to Walker Drug and they even cut him off at one point. I think it was frowned upon, even when I got into my store, because I discounted and I got a lot of heat for that. I had competition from every chain within two miles of me. All the customers had so many choices. I felt I had to compete and not give them a reason to go down the street.

DAD ON THE JOB

One thing there was never a question of throughout the time that I worked for Dad was that he believed in being straightforward and he believed in the employees being straightforward. I remember he was very adamant when we would get a new employee who had worked for someone else in the business, we would never use proprietary information or knowledge brought from another company for our benefit. He was very clear that we were never going to do that. There was never a time I felt that we ever crossed that line or ever did anything of that nature. He has always subscribed to high ethical and moral standards and to this day he still does. And he expects everyone around him to do the same.

He left Kmart in 1986. Qualitest was the business he started at Kmart. It was started as sort of a generic control label for Kmart. At that time, the generic business was sort of the Wild West. People were buying from different manufacturers. The drugstores and the Kmart stores were buying from different distributors and different brands. He wasn't sure if they all had liability insurance and if the quality was good.

So he started Qualitest as a way to, number one, really control the quality of the product; number two, make sure all the vendors had liability insurance; and number three, he really believed that if you got a generic for a product at one Kmart it should be the exact same product you would get in another Kmart. From a control and consistency standpoint and even from the standpoint of being able to get supply, he was trying to bring it all together under one label. If it was a yellow round tablet, that's what it would be no matter what store you were at. Bringing that together was a great idea. It needed to be done. He was really sharp in doing that. Very few people had done that at that time.

Dad asked me to move back and help in the [Qualitest] business. When I started, they only had approximately 20 employees. It was sort of like having my own store again because we were working from six in the morning to nine at night, all the time. We had to do a little bit of everything because there was not a lot of help. The business was really exploding and growing. It was doing real well. It was fun.

One of the greatest lessons I learned from Dad is that in business, you don't have to give in to everything and you don't always have to win. It's not "business at all costs or any cost." You don't always have to say yes. Because many times, I would think, "Why aren't we doing this deal" or "Why wouldn't we do something?" There's no reason to do a bad deal at any cost because we walked away from a lot and still did very well.

One thing Dad always preached was that the customer has to do well but the suppliers also have to do well and have to be kept healthy. If it's not a good deal for everybody, then it's not a good deal. You want to pay your employees, suppliers and contractors. They need to make a good living and have an incentive to come to work. He lived by that. He wanted people to enjoy a good living and make money. He wasn't trying to necessarily do what would have been the most profitable. He believed everyone should be able to make a living and he wanted to allow as many people as he could to enjoy that.

DESCRIPTIVE REFLECTIONS

Dad is humble, gracious and extremely competitive. I really see Dad doing nothing different going forward. I think he's always trying to build and grow. And, I really see him doing nothing different. He really loves the challenge of running a business. I think he'll do that forever. He'll do just what he's doing right now. I don't think he'll ever change. He's never going to retire. I can't ever see that happening.

The Personal Narrative of
Mike Propst
The Second Oldest of William (Bill) Self Propst, Sr.'s Children

Retired (Maybe)
Former Partner
McDonald Brothers Commercial Construction

When I was young, Dad worked all the time. He wasn't around that much. He worked in the store from 9 to 9, six days a week and usually on Sunday, too. When we moved to Michigan, that was probably the first time that he was home and part of our lives all the time.

What I value most about my dad is that family is so important to him. We're a very close family, doing a lot of things together as a family. There are four siblings and a bunch of grandchildren; yet, we do a whole lot together. My mother comes from a family of six siblings. Her big thing has always been 'family' and staying close to everyone so that helped, too, that she was very focused on the family being close.

Dad doesn't ever want any recognition or attention for the things he does. He called me one day and said, "We've got to go to the city council meeting."

"Okay, what for?"

"Be there at…" You know, this time, this date.

"Okay."

I went in and I learned that he had given money for the renovation of the civic center [Von Braun Center in Huntsville]. Someone asked him how much he had given, and he would never say. Finally, the mayor did. But he didn't want anyone to know. He didn't want the recognition.

Same thing happened another day. He called and said, "We've got a meeting at Samford University," at this date, this time.

"Well, what's this about?"

I get down there and there's a building with his name on it. That's just the way he is. Years ago, he and my grandmother redid one of the pharmacy labs in honor of my uncle after he passed away.

They have heart disease in their family from a very young age. Uncle Michael had his first heart attack at age 40 or younger. He had three or four heart surgeries and died mid-40s or late 40s. Dad had his heart attack at 55. I think he had five bypasses. Quite honestly, I never thought we'd be looking to celebrate his 80th birthday. It's a double-edged sword, his heart condition and his diabetes. Unfortunately, they go together.

When he had his heart attack, he didn't go to the hospital until the next day. Basically, he walked the floor all night thinking he had indigestion. I think, at 6 o'clock the next morning, my mom had Charlie Warren come over and take him to the hospital. He lost a significant amount of his heart muscle. Even with all these challenges, Dad has worked hard and done well. He's done well because he's worked hard. No doubt about it. Nobody gave him anything. Everything he's got, he earned and he made.

I have people ask me at times, "Does it bother you that your father has given money for a civic center and things like that?" I say, "Absolutely not. It's his money to do with what he pleases." I'm just glad he can afford to do that. I'm happy for him and happy for the community.

He's done a great deal for the community. Those things that are public is all the public knows about. But he's done so much more. Like, he had a fella that worked for him when we lived in Huntsville, worked at the drugstores, made deliveries, and babysat my sister and me. You know, he was part of the family. We went to Michigan and came back, and he couldn't wait to work for Dad again. At that point, he was where he probably shouldn't be working, but Dad put him to work. He made deliveries, ran errands and got the mail, that kind of thing. As he got older, his driving was getting to the point he wasn't as safe as he should be. So, Dad said, "I'm going to have to retire you." I'm pretty sure that from the time he retired, to the day he died, he had a check every week. Dad is generous to a fault. Most people don't see that side of him.

MENTORING

He's had folks that have worked for him over the years that started when he first came to Huntsville. He's taken people that weren't college educated, no real skills, no career path and they have worked for him over the years. He's had people that have gone from working in shipping and receiving, to running departments and things of that nature. They basically learned the trade over time, and he's put his trust in them to do that. There have been a lot of cases like that. He doesn't give that opportunity to people who aren't earning it. He expects quality work.

Back when they were just starting, they would work six in the morning to midnight and be back at six the next morning. When he bought his plant at Charlotte, he would leave Sunday afternoon, go to Charlotte, work all week, and come in

Thursday night so he could be here to sign checks on Friday. Or he'd come in here Friday night and sign checks on Saturday, then he'd go back to Charlotte. He did that for a year, or longer.

You know, when I was growing up, he didn't have the money he has now. We were like everybody else, struggling to make ends meet. He taught me very young, you have to work hard and work smart to get ahead in life. I did some work for him for roughly one year. I built a building for him. It was the first of the pharmaceutical manufacturing buildings here in Huntsville. It was a liquids facility. I had my own construction company just for the year it took to build that building. Other than that, I was a partner with my uncle. S.O. McDonald, in his construction company, McDonald Brothers. He is my mother's brother. I worked with him since 1989. Last January, we decided to get out of the business and shut down. I don't know if I'm retired or unemployed. [laughing] I haven't decided yet.

You know, Dad wasn't ever afraid to take chances. At the time he made the move to Kmart, he could have stayed in Huntsville. He had three or four drugstores. We could have stayed in Huntsville. He could have had a good life and been successful; but instead, he decided to take the chance. He went to Kmart to basically put pharmacies in all of their stores and run that department. That was a big step, to go from Huntsville and a handful of stores to Kmart…huge step. He took a huge risk. He knew that for him to get to where he wanted to be, that's what he needed to do.

By the time he got the liquids facility and the pill plant here, he had the manufacturing plant in Charlotte, Vintage Pharmaceuticals. He couldn't force himself to close it. He said, "I can't close it at this point in time. I've got people who have spent their entire lives there."

FAMILY TIME

As a family, we do all these great trips now. It's really nice. For me, there were a lot of trips that they went on when I was working that I couldn't go on. That's why I haven't decided if I'm retired or unemployed. I wanted to be able to go somewhere if they decide to go somewhere.

DAD'S LEGACY

Treat people like you want to be treated. You have to work hard for what you want in life.

DESCRIPTIVE REFLECTIONS

I want people to know Dad for the great and generous person that he is.

The Personal Narrative of
William (Bill) Self Propst, Jr.
The Youngest of
William (Bill) Self Propst, Sr.'s Children

President Big Spring Entertainment

I've spent my entire career working with my dad. I never really wanted to do anything different. I actually started working for him on one of my college breaks over Christmas. He told me to come out to the warehouse because he needed some help, so I ended up working with him every summer through college. Of course, even as kids, we were always working. My brothers had a lawn service when they were in high school. I started out working with them. When they went to college, I inherited the lawn service. I was cutting 25 yards a week and making $600. In the 80s that was a lot of money, especially for a high school kid.

When my dad bought Qualitest [from Kmart], he spent a year in Alabama by himself. Mom and I stayed in Michigan so I could finish high school. We moved back to Huntsville just as soon as I graduated, and I went straight to Auburn. We're all back together now, living within a stone's throw of each other.

Stubborn, Strong Willed, Intimidating & Opinionated

My dad is who he is because of how he grew up. He and his mom were two peas in a pod. He'll say she was stubborn and strong-willed. Lord, they were just alike. My dad grew up with nothing, but he's always worked hard. He'd outwork anybody. His mom taught him that and he's always taught us that. That's definitely the one thing he instilled in all of us. You've got to work hard to earn what you get. Nothing's given to you. Two other things that were a priority for him, honesty and ethics.

Dad is a kind man. Most people think he's a bear, and he can be. Back in the day, he was intimidating. He is still intimidating to a lot of people. Just with his stature alone, he intimidates a lot of people. Sure, he can be rough and gruff at times, but at the end of the day, the people that really know him realize he's a teddy bear. One thing about my dad: you always know where he stands. He's not going to sugarcoat it. If you've done something wrong in his eyes, he's going to let you know.

HOLIDAYS WITH THE FAMILY

Our holidays have always been about getting the family together. For us, that meant a long car ride back to Alabama for Thanksgiving and Christmas, Mom and Dad, four kids and two dogs in a station wagon headed south. Now our tradition is a Christmas Day breakfast. We all go to Mom and Dad's house. I'm kind of in charge of bacon, sausage and eggs. Dad's in charge of country ham. My mom cooks biscuits with blackberry jam and grits. We're a pretty tight-knit group. My sister and I were real close growing up because we spent the most time together. Mike and Trey were grown up and gone.

DAD'S COMMITMENT TO HIS WORK & HIS FAMILY

Dad had a heart attack at 55 requiring five bypasses. It was his good friend, Dr. Charlie Warren, an OB/GYN, who took him to the hospital. The joke is that he is Dad's family doctor. There he was, having a heart attack at home and he didn't want to go to the doctor. That's his hard-headedness that he gets from his mother. He kept insisting, "I don't need to go to the doctor.

THE ONE CONSTANT

"Dad is the one constant I've always had. We work together. We socialize together. We travel together."

- Bill, Jr.

I'm fine." All the while he's having these chest pains and taking Lortab and Percocet.

So, the next morning he calls his OB/GYN friend who says, "We're going to the hospital." Dad refuses to call an ambulance. "Let me get up and get my shower, and get shaved and dressed." He puts on his dress slacks to go to the hospital. He just takes his merry time getting there.

This was back in the day when he's thinking about our drug business and all that he's got going on and what he needs to do. So he's calling people up to ICU, including his attorney, so he can create a will before surgery. He throws an absolute fit for a telephone, which was a no-no in ICU. Of course, he got his way. We all laugh about that. Here he is laid up in ICU and he's barking orders at everybody. It's just kind of who he is.

DAD'S COMPASSION

That story gives you some idea why I say there's no way Dad could retire. He doesn't have it within him to sit at home. I think he likes the routine of working. He loves people. He loves to socialize. He can talk to somebody for hours, a perfect stranger - and just converse on any level, on just about anything. At this point, he really likes the social interaction.

In our drug business days, he was always so compassionate, concerned about the well-being of his employees. He made sure we had the absolute best level of Blue Cross/Blue Shield health insurance, the kind that offered vision insurance too. We charged $5 a month for single coverage. For family coverage, we'd charge just $30 a month.

JOHN WAYNE

"Dad watches a fair amount of TV. He loves westerns. He'll say, "If John Wayne could just make a few more movies..."

He'll watch Fox News or CNN. He's conservative, but he's not unreasonable. He just shakes his head at things that go on in the world today."

- Bill, Jr.

My dad said, "I really don't want anyone to have to pay for insurance, but I want them to know it's not free." He made sure they had a 401K plan too, and he encouraged them to use it. He's always been concerned about the employees. By the time we sold out, we had 715 employees. We had a lot of super, super loyal people. If we called some of them today and told them we were going back into the business, they'd say, "When can I start?" Paul Higdon would be one of them. John Schultz too – super, super loyal.

FAMILY TIME & WORK TIME

Dad was probably a lot tougher on his kids than he was on anybody else. I think he expected more from us, which pushed us more and drove us more. It was never an 8 to 5 job. We'd get to work 6:30 or 7 o'clock and we might not go home until 7 o'clock that night. We all spent a lot of time on the road, a lot of time away from home. I personally spent a lot of time in Charlotte, and it was tough being away. I missed a lot of time with my kids. While we were spending time away from our own families, my Dad kept viewing it as, "Hey, we're spending time together." I think it's just in our blood. If we go on vacation somewhere, we talk about work. Work just never leaves you. We enjoy it.

WHAT MAKES DAD TICK

Dad likes to build things, whether that's building a company or physically building something. In the drug business the thing he used to like the most was the machinery. He liked the tablet machines and he loved packaging. He said, "I love taking a box of bottles and pouring it into a hopper and watching that hopper spin that bottle around and stand it up straight and put it on that conveyor belt. It comes down that conveyor belt and it stops at this machine and it fills up with tablets and puts cotton in, puts the cap on and puts the label on and it comes out in a box." He loved doing that.

WE ALWAYS HAD SUCH GREAT RESPECT FOR THEM

A really strange thing - I was more worried about Dad being happy about my house when I built it than I was if I was happy with what I built. I guess it paid off. He loves my house. I've told him that we could trade houses. My house would be so much easier for my parents to live in as they age than theirs would be. He hasn't taken me up on it.

It's funny how we always want to please our parents. When I was in high school and middle school, I was never worried about getting in trouble with the school. I was worried about getting in trouble at home, because the punishment at home was going to be ten times worse than my punishment at school. It wasn't about the spanking. It was more that the punishment was disappointing your parents, upsetting them, or worrying about them looking down on you. I guess it's because we always had such great respect for them. It's just what they instilled in us.

DAD WORRIES ABOUT US HAVING TOO MUCH

One thing we have done a lot of lately, that has taken a lot of time, is estate planning. My dad tells me it is really hard.

You work your entire life to accumulate wealth and when you get it, you work the rest of your life trying to give it away. He says he struggles with that, and that mentally, it's a tough thing. He worries about us having too much. He especially worries about his grandkids having too much. He says if they get everything they want right now, they don't have any appreciation for it. He wants them to go to school, go to college, get a job. He wants them to be good citizens in the community. If they can't do that, then he doesn't want to help them with any bad habits or bad behaviors. He's very, very mindful of that.

Of course, he says we're all spoiled, and we are. We are just beyond blessed in so many ways, it's unbelievable. But, I think for the most part, we're all very, very grounded. Are we spoiled? Yeah, we are. But it could be a lot worse. I'm not saying we deserve what we have. I'm just saying we've all worked hard.

THE CHRISTMAS TREE FARM

When Dad worked at Kmart, he always wanted to do better. He always wanted to provide more for his family. There were some things Kmart didn't afford him to do from a financial perspective. We lived on 40 acres, and 20 acres of it was by a corn field. He would say, "I can lease this to this farmer and get next to nothing for it so I'm going to plant some Christmas trees." He got this guy to plant these Christmas trees. For a while, we didn't do anything. We didn't know anything about Christmas trees. Christmas trees don't just grow in that shape. It takes work to get them there, every year. You have to spray pesticide because every spring they'd get these army worms. Then, every June, through the 4th of July, they had to be trimmed. Basically, you take a machete and go around the tree shaping it. Every single tree. The later you waited to trim that tree, the tougher that new growth would be. Everywhere that you'd cut a limb, it would sprout three to five more branches. It would make the tree fill in and get full. It never failed, by the 4th of July, when all my friends were at the lake, I'd be out trimming Christmas trees. It was a good lesson. The first or second year we sold Christmas trees, if we hadn't had the trees, we wouldn't have had Christmas.

A PERFECT EXAMPLE

I've always said no one ever knows if you have a dollar to your name or $100 million to your name. How much money you have shouldn't change the real person that you are. And I think my dad is a perfect example of that.

- Bill, Jr.

When we built our house on that land, we had to move into it before it was finished so we ended up with plywood floors, without any floor coverings, for two or three years. We always joked about it. When we first started out, we had this big wood-burning fire place with an insert in it. You could get this hot roaring fire going on that steel metal insert. It would heat up and keep the house warm, so we would fill the wheelbarrow with wood and wheel it straight into the house. We ended up putting that big wood-burning furnace down in our basement and tied it into the ductwork. We would burn something like forty cords of wood a year. Not only would we burn a bunch of firewood, we'd sell a bunch of firewood as well. We had some great times at that house.

DESCRIPTIVE REFLECTIONS

You know the thing I think describes dad the best is how he raised us. I think he's raised us well. He's taught us all that nothing comes easy, that nothing is free in life. (Becoming emotional as he reflects on life with his father, Bill, Jr. pauses before continuing): And, he has taught us to work hard.

Paul Propst, age 35, 1950.

William, age 7, with Bob Maxwell and neighborhood boys, 1945, Ensley, Ala.

The Personal Narrative of
Rebecca Taylor Larrowe
Lifelong Family Friend

I have known the Propsts a long time. I first met Bill in the late summer of 1963. He and my now-deceased husband, Herb Taylor, were best friends. They grew up together in Arab. Bill actually lived with Herb and his family for a little over a year when his dad, a Methodist minister, was transferred. My husband was a radio announcer in south Alabama. Bill came down there to visit one weekend, and I met him at the station. We were at their wedding and they were our first babysitters for our oldest son, so we could go to the laundromat. They weren't even married at that time.

There are so many stories I could tell after all these years. I always liked going to the grocery store with Bill. We took a weekend trip with them when they lived in Michigan and they built a house at Petoskey, Michigan. We flew there with our two boys, got in their car and drove with them to Petoskey. They were still furnishing the house. They didn't even have pillows. So we had pillows and lamps in this one station wagon with six children and four adults. That thing was full. That was well before seatbelts. We stopped at the grocery store and ended up holding bread and milk in our lap and a child, of course. We were like that for probably a couple of hours... in snow and ice. When Bill goes to the grocery store he doesn't get just one cart of groceries. If he needs one head of lettuce, he's going to buy three. Always. He just doesn't want to run out.

Being a preacher's kid, they're used to a lot of people being at the table. I think that's what Bill loves, to just sit around the table and talk. He's regimented. He goes to lunch at 11 a.m. every day. He wants to eat between 5 and 6 in the evening. But then he'll sit there and talk to you for hours after that. When we go on trips, when we get done with breakfast, [laughing] it's time for lunch.

Bill is so giving, kind and generous with everybody. I've watched him with friends who've had cancer. He'll go over to their house and take food. Boots [Ellet] who used to have the restaurant here [called Boots Restaurant] wasn't sick long. He had ALS. Bill and Eloise would go over there every Sunday. They'd take his wife, Joyce, some food. Breakfast or something.

He likes to hear about a need and meet that need, rather than so many people coming to him for money. When he finds out about a need that nobody asks him about, he loves and has joy in meeting that need.

DESCRIPTIVE REFLECTIONS

Bill is happy. He laughs. But he's serious. He's real loving and sentimental but doesn't want anybody to know that. I think he likes to keep that under cover. He'll push my husband's wheelchair when we go out to eat so I think he has the gift of helping. I really think he does.

THE PERSONAL NARRATIVE OF

Benny Nelson

BUSINESS ASSOCIATE, LONGTIME FRIEND AND
FREQUENT LUNCH PARTNER

I came to Huntsville in 1944. We lived just north of Drake [Avenue]. It was called Donegan Lane back then, which was just a one-lane road... where everybody went to park. I've known Bill for a long time. When he was in the drugstore business, I didn't know him very well. I just knew him socially from Boots, a local steak restaurant with a little sports bar on one side. It was kind of a gathering place after 5 o'clock. The owner, Boots, was one of Bill's really good buddies.

When Bill came back and built his facility here, I had a corrugated box plant so I sold packaging to him for his manufacturing plant. [laughing] He'd beat me down [on my prices]. I used to make some money, but I didn't make much after I dealt with Bill Propst (continuing to laugh).

We don't talk much business anymore, but you can sure learn a lot about someone not talking about business. What Propst and I do most of the time - is go eat. After all he's done, he's still just Bill. Once a week, we sit at the Furniture Factory and have two beers, Ultras because Bill is a diabetic. For lunches, we go to G's, Greenbrier or Walton's.

DESCRIPTIVE REFLECTIONS

He's very loyal. Very loyal. He's honest and hardworking. He doesn't like a lot of fanfare. He's a humble guy, but he's done a remarkable job here in Huntsville, especially considering the number of people he's employed. He's been involved in a lot. He's been in the steel business, drugstore business and of course, the business of discount drugs.

Bill's just as solid as you can get. He hasn't always had a lot of money. All that he did, he did on his own, going out on a limb several times.

He's pretty hard, too. Listen, when he had his business in North Carolina, he'd get up at four o'clock in the morning to catch a flight out of Nashville - five or six of them would go up there once a month, every month, for the weekend. They would drive to Nashville and take a flight over to North Carolina. To fly out of Huntsville would have cost him another $1,000, and he knew the value of the work it took to get that $1,000.

Bill really cares about people. They mean a lot to him. He doesn't like to be around a bunch of cussing and talking rough, locker room talk. He doesn't want to hear it. That's not his cup of tea.

He always tells the story from his youth about a big house that was in the area where he lived. He and his brother would walk by it every day. His brother would say, "One of these days, Bill, we're going to get something just like that. It's going to be a big house, with big columns." I imagine it looked a lot like the house he and Eloise live in now.

It makes you think, what if he hadn't ever gone back to school to get his pharmacy license?

THE PERSONAL NARRATIVE OF

Dr. Charlie F. Warren

LIFETIME FRIEND & DOCTOR OF
OBSTETRICS AND GYNECOLOGY

I moved here in 1965 from the Air Force. I think I was physician number 88. Now there are 700 or so physicians in this community. It's really grown. Bill had a drugstore on the corner of Whitesburg and Airport Road. That's how I initially met him. We would sometimes have a sandwich or something. He'll tell you that he always fed me because we were always eating sandwiches at his store. We've been friends ever since.

I would go to that drugstore and he would have toothpaste stacked almost to the ceiling. I asked him what he was going to do with all that toothpaste. If my memory serves me correctly, he'd sell three tubes for a dollar. He said, "That's my leader." You could tell he had the ability to market, not only to be a good pharmacist, but to market the other stuff in the drugstore.

Back in 1965, he was like the rest of us just trying to get started with limited funds. He could make it all work. You could tell that he was going to be more than the corner drugstore. He was going to expand his horizons. He was the kind of guy that you knew was going to be successful. Probably neither of us had the vision to be where we are today. You're young trying to get your career started and things were just different in the 60s. It was a different world as far as marketing. We didn't have these huge stores and chains. We had

CVS and Walgreens and similar [stores] back then, but they were not massive like they are now.

As he grew, he began to get other drugstores in the city and then he approached Kmart, which was moving to this area. He began to put drugstores in Kmart; they liked what he was doing and the return they were getting from the square footage that he required. He subsequently sold out, moved to Michigan and went to work for Kmart. He was there for a number of years. We stayed in touch. When he came to town, I'd see him and Eloise at Boots' restaurant.

I lived up on Covemont at the time of this particular story and there was a vacant lot for sale near me. Bill had tried to buy it and was not successful for some reason. I contacted the physician who owned the lot. I subsequently bought it. Bill sent me a check to pay for it, but I left it in my name for five or 10 years. He trusted me enough, I guess. So I always told my children if something happens to me, "that's Mr. Propst's lot." Subsequently, it was changed to his name.

I guess the one thing that binds us together is our confidence in each other. I had confidence that he was good at what he did and he had confidence that I was good at what I did. I don't know what else would make us better friends.

So, I've been through a lot of years with Bill. They've all been good. There's probably not a more kind-hearted fellow in the world than William Self Propst. He takes care of his employees. He takes care of his friends. He's just a very generous man. He's been through a lot, health-wise and otherwise. It never seems to stop him though. He just keeps going, even through his heart attack.

I was involved when that happened. As a matter of fact, that morning I was going to work in my pickup truck and Eloise called me and said, Bill's been up with some indigestion.

I went by to see him and I realized it was not indigestion, so I brought him to the hospital in my pickup. He ended up having some cardiac work done. He subsequently did well. He's had two or three other little episodes, but they don't keep him down. He just gets right back up and keeps going.

Another example of how tough he is, a few years ago he called me and said he thought he had a problem. He said, "Get me in to see somebody." I had been his

> **QUICK WITTED LUNCHES**
>
> To be at lunch with him is fun because we banter back-and-forth. He's super quick-witted. I've known several people like that, but I've never known anyone with quite the same ability to so quickly come back at you.
>
> - W.F. Sanders

doctor for years, but when he had that heart attack, I finally told him he needed a doctor better suited to his needs than an OB/GYN. So I called my friend who is a doctor and got him in. He called me back to say, "He has a ruptured appendix." Shocked, I said, "You're kidding."

I found out, after the surgery, that Bill's pain had started while he and some others were in Las Vegas. They caught the red-eye to Atlanta, flew all night, missed their flight to Huntsville, rented a car and drove to Huntsville, all with a ruptured appendix. That's how tough that dude is.

A lot of people retire when they get to be our age, or well before it, but they seem to be bored. I don't want to retire and be bored. I enjoy doing what I do. So Bill hasn't retired, W.F. [Sanders] hasn't retired and I haven't retired. I guess we're the hold-outs. I just think you have to do something meaningful or you get bored. I think it's more difficult to retire than it is to begin a career. It's hard to make that call, unless your health helps you make that call. Bill doesn't have the stamina he once had but he still works and under conditions in which a lot of people would retire.

He was kind enough on one of my birthdays recently to send all my family on his airplane to the Greenbrier in West Virginia. The plane stayed, the crew stayed and waited and then brought us home four or five days later. I thought that was really a great thing for him to do. I really appreciated it. That's royal treatment. It really is. But that's just the way he does things.

He gives turkeys and hams to people at the holidays. Even the nurses that work for me, he gives them a ham. We occasionally do things for him, too. I've delivered most of his grandchildren. So, I've known the family real well for all these years. They're all great people.

DESCRIPTIVE REFLECTIONS

He's kind. He's generous. He's a caring individual, a very considerate person. He'll do things very softly and quietly that you don't even think he's concerned about. I think that's a great quality. I think he's been a dear friend and a good influence on my life.

He's a real asset to the city, too, very generous. He doesn't carry his wealth on his shoulder. You'd never know he had any money. He sure doesn't brag about it or make it apparent otherwise.

He never forgets anything that he can tease me about. He never forgets anything. He always hammers me about something, which is okay. That's part of it, you know, we have fun. He just never forgets any little misadventure you've ever had.

Being a friend of his, watching him progress, watching him with his success, it's been a really great experience. Key to his success, I think, is his ability to communicate with people and to inspire them to do well. I think it is his generosity, too. Everyone who's ever worked for him has always complimented his generosity and his consideration for them, and for everyone in the organization. He's a good man. I don't want to make out like he's a saint, but I don't know of a more generous, considerate person than Bill Propst.

Most people don't know Bill as we all know him. He's an astute business man; he's also a very intelligent pharmacist and he knows medicine. He is a unique individual.

He doesn't make a big to-do about anything. He's just very quiet and gets it done. And that's enough said about that fella. I think that's good.

Papa Self, 1949.

Mama Self holding two month old William Trippi, 1949

William (7), with brother, Michael (9), and Mother, Margaret (27), 1942.

William, age 8, 1945, Lake Junaluska, NC.

ICONIC & UNFORGETTABLE

Professional Pursuits

William (Bill) Self Propst, Sr.

"Talk low, talk slow, and don't say too much."

John Wayne

A Preface

The Iconic & Unforgettable Professional Pursuits of

William (Bill) Self Propst, Sr.

Huntsville / Madison County's

Vanguard Business Leader

Not unlike the legendary star of his favorite old western movies, John Wayne, Bill Propst, Sr. is a man who says what he means and means what he says. As referenced earlier in this book, Bill Propst, Sr. is known by his family for saying, "John Wayne really should make a couple more movies." From that, it's an easy assumption to make that these old classics, and their star, resonate with Bill because of the sincerity of Wayne's no-nonsense approach to protecting and honoring a way of life he valued. Bill's approach has been similar.

In the pages that follow, you'll find illustrations of the five major categories, in chronological order, of Bill Propst, Sr.'s professional life. Bill's drive to make something of himself is quite evident from even his teenage years when his overachieving ways quickly found him co-owning a steel company. Learning early in life that sometimes the best of things happen after closing the door on one chapter in life for another, Bill sold his interest in his steel company while still a very young man. He then transitioned into the more typical path of a man in his early twenties: he returned to college to follow the family tradition of entrepreneurship in the field of pharmacy.

If Bill were a man who had finished college and just gone to work as a pharmacist, this book likely wouldn't even exist. As the reader is soon to learn, Bill is a man with drive and incredible stamina, a visionary who likes to build things, a goal setter who quickly creates plans to reach his goals and doesn't hesitate to put them into play.

Post pharmacy school for Bill Propst, Sr., quickly found him owning his first store, and then another and another. At one point, Bill owned and operated five stores in the city he had come to call home, Huntsville, Ala.

Being a natural marketer and businessman, Bill quickly appreciated the need to make his stores stand out from the others in town. Through a shrewd and concerted set of efforts, Bill did just that. Completely transforming all five of his stores into reliably well-stocked, discount pharmacy stores, and offering other services as well, Bill gave his customers a reason to prefer Propst Drugs.

Relationship-driven, Bill worked to maintain trusted friendships with his vendors as he continued to tweak his formula for a successful model of the discount pharmacy. Bill's well-intentioned efforts soon worked in his favor as the stars above lined up to present him with a little nugget of information that the wise and prudent Bill Propst would have the vision to turn into an opportunity. One of Bill's trusted vendors took him to lunch one day and revealed the reason why his own sales were suffering: a discount store called Kmart, known as "The Saving Place," had come to Florence Ala. As the sales rep revealed to Bill during that fateful lunch, this new store with a discount image was selling Maalox cheaper than he could purchase it wholesale.

As soon as their lunch bill was paid and the gentlemen went their separate ways, Bill drove directly to Florence and the "The Saving Place." Little did even he know how this one initiative would launch a season of hard work and great success for young Bill Propst, Sr. and his family of six. Bill was on the verge of initiating yet another brand new concept, the inclusion of a pharmacy, along with all the typical health & beauty aids of a drugstore, into the square footage of the big-box store known as Kmart, "The Saving Place." In rapid succession, in one Kmart after another, a Propst Drugs K was opened. After several were opened and Kmart asked for another 98, Bill made a bold move. He sold his stores to his landlord, Kmart, and joined the company in Troy, Mich. as the Director of Pharmacy.

While at Kmart, Bill further honed his marketing skills right alongside his business acumen. Installing and managing 1,480 pharmacies across the country presented Bill with plenty of reasons to create a mechanism to regulate the safety and quality of the generic products being sold in his pharmacies and to standardize their branding. To this end, Bill's next creation of significance was born. It was known as Qualitest. And it was soon to put the Propst name on the map of millionaires.

Working at Kmart meant a big change for the Propst family, living in Michigan. From the moment they all left, they knew they'd be returning to Huntsville. Eventually, the inner calling to pursue a new season in Bill's professional life was as much of a catalyst to move home as was the never-wan-

THE ICONIC & UNFORGETTABLE

ing draw of family and close friends left behind in Huntsville. It's hard to keep a visionary locked inside the cogs of a large corporation. So what did he do? Bill, very craftily, used Qualitest to maneuver his way back home by bringing Qualitest to Huntsville, ultimately paving the way for far greater things for the Propst family.

Qualitest was a distribution company, efficiently delivering generic drugs to customers across the nation. The typical businessman would feel accomplished and stop there. However, Bill Propst, Sr. is a man that doesn't rest on his laurels. Bill is a man perpetually in creation mode, and an untiring man always willing to back up his dreams with long days and even his own sweat and muscle when needed, whatever the work demanded of him.

Understanding the need to control his supply line, Bill created Vintage Pharmaceuticals, which would serve as the manufacturing arm of his new enterprise. Along with Qualitest, the two were a highly valued pairing. A pairing which, when sold, took the legacy of Bill Propst, Sr. from being an impressive one to an epic one, certainly one that is Iconic & Unforgettable.

At 71 years of age, Bill sold his pharmaceutical empire before realizing all of his dreams for it, but he never looked back. Bill is, unquestionably, a forward motion kind of man, even at his age now. In 2017, during the conducting of the many interviews that led to the writing of this book, Bill coasted into a brand new decade. With that birthday, celebrated quietly at the beach with his family, he finished eight full decades on this planet. Each day within each of the years within each of the decades was lived with a zest for working, building and creating.

2018 now marks the tenth year in Bill Propst, Sr.'s latest

creation, Propst Properties, a real estate business. Initially formed to focus on the building, buying and selling of retail centers, this endeavor, being flexible to the demands of the market, now finds its greatest economic comfort in the residential arena.

Through each of the professional illustrations to follow, the reader will find more than a list of dates and minute details about Bill's many pursuits and enterprises referenced above. Indeed, in the life story of William S. Propst, Sr., one might even say, the minutia of facts are so unimportant. His is not a story told by numbers, except for, maybe, the singular story of his current bank accounts and assets. But that is a story that limits the definition of Bill Propst, Sr., and it is certainly not how this particular man would ever want to be known. In this section, the reader finds something far more important. Here, the reader finds demonstrations of how Bill Propst, Sr. applied himself and epically built his wealth. The reader finds demonstrations of Bill's sense of loyalty, a pride for protecting a strong work ethic and the stamina to support it, an uncompromising dedication to his family and friends, a joy-filled spirit, a generous nature, a heart for mentoring, a no-nonsense style of communicating and, mostly, evidence of the selfless man with a servant's heart who will always choose to do what is right over what is easy and who will always choose the needs of the many over his own. Indeed, in the pages to follow, the reader will discover the essence of the vanguard business leader who brought the pharmaceutical industry to Huntsville, Ala., William (Bill) Self Propst, Sr.

"Carl and I both put up $185, all the money collectively we had, and began calling on contractors in town asking them for their business."

William (Bill) Self Propst, Sr.

The Personal Narrative of

and

Excerpts From The Personal Memoirs of

William (Bill) Self Propst, Sr.

Regarding

Lambert & Propst Steel Company

While at Huntsville Steel, Carl [Lambert] and I continued to call on the local contractors and bid jobs, and most of them slowly began to trade with us. But there was a feeling in the air at work that I just could not put my finger on.

Grandmother Propst was in the hospital in Sheffield in critical condition, so early one Friday afternoon I took off work and drove to the hospital. Mr. Hatcher with N.S. Hatcher Company and Tri-cities Construction Company, which owned Huntsville Steel Company, called late that evening and asked me to go with him to Huntsville the next morning. As it turned out he wanted to take an inventory - which we did - and it must have been okay because we never heard anything about the calculated results. Here again, something didn't seem right and it appeared to me that pressure was being increasingly applied to Carl.

In the spring of 1956, Mr. Hatcher sent Carl a letter drafted by Mr. Hatcher's attorney telling Carl that in the future Carl would be entitled to 10 percent of the profits as a bonus each month as reflected on the Profit and Loss statement compiled by the Sheffield office. Carl then agreed to give me an amount equal to 30 percent of the total bonus he would receive and he would keep 70 percent.

When the Profit and Loss statement came the following month, it reflected an $18,000 profit. Consistent with the agreement, Carl wrote himself an $1,800 check. The following month Mr. Hatcher flew over and told Carl he should put the money back into the company until he, Mr. Hatcher, got all of his investment back.

The agreement was not an Equity Agreement, but an unsolicited bonus agreement that Mr. Hatcher had voluntarily given without input, discussion or comment. From that point on, Mr. Hatcher began to put more pressure on Carl. In retrospect, I believe the bonus should have probably been paid on an annual basis but that was not the way the agreement was written. I can assure you when Carl resigned, he would have never been able to collect even a small part of any amount due him. After Carl resigned, I worked three more days specifically to complete a job that had been promised to a contractor. Rest assured it was a very profitable job, but Carl never received a check for his portion of the profits that month.

I had previously told Carl I was thinking about quitting and going into business, but while I was adept at using the AISC handbook to size beams, etc., I knew I didn't have the engineering knowledge, education or the experience necessary to handle the bigger and more complex jobs. I asked Carl if he wanted to go in business with me. We agreed he would handle the sales, engineering, drafting and accounting, and I would handle the fabrication and erection.

Before we went into business, I was talking to Mr. Rutland Cunningham regarding my status of being a dependent of my parents. He advised me to get my dependent status removed and explained how it could be done. Doing so would prevent Daddy from being responsible for any of my debts and legal actions that could be filed against me. I would be able to legally sign contracts and be totally responsible for my own actions. In fact, I could legally do everything a person 21 years old could do, except vote. Mr. Rogers, an attorney in Florence, drew up the papers and filed them with the court for me. When I received the court order, it really gave me a lot of comfort and relief. I was always grateful for Mr. Cunningham's advice and vouching for me.

It's very difficult to go into business when you don't have much money. Carl and I each put up $185, all the money collectively we had, and began calling on contractors in town asking them for their business. The gentleman who was managing W.W. Scott Company had previously suggested we open our own business. He called us one afternoon and told us of the availability of the old Rodenhauser Florist barn located on Clinton Street across from OK Rubber Welders. We quickly rented the building for $25 a month and everything began to fall into place.

We then called Mr. Wells, the electrician to whom we had given his first job, and explained our financial condition to him. The next day he came over, wired the building and told us to pay him when we could. Bill Sexton sold us all of the welding supplies, acetylene, oxygen, cutting rigs and other items we needed, also telling us to pay him when we could.

We bought two used welding machines from a used equipment dealer in Nashville for $150 each. Leroy Putman of Putman Construction gave us our first job fabricating the steel for Reynold's Clinic. O'Neal Steel in Birmingham sold us the steel for that first job on an open line of credit.

We had promised delivery of all the steel on Thursday. Wednesday night Carl held a light while I painted the fabricated steel with a paintbrush since we did not have a spray machine. We didn't have a truck, so a friend, Mr. Taylor, came over Thursday morning and hauled the steel to the job site for us.

On Friday at the end of our first week in business, Daddy came over from Florence to see how things were going. He took some pictures, went with us to eat lunch, said he had to get back home, and pulled up to the Shell station on the corner of the street adjoining our property. In a few minutes, he came back to the shop, told me he had left his billfold at home, and wanted to know if he could borrow $20. When I told him I didn't have $20 he smiled and handed me a check for $1,000. Thank goodness, what a relief, neither Carl nor I had any money, and I had not known what we were going to do because our help, Leo Brown, had to be paid since he lived paycheck to paycheck.

The first two weeks, Lambert and Propst did real well and made, on paper, a little over $1,900. Remember what Mama had always told me? "A man has not made any money until he collects." That was soon to apply to my life.

CHECK DELIVERY ON TUESDAYS

Leo was a very hard worker and could fix almost anything at work. He worked hard and I later learned he also played hard.

Apparently when Leo got paid on Friday night he would frequently go to some beer joint, drink, stay out all night, and by the time he got home the next day, he would be dead broke or at best have only a very few dollars left. The next Monday or Tuesday he would need to borrow money for lunch and gas.

I finally realized what Leo was doing each Friday when we were scheduled to work one Saturday morning. Leo came to the apartment about 6:30 that morning and told me he knew he was supposed to work that day, and he told me he was drunk, but if I still wanted him to work, he would. Of course I didn't. He had been drinking Peach Brandy, had run out, and wanted me to go buy him another half pint when the liquor store opened, which I did and then I took him home.

That was the first time I had ever seen where Leo lived and the shack he called home. The place was literally a shack up on poles high enough off the ground so it would remain above the water when the Tennessee River flooded. I thought about this situation for several days and finally decided it would be best for Leo and our company if we would change the days we paid the employees. We were currently paying the employees for the week each Friday afternoon. I decided to change the work week pay period to Monday through Sunday with check delivery on Tuesday. Moving the payday to Tuesday would allow the overtime, if any, to be calculated for the week. I also had come to the conclusion if we paid in the middle of the week, it would be less likely employees would go out and spend their money before buying the basics since party time was normally reserved for Friday and Saturday nights.

A few days later, Leo's wife and daughter came to pick Leo up and I went out to the car, as I often did, and talked to them. I told his wife we were changing the day we would pay each employee from Friday to Tuesday and I thought it would be best for her to come pick him up Tuesday afternoon, go to the grocery store, cash his check, buy groceries, and get some cash to get her through the week. From that point on, Leo was a different person and his family seemed to fare much better. Leo even stopped needing to borrow money for lunch and gas and just simply getting by each week.

A grocery store located just a few blocks from the shop caught fire and was rebuilt. While much of the lumber was not burned but simply discolored, the decision had been made to completely rebuild with all new materials. Since the contractor was just going to take the scorched lumber to the dump, he gave it to me just to haul it off. I gave the lumber to Leo who had just bought a small farm. He was able to buy in Valhermosa Springs without paying anything down and simply make monthly payments. The farm Leo bought was located just a short distance south of Huntsville at the foot of the mountain not far from where Leo had been living, but on acreage that would not flood. Leo, with help from his brothers, built the house with that wood I helped him get, working on weekends sawing the two-by-sixes to two-by-fours. The improvement in the living conditions in this house compared to the place they had previously called home was like the difference between daylight and midnight.

EVERYTHING APPEARED TO BE GOING WELL

In 1957, Lambert and Propst Steel Company appeared to be doing well. For the first time in my life, I had some money in my pocket and appeared financially able to do many things I had wanted to do without having to worry. Redstone Arsenal was booming, the city was growing by leaps and bounds, business was good, and the prospects for the future appeared bright. We had purchased quite a bit of new equipment for the business. On the personal side, I bought a new 1958 Ford convertible that turned out to be a real lemon, and Carl bought a new Chevrolet convertible.

Everything appeared to be going well with Carl running the office, supposedly paying the bills, calling on contractors and being responsible for the engineering and drafting, while I was running the shop with the responsibility for fabrication and erection. I also frequently assisted with estimates and bids.

General Carter, the commander of the Tennessee Air National Guard called a two-day meeting at Berry Field in Nashville of a select group of officers that included Carl. At that time, the majority of our work was required to be done outside with very little fabrication to be done inside. That day it was raining. We completed the small amount of work that could be done inside and began to clean and service equipment.

I went into the office to get something out of the file cabinets. When I opened the top drawer of one of the cabinets, I couldn't believe what I found. The drawer was filled with invoices with some envelopes opened and some that had not been opened. Apparently the invoices had just been thrown into the cabinet as they were received. Some partial payments had been made and the date paid, check number, and amount of payment had been recorded on the invoices. Many of the statements had been stamped "Past Due."

It took me almost two days to make files for each firm and each job and record each invoice in a ledger. Thank goodness Carl had written needed information on most invoices when he made a partial payment. That really assisted me in the entry process. Over the weekend I went through the same process to determine our position on all of the accounts receivables. What a mess!

Due to the amounts and dates of the payments received with no record of the contract or job to which the payment should have been applied, it made it more difficult to determine precisely the outstanding balance on each contract, but I could at least get a grand total of the balance due from each contractor. Many of the receipts each week were payments for the same dollar amounts. It finally dawned on me what was happening and my fear was later confirmed. Each week, Carl would go to a contractor and try to collect some money. The contractor would ask how much do you need and Carl would tell them he needed enough to make the payroll so guess how much they would pay him? When one of our suppliers began to push for payment Carl would ask the contractor or contractors for enough money to satisfy the supplier for the time being with a partial payment. Of course the contractor would always pay as little as he could.

When Carl returned, he and I had a very serious and heated discussion regarding future requirements for our bookkeeping, billing, collection, payment of invoices and statements. It took us several days to review and verify the accuracy of my accounting to be sure it was correct. When everything was verified, I started visiting the contractors to collect the past due amounts. I made my first stop at Putman Construction and when I told Leroy Putman I needed some money he asked, "How much is your payroll." I told him to forget the payroll; I had to have some real money because I had to pay some bills. Leroy asked "how much" and I believe it was around $62,000. He said, "Why, I don't have that kind of money." I told him to go to the bank and get it because I had to pay some bills. After a few minutes of discussion, Leroy called his bookkeeper in and told him to write me a check for the past due amount I had requested. After collecting a major portion of the money of the past due accounts, Carl and I sat down and paid bills and brought the majority of the accounts current.

Shortly after Beverly and I got married, a number of contractors began to show signs of trouble. Once again, I discovered Carl had become lax and let our accounts receivables become aged. One of our major customers was building quite a number of houses in Blossomwood, one of the most popular subdivisions in the city. They were not only building houses but had numerous service stations, two office buildings and a church building, all in varying stages of construction. When I discovered how much they owed us and how long it had been since they had paid us with even small partial payments, I knew something had to be done.

I began to call on the owner on a regular basis with only limited results. I then stopped work on every one of his jobs that were in progress at that time. I finally decided I had to do something different to get his attention. I started setting my clock each night for 3 a.m., and I would call him. The Alabama Legislature later passed a law making it illegal to make collection calls after 11 p.m. Each night when I called, he would ask what I wanted and I would tell him I was just laying here worrying about these bills and I knew he would want to help me worry. Every time I called, he would tell me to come by the next day and he would give me a check. The only problem was those checks would only be for $2,000 or $3,000 - just a small portion of what he owed us.

We had never borrowed any money, but we needed a few thousand dollars to get us over a hump, so I went to State National Bank who required the firm in question to cosign the note. Two weeks later, the customer filed for bankruptcy protection and I was surprised to find that State National Bank was a major creditor.

One of the jobs we had stopped working on was his church project. One afternoon, a number of the members of the board came to the office and guaranteed us payment in full if we would finish the job. Taking them at their word, the next morning Leo and I started at 7 a.m., worked all day, through the night, finally completing the job around noon the following day.

I really felt good that we would collect from the church due to the board members' promise and the fact we had completed the job. I went home, took a shower, and Carl drove us to Atlanta while I slept going to and coming back from Atlanta. We had previously given a verbal commitment to purchase a Universal Iron Worker from a company in Atlanta pending our inspection and approval. Following our inspection, we consummated the deal due to our belief we would collect from the church. This machine would punch holes in steel beams, plate and angles, shear plate and angles, improve our quality, reduce our fabrication time, reduce oxygen and acetylene use, and therefore greatly reduce our expenses.

When we went to collect from the church, we were told the church had been advised by their attorneys that they could not pay us without risking the possibility of the church being required to assume all of the contractor's debt. So much for a religious group's guarantee!

In the next couple of weeks, several contractors sought bankruptcy protection. Carl and I collected everything we could, paid our bills and split the remaining amount with each of us receiving just $7 and change. When you only have a few dollars, don't know where or when you will get more money and have a wife and employees who are dependent on you, it is a terrible feeling. Depressing does not begin to describe it.

On the way home, I went to the liquor store and bought a fifth of Early Times Whiskey then stopped at a convenience store and got a carton of Coke. Beverly had really labored that afternoon to cook a great meal and should have been complimented, especially considering the apartment was not air-conditioned. I was not in the mood to eat since I had to come up with a way to provide for her and our employees. In any event, I was in bed between seven and eight o'clock in terrible shape.

The next morning, a little after 4 a.m., I got up and took a long shower. I started putting my coveralls on when Beverly asked what I was doing and I told her, "I am going to work. I certainly can't make any money laying here." I left the apartment about 4:30 a.m. and was driving down Governors Drive when I saw the lights on in the Dwarf Restaurant, a building that we had supplied the structural steel for. I decided to see if Jay Moss had arrived early and if so, I might get lucky and get a cup of coffee. Sure enough, Jay was there and I got a cup of coffee but I did not order breakfast. We talked for a while discussing the bankruptcies, etc. In a little while, a waitress brought me a huge breakfast, country ham, eggs, grits and biscuits. I told Jay I had enough money to pay for the coffee but not for the breakfast. Jay told me not to worry... breakfast was on him.

I got to the shop between 6 and 6:30 a.m. that morning and to my surprise, Homer Scott, the superintendent for Walsh Construction, was sitting in the driveway in his truck. Homer was really glad to see me, especially since it was Saturday and he had a number of brick mason crews scheduled to work that Saturday and Sunday. At the last minute, he had discovered someone had forgotten to order the steel that would be needed for both days, Saturday and Sunday. Homer gave me a list of beams and angles needed and the required lengths of each. I located the materials needed and cut them to length while Homer loaded some of the lighter items on his truck and then both of us loaded the heavier items. Since we had Walsh Construction on C.O.D., Homer paid me a little less than $2,000 in cash. What a relief! I drove home whistling and singing and in a great mood since a huge weight had just been lifted off my shoulders. Unfortunately, at my house things remained cool for a few days.

FROM THE STEEL BUSINESS TO SHOW BUSINESS

For me, things became progressively more unacceptable at the company. I suppose I was just being picky, but Carl's work schedule and his failure to timely manage the accounts payable and receivable began to bother me more and more. I finally came to the conclusion that as long as Carl had a nice car, new sports coat, a new pair of shoes, and $20 in his pocket, he was happy and owing others did not seem to bother him. With that thought and other things considered, I concluded I would never be able to be successful with Carl as a partner, and so I decided to sell. Carl's brother in law, Woodrow, who was an attorney with an outstanding job with Dupont and who also owned a construction company, drove down from Nashville, woke me about 3 a.m., and said he wanted to buy me out. I got up and we went to the office. He reviewed everything, we agreed on the price, and he drew up a contract and wrote me a check. Part of the deal was for me to continue to work there as long as I liked, maintaining the same responsibilities and salary. I was home around ten o'clock that morning and once again, I was the most relaxed I had been in a long time.

In January 1959, Beverly and I moved to Nashville and I joined the group known as the Keynotes. What a mistake! We rented a house on Battlefield Drive just north of David Lipscomb College. I got a job at Englert Engineering Company and Beverly got a job at one of the banks. One of my big mistakes was letting two of the group, Doug and Herb, move in with us on a temporary basis. A young woman just does not feel comfortable with other men living in the same house, and besides, at times it can be very awkward. I really did everything I could to make the group successful, but it just wasn't supposed to be.

I did not have a deep bass voice but it was deep enough for the harmony. The other members had outstanding voices. I was elected to handle all the business items. I knew if we could have just one hit, we would have plenty of money in a short period of time and a lot of opportunities, if we were just lucky.

We were in the drugstore across the street from David Lipscomb one afternoon when one of the members of the Jordanairs came in. We all talked for a while and he asked if we would be interested in doing back-up work for the Grand Ole Opry. The Jordanairs were not only doing back up work for the Opry, but they were also doing the backup for Elvis Presley. Quite often they would not be available for rehearsal, or for that matter, sometimes they could not be available for the Grand Ole Opry show on Saturday night.

As it turned out, the minimum compensation we could expect would be $1,000 a week for the group, $250 each. It didn't take long for me to do the math since I was making $90 a week at Englert Engineering. We had a long discussion about the pros and cons, and then we had a vote. I voted yes and the others voted no. Their reasoning was it would hurt the Keynotes' image to be associated with country music. My position was we are just getting started again so we don't have an image. I quit, and as you can imagine I was terribly disappointed, but I had known from the start it was a long shot. It takes more than harmony to be successful in show business.

A KEPT PROMISE:
A FORTUITOUS AND LIFE-CHANGING DECISION

Beverly and I moved back to Huntsville and I went back to work for Lambert Steel Company. I had promised Mother that someday I would graduate from college, so I decided there was no better time than right then for me to go back to school. I had two uncles who were pharmacists and both had done extremely well financially, even during the depression. In addition, my brother, Michael, was in pharmacy school at

THE HISTORY OF HOWARD COLLEGE'S PHARMACY SCHOOL[1]

"For 90 years, McWhorter School of Pharmacy has been at the forefront of pharmacy education. Our school was founded as part of Howard College in 1927, with a handful of students and a small number of faculty. The stock market crash in 1929 and new accreditation requirements forced Howard College to close the pharmacy school after only two years. However the Alabama State Board of Pharmacy and the Alabama Pharmaceutical Association pushed the administration of Howard College to reopen the program in 1932, and by the late 1930s, the school was the largest pharmacy program in the South.

The McWhorter School of Pharmacy remains one of the most influential pharmacy schools in the country, with graduates who are transforming lives in a variety of settings, from acute care to retail to executive management with some of the world's leading pharmaceutical companies.

Over the years, our program has continued to grow and thrive. When Howard College became Samford University, we relocated to the new campus.

- Jonathan Parker, Samford University Director of Pharmacy Admission

Howard College, known now as Samford University, in Birmingham so I decided to go to pharmacy school.

Due to the financial strain going to pharmacy school would put on us, it took a lot of soul searching to make the final decision to enroll in the pharmacy school at Howard College. Part of my decision was because of the options available with a pharmacy degree. I could always work as a pharmacist and make a decent living, even in bad times. Also, if I decided to go to medical school, I would be able to work part time and earn a top dollar

---

1. Jonathan Parker, "History," Samford University Director of Pharmacy Admission, Accessed April 2018, https://www.samford.edu/pharmacy/history.

hourly rate. I could always go into some kind of business and have pharmacy to fall back on if things didn't work out. One could become a pharmaceutical salesman or you could also go to work for the government as a narcotic agent.

I enrolled in Howard College in the summer of 1959 and, if you can believe it, I took organic chemistry. The lectures were scheduled from 7 to 11 a.m. five days a week with the lab work beginning at 1 p.m. I had been out of school for four years and that makes a tremendous difference in your ability to concentrate. I had to learn how to study again. I had a very difficult time for the first two weeks and went to Dean Woodrow Byrum's office several times to tell him I was quitting. He would always say "Now William, you just stay in school and soon it will be just like opening a book and it will become easy," and he was right.

CARL

Carl and I remained friends until his death many years later. I have always been grateful for the many things Carl taught me, some intended, and some not intended. We always ran around together and while I was in pharmacy school, we would go to football games, etc., and I would also work for him between semesters and other times when he needed me on the weekends. When I was in Huntsville, I was always welcomed to stay at his apartment. Years later after he went out of business, he worked for me at the drugstores until he got a job as an engineer at Cape Canaveral in the space program.

"I asked him, 'What is a Kmart?'
He told me it was a large discount store."

William (Bill) Self Propst, Sr., February 1968

The Personal Narrative of

and

Excerpts From The Personal Memoirs of

William (Bill) Self Propst, Sr.

regarding

Propst Drugs & Propst Drugs K

Right out of pharmacy school I worked for H&H Walgreens until the management exercised some very poor judgement and most of the pharmacists left. In 1963, I went to work for Luther Latham at Latham Drug in Arab, Alabama, about 30 miles south of Huntsville. While working at Latham Drug, Luther and I developed a friendship that spanned many years, until his death in 2011. I told Luther up front that I wanted to open my own store so he could consider me a short-timer. Luther suggested we go into business together. He signed the lease and paid $6,300 for the opening order we received from the drug wholesaler, Walker Drug. The store, Propst Drugs, was opened October 30, 1963, in Dunnavant's Mall.

It was a very small store, 3,000 square feet, but it had a very busy snack bar that generated enough volume and gross profit to make the $2,300 payments we had to make each month, plus we still showed a very small profit. The poor volume on the prescriptions and health and beauty aids were the result of several things.

First, the location of the store in the shopping center did not face Governors Drive as it should have. Had the store faced Governors Drive, it would have had the potential of being a great 24-hour drugstore since that particular location was the centermost point of the city.

Second, I listened to other independent pharmacists in the area who told me how to price my merchandise, and as a result, the store was opened as a full-price store. I failed to consider why anyone would pass several other full-price stores to get to Propst Drugs, another full-priced store. Where's the incentive?

Third, when we opened, our shelves were not full. Although we had a good assortment, we had just a few bottles of each item.

One of the things we did have was a good credit rating. While we were making our payments, I got the opportunity to open another store on North Parkway with a very good pharmacist, Jerry Brown. Jerry was the manager of Plaza Drug, a store located just a short distance down the street from the new Propst location. We opened that store in the Pearsall Shopping Center in the fall of 1964. At that time, we were also able to employ a third pharmacist who worked between the two stores.

The Propst Drugs at the corner of Whitesburg Drive and Airport Road opened April of 1965. It was the third Propst Drugs and in one of the best locations in town, but the center did not have a true anchor tenant. Therefore, it lacked the anticipated customer traffic when it was first opened.

Bill Conner, one of the partners in the shopping center, became a partner in the drugstore with me. Even though the location was far superior to our other locations, the store volume started a little slower than originally expected. The store was just poorly laid out with the counters and aisles in the wrong direction, a snack bar that the community was not capable of supporting, and the full-price image of Propst Drugs. In spite of the negatives from the opening day, the store produced better sales and gross margins than each of our other stores.

Mr. Cummings, the Dunnavant's Mall landlord, built a small shopping center at the corner of Oakwood Avenue and Andrew Jackson Way with M & J Super Market as the anchor tenant. Once we signed the Oakwood lease with Mr. Cummings, we sold the Pearsall store to Jim Marsee and opened Propst Drugs in the Oakwood Shopping Center. That store also started slowly, but even then, we were able to make our payments and squeeze out a small profit.

One of the problems we experienced with the Oakwood store was the design of the building. The back of the drugstore did not extend to the back of the M & J Super Market store and that created an offset and a blind space behind the drug store such that a car could park and not be visible from the street. This blind space made it easy for burglars to burglarize the store and make a fast getaway.

The store was burglarized five or six times in a very short period of time. After one of the break-ins, we experienced a setback or two. When we filed our insurance claims, they were denied because the agent had failed to send the payments to State Farm. As you may have suspected, the State Farm agent had skipped town.

Luther and I sold the Dunnavant's Mall store only to see

the new owner file a Chapter 11 bankruptcy petition. I had to take the store back at the worst time of the year for a retailer to purchase merchandise, the Christmas holidays. Ken Jacobs came to work as the store manager and I later verbally made him a partner in that store and the others, a commitment I fully honored.

The local H&H Walgreen stores went into bankruptcy and I really wanted their Five Points location. It was a great location and had produced outstanding volume. The owner of the building was Mrs. Lucile Lanza, my ex-mother-in-law. I went to Lucile, and really to my surprise, she signed a lease with me.

After I signed the lease, I contacted the Referee in Bankruptcy and asked him how much he wanted for the fixtures, equipment and merchandise in the store, and he said $40,000. I offered $12,000 and when he turned me down, I informed him I had leased the building and he needed to remove his fixtures and merchandise. He filed an action in federal court. The court awarded me the store for $18,000. The only thing standing in our way at that time was we didn't have the $18,000.

Homer Scott, the owner of Quality Construction, a long-time friend of mine, bought one third of the store for $18,000. Homer, like most people who have not been in the retail business, thought when you open the doors of a drugstore the money begins to just pour in. It wasn't long before Homer offered to sell his interest and we paid him $26,000 dollars. Homer was extremely happy with the deal and years later when I was trying to buy the Big-K discount stores, he committed to a substantial amount of money.

By the time we got the Five Points store opened, it had been closed for six or eight months. Much of the merchandise had expired, the customers had, by necessity, started trading with other drugstores, developed habits, and attained some kind of comfort level with the personnel in those stores. Due to the customers' change in habits and the high-price image of Propst Drugs, the store's sales started off slowly.

The biggest problem I ever had was trying to figure out if I was going in the right direction when I went discount. When I opened my first store, I listened to other pharmacists about how to price things. But, by 1965 when I had five stores in operation, I took a closer look at my pricing. That year we had a really dry summer, smog too. It just didn't rain much, so business was slow, giving me plenty of time to think.

What is the purpose, what pulls a person to a Propst Drugs? Our stores are well-located, good looking stores with free delivery and charge accounts. We had a good assortment of merchandise, but without good depth. If you go into a store and you see two tubes of Crest toothpaste, you're not too impressed, are you? If you see 24 pieces, you think it's going to be fresh. That's just the logical thought. So besides depth, what else did we not have? It came down to price.

Well one night I had this guy come in the store who was selling bandages and braces for Futuro. His name was Wally Brooks. We'd talked before, at the Christmas show in Birmingham. Wally wanted me to buy a big display. I asked him, "Do y'all sell direct?"

He kinda danced around, hemmed and hawed, so I said, "Either you sell direct or you don't."

"Well, we do some."

"Well, if you'll sell me direct, what is the discount?"

"Twenty percent off the wholesale price."

"If you'll sell me direct, I'll put a display in each of

my stores and put some in my warehouse for overstock."

He finally decided he'd sell to me and he did. I found out later the reason he was reluctant was because he knew that the wholesalers were going to get upset with him for selling directly to me and not going through them.

Sure enough, a couple of weeks later, Wally called. Walker Drug in Birmingham and Duff Brothers in Chattanooga were giving him a hard time for selling direct. While we were talking, I said, "Do you know anybody else that sells direct that I need to talk to?" He gave several names so I began to ask each salesperson as they came in if they sold direct and if so, what the discount was. I started buying direct on many items.

Back then if you bought an item from a wholesaler that sold for $1.49, you'd only pay $1 for it and you would make a third. So, I got to thinking about it. If I could pay $1 and sell it for $1.50 and make a third, then if I pay 80 cents and sell it for $1.20, I'll make a third. Then, I got to calculating and said you know, from $1 to $1.50 is 50 cents. From 80 cents to $1.20 is 40 cents. I'm missing a dime here. So instead of pricing it for $1.20, I priced it at $1.28, to keep most of that dime.

I decided we'd go direct and the wholesalers about had a fit. They tried to prove to me how wrong I was. I even had one partner to whom I eventually sold my part of his store, because he didn't want to go along with what we were doing. That was Jerry Brown, at the Oakwood Avenue store. Jerry and I discussed our direction and it was finally decided that I would sell him my interest. Part of the deal was Jerry would change the name from Propst Drugs to Peoples Drugs.

When you start tinkering, you better think about everything that can go wrong. Although I had not declared our intention to go discount, I really decided that was the direction Propst Drugs needed to go. As you might expect I was a little nervous about my decision, walking on new ground coupled with the lack of assurance of success. I had no fall back capital and I was concerned about what would happen if we got cut off from a major manufacturer and were unable to sustain the discount prices and our intended direction. I also anticipated some type of behind-the-scenes action from wholesalers, but I just didn't know what those actions would be.

The big question the wholesalers had for me was where would I be if our traffic and sales did not increase. To me it was simple, since I would be buying the items at a cheaper price. If business did not pick up, I would simply re-sticker each item with the original price as if we had bought the product from the wholesaler and instead of the 50 cents mark up on each sale, we would realize 70 cents and make more money than we had previously made. I concluded the prospect of failure was negligible, so I decided discounting was the way to go.

The question I had to answer with our current financial condition was how do we increase the inventory, reduce the prices, and remain even slightly profitable in the short term. It was up to me to come up with the manufacturers from whom we needed to purchase product and find a way to take our discounts without borrowing as we increase our inventory.

Proctor and Gamble refused to sell to Propst Drugs on an open account because of our slow payment credit history, as reported by a wholesaler. I called Luther and since he had an outstanding credit rating, he placed the order and had the merchandise shipped to Propst Drugs and billed to Latham Drug.

It wasn't long before we were buying direct from most of the major companies, except Clairol, but we were able to buy that line of product through Berry Wholesale in Nashville, Tennessee, at very favorable prices. Even better, we could purchase only the quantities of each item we needed without a required minimum order and that permitted us to deep cut the Clairol fast-moving items like Nice 'N Easy haircolor and at the same time maintain a good turnover rate.

If everything worked as I had calculated, the number of customers visiting our stores would increase substantially, and therefore, so would our sales. If we simply sold the same number of units, we would still have the same amount of gross profit dollars and the customer would have saved money. If customers recognize the savings they could realize at Propst Drugs, they would tend to visit the stores more, buy more items, and also tell their friends. If those assumptions were correct, Propst Drugs' sales would increase, profits would increase, and the Propst Drugs image would greatly improve.

I knew there were some other things that had to change in our operation. The first change had to be our buying habits. At that time we were getting same-day delivery from the wholesalers on items we would in the future be primarily purchasing direct from the manufacturer with required lead times. Second, to establish a discount price image, there had to be certain items deep cut every day, called loss leaders. Third, the depth of merchandise on the shelves had to be increased, but done gradually due to our financial position. Fourth, we had to find a more economical way to advise and convince the general public of our new pricing policies and their potential savings.

To emphasize our new pricing we had bright, reddish orange, arrow shaped, shelf tags printed with the words "Regular Price," "Propst Price," "Compare" and "Save." These were mounted on the face of the shelf with the arrow pointing to the item above where the price had been reduced. Those bright tags not only advised of a reduced price but they also gave the stores a promotional appearance everyday. I knew changing our image would be a gradual process because we did not have people standing outside peeping in the window to see if we had lowered our prices.

The first major test of my discount theory came when we started discounting photo finishing, which was a big business back in those days. To attract attention and quickly get out the message of our new pricing on photo finishing, we had very large signs painted on the exterior windows of each store. They were visible from the street and parking lots so that potential customers absolutely could not miss them. Each sign was very simple "Discount Photo Finishing." The sales of photo finishing, film and flashbulbs skyrocketed. While the gross margin percentage was reduced, the sales on all items related to photo finishing increased so the gross profit dollars dramatically increased. These results appeared to validate my pricing theory. Now the question was, "Can we get a similar result with the sales on our other merchandise?"

As we received the merchandise purchased direct from the branded manufacturers, we immediately reduced our sales price on each item. The sale prices of some of the fast-moving image items were reduced more than the prices of the slower moving items. After several months of gathering experience, we reduced the price on all items, even the lower-margined, slow-moving, but necessary, items that we purchased from the wholesalers.

This pricing of leader items was done strictly for impact and to enhance our desired pricing image. Some leader items were priced at or near cost. It soon became glaringly evident that we did not have sufficient turnover information on those items we were now buying direct and we began to sell out of a number of the items we had purchased direct. Rather than simply be out, it was necessary to temporarily purchase those items from the wholesalers. We continued to price each item received from the wholesaler at the reduced price we had established and that temporarily reduced our gross margin. It took several months to adopt a better system of purchasing, obtain needed turnover data, increase our inventory levels and make other necessary adjustments.

In those days, the traditional method of marking the price on each item in a drugstore was by using a grease pencil. Marking with a grease pencil sometimes would deface certain types of packages, especially gift items like Chanel perfume. When marking merchandise with a grease pencil, it takes a lot of time to check in an order and write both the coded cost and the sale price on the merchandise.

One day I was at Gerber's Department Store in Memphis picking up a large order when I saw them marking some merchandise with stickers that were printed on a small machine that was manufactured by Monarch Marking Systems. When I inquired, I found the company sold a machine that had two dials, one to set the regular price, another to set the Propst discounted price, with both prices being printed on the very small ¾-inch sticker. This machine also permitted quick, easy dialing of the price changes from one price to another, rapid label production time, and a neat appearance. Each roll of stickers had an easy peel wax-like paper backing that permitted each sticker to be easily and quickly placed on the merchandise.

The color of the labels selected was a bright reddish orange that would almost glow in the dark. Preprinted across the top of each sticker were the words "Regular Price," and in the space directly under this print was room for the manufacturers suggested retail price. In the center of the sticker were the preprinted words "Propst Price." In the space below this line of print was the space for the Propst discounted price to be printed. Having the regular price and Propst price on the same small label made it easy for the customers to see how much we had reduced the price before they made a purchase. This subtle comparison was effective before and after a purchase.

The sales volume in each Propst Drugs began to increase slowly. Christmas Day, 1966, we were the only stores open in Huntsville. I ran one hundred radio spots on each of two radio stations, WAAY and WNDA, with the following message, "Propst Drugs is open, film, flash bulbs, batteries, bread and milk all at our everyday low price." It seemed that every person in town came to one of the stores that day. Since the majority of the merchandise was accented with the bright orange arrow mounted on the shelf and each individual product was marked with the bright colored stickers, many customers asked, "What kind of sale are you having?" Of course our response was, "We are not having a sale. These are our regular everyday prices." From that day forward, the sales in two of the stores, Five Points and Whitesburg, increased dramatically. The sales in the other stores increased only slightly, but continued to steadily grow. For the first time, there seemed to be excitement in the stores and there was definitely more traffic.

Since H&H Walgreen stores had post offices in their stores prior to the bankruptcy, Propst Drugs had initially been unable to get a contract with the Postal Service, so we installed mailing stations in our stores. We not only sold stamps and money orders but we also accepted packages that we delivered to the post office each day. When H&H Walgreens went bankrupt, we were fortunate enough to be able to negotiate a

U.S. Postal Service contract to put a substation in each store. Advertising, discounting prices, and placing post office signs at each store really increased the traffic in the stores. With that increase in traffic, our sales increased notably.

The Propst Drugs stores were now promotionally priced, conveniently located, easily accessible, with fast, friendly, courteous service, well-stocked, clean, well-maintained, and had the added benefit of a U.S. post office in each store. The combination of these factors made Propst Drugs extremely attractive to customers as reflected in our increased sales and the resulting profits.

One morning in February 1968, about eight o'clock, before the Whitesburg store opened for business, two salesman came into the store, representing G.D. Searle and Clairol. They suggested we go to EZ delicatessen, a few doors from the drugstore, and drink a cup of coffee. It wasn't long before the salesman with Rorer Pharmaceuticals joined us.

Since the Rorer salesman lived in Chattanooga, Tennessee, he normally called on us every six weeks. Since he had called on us about two weeks before, I asked what brought him to town. He told me his volume was down in his territory and he needed me to buy a hundred cases of Maalox. I reminded him I had just bought a hundred cases and asked why his volume was down since the salesman that he replaced had never had a problem with a lack of sales volume. He told me that the salesman he replaced did not have a Kmart in his territory as he did now in Florence.

I asked him, "What is a Kmart?" He told me it was a large discount store. He went on to tell me that Kmart buys Maalox from McKesson in Memphis for $1.07 per bottle and sells it for 97 cents. I suggested he call on Kmart and tell them I would sell them 100 cases at a time for 96 cents a bottle. He said he couldn't. If any of the pharmacists in Florence found out that he had called on Kmart they would stop buying from him.

After the other salesman left, the salesman for Clairol and I rode over to Florence to see if I could sell Maalox to Kmart. While we were waiting for the manager, I was looking around the store and was amazed at the traffic. The assistant manager finally joined us and explained the store manager was out of town. We talked for a few minutes and then I told him the thing for me to do was not to just sell Maalox to Kmart, but I needed to put a pharmacy department in the store. He smiled and told me Kmart was not interested in pharmacies. I asked the name of the person I would need to talk to about opening a pharmacy and he gave me the name and telephone number of the Kmart Regional Manager in Atlanta, Mr. Boles.

I called Mr. Boles and he referred me to Mr. W.R. Marshall, the vice president in charge of licensees in the Kresge Corporation's home office in Detroit. I didn't know much about the company, but I was beginning to realize it was a very big company.

I called Mr. Marshall's office about 4:45 p.m. Eastern time. His secretary, Margaret, answered the phone and wanted to know my name and the company I represented. When I told her Propst Drugs, she advised me that Kmart was not interested in pharmacies. I quickly thought to myself, if I saw her in the middle of the street, I wouldn't know her and she wouldn't know me. I told her I was paying for the call and I didn't believe Kmart had gotten as big as it was without listening. I then asked if I may speak to Mr. Marshall for just a moment, and if he has no interest in what I was going to propose, I guaranteed her I would never call again. Margaret then said, "Hold on, I think I hear him coming."

Mr. Marshall picked up the phone and quickly told me that

Kmart was not interested in pharmacies. I asked how much volume Kmart did in pictures and picture frames, the area I thought would be the best location for a prescription department in Florence, Alabama. He replied, "Oh, I don't know, I don't have those figures in front of me." I ask if they would do about $50,000 a year? He said, "I believe that might be a good number." Then I asked if they would net five percent and again he said he thought that was a good number. I then said, "Five percent of $50,000 is $2,500; will you take six percent of a $100,000?" He then wanted to know if I wanted to carry items like Bayer aspirin. I told him no, I didn't want anything that Kmart currently stocked; I just wanted what Kmart doesn't stock. He said "Why don't you come see me sometime?" I asked, "What about tomorrow morning?" He said, "Why you can't get here by then."

I asked if he would see me if I did. He assured me he would. I rushed to the airport and the attendant was literally in the process of closing the door to the plane for the last Southern Airways flight to Atlanta that would connect with Delta and get me to Detroit that night. I arrived in Detroit around midnight and checked into a Holiday Inn near the airport. I was afraid to go to sleep for fear I wouldn't wake up in time to get to the Kresge building early the next morning. I absolutely had no idea where I was, how far it was to the Kresge building, nor how long it would take me to get there.

The next morning I caught a cab to downtown Detroit. The cab driver took me to a Kresge store downtown that just happened to be the first store Mr. Sebastian Kresge opened in Detroit. Something just didn't feel right to me, so I told the driver to wait while I knocked on the window and asked someone how to get to Mr. Marshall's office. A clerk came to the door and gave us directions to the Kresge headquarters building.

Mr. Marshall and I had a good meeting and he appeared to be

receptive to my proposal. I believe part of the reason for his interest was the Kmart in Florence was far from being one of the company's better stores. Since pharmacy would be a new department, the company knew absolutely nothing about it so I was confident there would be more than one conversation and more than one person would be involved in making a decision. I was also quite sure it would be necessary for them to run a credit report on Propst Drugs and I was right.

A few days later, Mr. Marshall called me about the credit report and I convinced him we were in better shape than what he was reading due to a number of errors on the report. I was then invited back to Detroit.

April 4, 1968 was my second trip to Detroit. During this flight, one of the Delta Airlines pilots announced that Dr. Martin Luther King had just been assassinated. I checked into the Holiday Inn just a block from Tiger Stadium in downtown Detroit, three or four blocks from the Kresge building. Believe me, it was very disturbing being several hundred miles away from home and wake up hearing a rumbling noise, only to find it is a tank moving down the street to quell riots. None of the restaurant personnel came to work during the time I was there, so all we had to eat was packaged snack foods and drinks from the vending machines. Both were quickly sold out.

It took three days to catch a cab to the airport. Each morning I would pack my bag and go sit in the lobby and wait for a cab to pull under the canopy of the Holiday Inn. When a cab would pull under and stop I would go out and ask them if they would take me to the airport. The answer for the first couple of days would be a very curt "NO." On the third day, a car pulled in and I asked if he would take me to the airport. The answer was a curt, "no" for the normal $15 fare.

So I said, "$50." Still the answer was, "No."

"$75." "No," came the answer again.

"All I have is $90."

"Get in the cab and lay down in the back seat."

I guess he didn't want anyone to see him with a white man in his car. I have always contended that the prettiest sight I have ever seen was Detroit in the rearview mirror of that airplane.

On my third trip to the corporate Kresge building, Mr. Marshall introduced me to Mr. Griffin, the VP responsible for the entire Kmart division of Kresge. He and I had a very good conversation and he agreed to give me a license agreement to put a pharmacy department in Kmart Store # 4087 in Florence, Alabama. I told him I didn't want just one store, and he agreed if I generated sales volume of $125,000 or more per year, I could have an exclusive agreement.

Following Mr. Griffin's approval, I was introduced to Mr. Wilcox, the head of the legal department, who wanted to know the name of my attorney. I was reluctant to go home without an agreement so I told him I would just wait until he finished drawing up the agreement since I thought it would probably be a fairly simple agreement. He completed the agreement that afternoon. I read it, we made a few changes, signed the agreement, and I went back to Huntsville ecstatic. In my hand was the license agreement for Propst Drugs K to open the first Kmart pharmacy ever opened in a Kmart store.

I now had the privilege of purchasing fixtures and installing a pharmacy department in Kmart # 4087 in Florence. The first hurdle came with the installation of the drain for the sink. The city would not give me a license until we were able to prove the drain from the sink in the pharmacy to the sewer had the slope of ¼-inch per foot that is required by code. I finally was able to overcome that problem, then build the platform, install the canopy, lay the tile, install the counter and shelving, stock the shelves, place the grand opening ad, and then, we were ready to go.

The grand opening ad announcing the new Kmart Pharmacy ran in the Florence Times on Sunday, April 15, 1968, a day we would normally choose not to run a grand opening ad. The reason we ran it was because we knew the new Sheffield Woolco store's grand opening ads would run the following Wednesday.

About 30 minutes after the store opened on Monday morning, Mr. W.W. Walker of Walker Wholesale Drug called me and asked how the opening was going. I told him things were slow but were really what we expected since the people in Florence did not know Kmart was opening a pharmacy until they read the Sunday paper the day before. Even if they had known they could get their prescriptions filled at Kmart, they would not have been holding a prescription over the weekend except maybe for maintenance drugs. If they were really sick and had gone to the doctor on Friday they would have gotten the prescription filled that day. Also, the doctor's offices were just beginning to open that morning.

Mr. Walker then told me every store in Florence, Sheffield, and Tuscumbia had called him to tell him if he sold to Kmart, they would stop buying from Walker Drug and he asked what I thought he should do. I told him I like to make the decisions about running my business myself and he had to do what he thought was best for his company. He then told me he would tell his salesman, Bob Lee, not to call on me anymore and we hung up. Here we were with a new venture 70 miles from our other stores without the drug wholesaler that we had depended on for years. I realized at that time that Walker Drug did not have a very high regard for the business in any of our stores.

For a short period of time, we would have merchandise for the Kmart store in Florence shipped to Huntsville and then either drive it over to Florence or ship the merchandise by bus and have the pharmacist pick it up. As you can imagine this had to be a stop-gap measure at best.

I talked to the salesman that represented Tennessee-Alabama Wholesale and told him if they would increase their inventory and give us a 10 percent discount off of the AWP (Average Wholesale Price), we would give them the bulk of our business on the items that we did not buy direct.

Before Bill Richards, one of the owners, and his sales manager came to see me, I went back and listed each of the purchases for each Propst store by month for the past year, the invoice numbers, dollar amounts, and the number of stops their trucks had made. Mr. Richards could readily see he had lost money dealing with Propst Drugs due to the low volume his company generated from each store.

Mr Richards badly needed volume and I needed a discount just as badly. After we had talked extensively about current and future business, Bill Richards asked me to give them a few minutes to talk and they went back to the cafeteria. In a fairly short period of time they came back to the pharmacy and we ironed out some minor points.

Tennessee-Alabama Wholesale would increase its inventory to what Propst Drugs agreed to be an acceptable level of supply as determined by the number of items ordered by each store versus the number of items received. We finally agreed that Tennessee-Alabama Wholesale would invoice each Propst store at the Average Wholesale Price (AWP) as published by the manufacturers in the Red Book.

The Propst stores would buy a minimum of $200,000 worth of goods each month from Tennessee-Alabama Wholesale.

Propst could deduct an amount equal to 10 percent from the invoice totals if payment was remitted on or before the tenth of each month. This minimum $20,000 discount each month was terribly important to our stores, especially when you consider, at that time, you could buy a new Chevrolet for $2,500.

I had two problems that I felt had to be resolved before I could make a final commitment. The Dunnavant's Mall stores owed Walker Drug $15,000 resulting from the Dunnavant's Mall takeover as a result of the temporary owner's bankruptcy. That past-due amount had been previously discussed and agreed upon with W.W. Walker, the owner of Walker Drug, and his sales representative, Jim Nabors. Our arrangement was that we would pay our current bills, and when able, we would make payments to reduce the balance. This arrangement would have to change if we were going to be moving our business.

Ken Jacobs and I discussed the situation and we decided to go to Birmingham to see if we could put the $15,000 debt on a note and pay $750 a month until the debt is paid in full. Ken didn't believe Walker would do it, but I knew they would because now we would be paying interest on that debt each month. Ken and I drove down to Birmingham early one morning, arriving at Walker Drug about 7 a.m. We presented our proposal and naturally, they agreed.

The next day, I received a note from Mr. Walker for $15,000 calling for a monthly payment of $750 per month that included five percent annualized interest. Accompanying the note was a letter telling me if we didn't intend to make the payments and honor the terms of the agreement to simply, return the note. That letter really infuriated me. We had always been up front with Walker Drug and had never failed to do anything we had told them we would do, including paying the delinquent amount at the Dunnavant's Mall store. After considering all of the facts, I signed the note and mailed it back to Mr. Walker without comment.

The other reason I was really bothered about moving our business was my friendship with Jim Nabors, the Walker Drug salesman. We had been friends for several years and I knew when I moved the business Jim would take it personally and be really upset. As predicted, Jim was deeply upset when I told him our primary supplier in the future would be Tennessee-Alabama Wholesale and Walker Drug would be one of our secondary suppliers. He failed to appreciate the position Mr. Walker had placed us in, giving us no choice but to make other arrangements, especially when one considered the additional discounts we would receive on future business.

Being a licensee in a large discount store like Kmart was a major learning experience. The first thing I learned was that the pharmacists in the area deeply resented a discounter. We also experienced pharmacists in independently owned stores making claims to the Alabama Board of Pharmacy claiming our pharmacists were committing illegal acts, especially where refills and transfers of prescriptions from their stores were concerned.

The claim was that when one of their customers presented our pharmacist with a prescription, that we simply typed a new prescription and filled it without getting a copy from their previous pharmacy. What they didn't know was that we called the physician and asked permission to fill the prescriptions, which is completely legal. What most did not consider was a Kmart pharmacist had nothing to gain by violating the law.

I saw one of the state board inspectors one day who told me about the complaints and he assured me he had checked us out. I told him about the Doriden sleeping tablets that most of the stores were selling for 65 cents a dozen even without a prescription. At the next pharmacy board meeting, the pharmacists in 13 stores were required to appear before the state board, fined, and put on probation.

There were several problems that we, as a licensee, had to quickly overcome in the simple daily operations of Kmart. How do you ensure that the price of each piece of merchandise is rung on the proper department's assigned cash register key. To address the problem, each department was assigned a specific label color and key number for a label to be place on each item to assist the cashier in identifying the proper key to ring the price marked on the sticker for each piece of merchandise.

The pharmacy department was assigned a white label preprinted with a brown stripe and "Key 5." A price sticker should be affixed to each piece of merchandise. Kmart general merchandise was marked with a yellow "KEY 1" sticker. Unfortunately, the cashiers were so accustomed to ringing merchandise on a yellow "KEY 1" sticker, sometimes when the store was real busy, merchandise would be rung in error on the wrong key. I do not mean to imply these miss-rings were deliberate, but mistakes seemed to happen more when the cashiers were extremely busy.

We quickly learned that in order to guarantee proper credit, we needed to ring everything we could on the cash register in the pharmacy department. On occasion, a customer would insist on paying for "KEY 5" merchandise at the general checkouts to prevent writing more than one check or some other reason. Sometimes one of the pharmacy department's employees would discreetly follow the customer to be sure the merchandise was rung on the proper key. Not only would this action be effective for that particular sale, it would also remind the cashiers to be more careful in ringing merchandise on the proper department's key.

A major hurdle we faced was other firms constantly trying to get a pharmacy licensee agreement with Kmart to open pharmacies in other parts of the country. Since Kmart had so many locations and were expanding rapidly, it was obvious that a small operator like Propst Drugs K could not open a department in all of the existing stores in a timely manner and most assuredly, could not keep up with the Kmart expansion program. Mr. Griffith adhered to our agreement that if the department did $125,000 in the first year, Propst Drugs K would be given exclusivity. One thing that could be said for Mr. Griffith and Mr. Marshall was both of them were honorable men and their word was their bond.

Carl Parker, an outstanding pharmacist, who was also very smart, honest, and blessed with a great personality came to work for us in Florence, Alabama. Carl quickly increased the business because of his understanding of pricing and outstanding manner in the handling of customers.

One Saturday soon after we opened, Carl had to attend a National Guard meeting, so I drove to Florence and was the pharmacist that day in Carl's absence. It didn't take but just a few minutes after the store opened that a crowd descended on the pharmacy and from that moment on, until we closed that night, the cashier and I worked as hard and fast as we could without any pause. About 10 a.m. that morning, I realized one person could not give adequate service to the customers, so I called Huntsville and asked Ken to send me someone to help, but he couldn't find anyone with experience. That night when the store closed, I got in my car and drove across the parking lot to Highway 72 and the traffic light. I was really tired and had 70 miles to go. When the light changed from red to green, the car behind me woke me up by blowing his horn.

That following Monday, we got Carl some temporary help and then as quickly as we could, we hired a second permanent pharmacist. At that time, there was an extreme shortage of pharmacists due to the academic changes that had been made and the failure of pharmacy schools to graduate pharmacists for one entire year.

In August, just a few months after we opened that first store in Florence, Mr. Marshall called and asked us to open three stores in Birmingham in September. The stores in Birmingham were opened with a pharmacist partner in each store. Randy Tribble was the partner in the Roebuck store and Fred Barnett was the partner in the Green Springs store.

The next time we met, Mr. Marshall wanted pharmacies to open in the early spring in the new Kmart stores in Chattanooga, Tennessee; Rocky Mount, North Carolina; Florence, South Carolina; Lafayette, Louisiana; Daytona Beach, Florida, and Overland Park, Kansas, Kmart's reasoning was a temporary mystery to me but I soon came to the conclusion they wanted to see if I could manage multiple departments especially those that were a considerable distance from our office. Kmart also wanted to determine if a pharmacy department could be profitable in different areas of the country.

In the fall of 1969, when I would go to Detroit, there would be meetings with Mr. Marshall, Walter Teninga and Mr. Griffin. After these meetings, I would normally be given a list of additional stores to open. Once I was given 38 stores to open and later I was given an additional list of 60 for a total of 98 stores to open. There was absolutely no way I could finance that number of stores without a major capital infusion. Besides capital, a company must have an experienced organization to open and operate that many stores and we were certainly lacking in that area.

I finally decided we must either go public or find a deep-pocketed investor, but even if we did find an investor, we still did not have the management personnel to handle that type of expansion.

There was a clause in my license agreement that prohibited Propst Drugs K from using the names Kresge, Kmart or Jupiter in any way except the normal manner of doing business. I felt I had to inform Kmart of our intended direction to go public due to that clause in the license agreement. I believed just the word Kmart and the discussion in the prospectus would be the thing that would sell the offering.

Some of the lawyers assured us it was not necessary to tell Kmart since going public was the normal manner of doing business. I didn't believe that was correct, since most people only take one firm public in a lifetime. I felt I was morally obligated to inform Mr. Marshall and Mr. Griffin of our intended direction.

My friend and Huntsville attorney, Eugene (Gene) McLain, and I traveled to Detroit. We met with Mr. Marshall and others on a Friday to advise them of our intended direction. It was a very cordial and pleasant meeting. I believe they really appreciated the notice. The following Tuesday morning I was working in the warehouse at the Five Points store when I got a phone call from Mr. Marshall. After a short pleasant conversation, he asked if I could be in Detroit the next Monday morning at Kresge's expense. I assured him I would be there.

After I hung up the phone with Mr. Marshall, I called Eloise and told her I would be home in a few minutes. When I got home she was in the kitchen. As I walked in the door, I told her to start packing because we were moving to Detroit. Thank goodness she didn't say no. I was confident Kresge was going to buy Propst Drugs K and part of the deal would require us to move to Detroit and for me to become a Kresge employee.

Sure enough, Tuesday morning they made me an offer for the business, coupled with an employment agreement, but I did not accept the offer. Kmart really wanted to just buy the fixtures and inventory, plus a very small amount for goodwill. The salary offered was also totally unacceptable. We were confident any offer would include a requirement to move to Detroit and the cost of living would be considerably higher than in Huntsville. It was certainly a difficult decision to consider moving to Detroit, a city that had experienced major rioting and unrest. Neither Eloise nor I wanted to move a considerable distance from our relatives, especially to Detroit, since everything we had read, seen on TV or heard, was all negative.

Gene and I returned to Huntsville. A few days later, I received a letter from Mr. Marshall stating in one paragraph, "There could be problems attendant to your moving, adjusting to being a corporate employee, and the salary with which you expect." I wrote him back stating, "I have considered moving my family to Detroit with some reservations. As you may recall, the only part of Detroit I have seen is between the airport and the offices you are now vacating for better surroundings. Adjusting to being a corporate employee would not be a problem, provided I would be on equal par with others in the same or similar position and have the same opportunities as those who have been employed by Kresge for some time. As to the salary, I am confident you would not expect me to lower my family's standard of living, which you have seen firsthand, while comfortable, is certainly not extravagant." They then invited me back to Detroit and we reached an acceptable and definitive agreement embracing all of the issues.

"Are you going to be home all day tomorrow, too?"

Eloise McDonald Propst

The Personal Narrative of

and

Excerpts From The Personal Memoirs of

William (Bill) Self Propst, Sr.

Regarding

Kmart & The Formation of Qualitest

The final inventories of the Propst Drugs K Pharmacy departments were taken in the stores January 17 and 18, 1970, and the deal with Kmart was consummated a few days later. When I received the check for payment for the full amount of the deal I flew back to Huntsville, deposited the money in the bank, wrote checks to the partners for their share, paid bonuses to the department managers, paid the bills we had received, and left the remaining balances in the bank for Ken to pay any bills that might come in at a later date. Since we had not been able to find a buyer for the Huntsville stores, I assigned my interest to Ken Jacobs with the agreement that I could come back to Propst Drugs anytime with the same ownership as I left. No money changed hands since I left all the money to pay any outstanding invoices.

I couldn't sleep the night before I reported to work on my first day at Kmart since I was concerned about the traffic and worried about being able to find the Kresge building. I got up around 4 a.m., got dressed and started to the office. It was an eventful first drive to work in the snow. I arrived a few minutes after 5 a.m., February 1, 1970. It wasn't long before Mr. Booker, one of the executive VPs, arrived and invited me up to his office. We had breakfast in the cafeteria and then I went to Mr. Marshall's office for a short time before my first meeting with Misters Neiman, Booker, Marshall, Teninga, Wardlow and Zane, all vice presidents or executive VPs.

We discussed a broad number of items from the location of my office, to pharmacy fixtures, personnel, expansion and the fact that I would report directly to H.B. Cunningham, the chairman and CEO. It didn't take long for me to understand the luckiest thing that came out of that meeting that day was that I would report directly to the chairman of the board. Even in that first meeting, I felt that some might be harboring some thinly disguised resentment of the "very young outsider" who had not come up through the stockroom as they had. It wasn't long before my suspicions were verified.

We were met with some problems right away. Several states created difficulties in obtaining licenses for a pharmacy inside a discount store.

The biggest issue, which affected operations for years, was the serious shortage of registered pharmacists due to the change in the curriculum of the pharmacy programs nationwide, from a four-year to a five-year program which resulted in zero graduates for one entire year across the country. Consequently, that presented problems in recruitment and appointments of pharmacists to district managers positions.

One of the first things I tried to do was to smoothly integrate the pharmacy departments into the store operation. I spent a major portion of my time trying to explain and convince store managers, district managers and senior executives how a pharmacy works, specifically the ordering system, expected inventory, turnover and the fact that 62 percent of the department's volume is generated from prescription refills. Most did not listen.

The pharmacies started off very slowly for a number of reasons. The most notable reason was the skepticism of the public concerning the quality of the prescription medications in a discount store due to the negative advertising and physician detailing efforts by the branded companies. Until there are several hundred prescriptions on file, there are only a few refills each day.

Public acceptance of private label products soon became more common, resulting in an explosion of over-the-counter products. Additionally, the prescription drug industry was also rapidly changing with new legislation regarding generic drugs. Kmart did not have a significant private-label program. And, therefore, only a handful of items had been private labeled.

I have always believed that each private-label product should possess all of the qualities of the branded product. By that I mean it should have the same formula, look like, act like, taste like, smell like, have the same viscosity, coloration and all the other characteristics of the branded product. The label should be designed in such a way that the customer can easily and quickly recognizes the private-labeled product as a direct comparison to the branded product. There must be, however, enough difference in the packaging of the two items to avoid legal problems.

There were many health and beauty aid items that needed to be private labeled and sold in every Kmart, even those without a pharmacy. I contacted Perrigo, the generic manufacturer from whom Kmart was purchasing their Kmart-branded vitamins, and asked them for a quote on vitamin C tablets, 250mg and 500mg, in bottles of 100. When I received the quote, I could not believe the high price. Eventually, we negotiated the price down to a reasonable price so Kmart could sell the item for less than $3 and double our money. I placed an order for $1,000,000 worth of a combination of the two strengths.

The second Kmart product I private labeled was a generic to Contac. Since I had learned the sales department had to review and approve any new product and package, I submitted a mock up of the Kmart Contac package. I had specifically used what I called the "robin egg blue" color similar to the Contac package. I submitted the package to the sales department. But, since I had not used the light green and blue colors Kmart normally used on private-label items, nor had I included the red Kmart Satisfaction Logo Key in the right hand bottom corner of the package, the sales department insisted I change the colors of the package to the Kmart colors. I was confident the product packaged in this way would have trouble selling because the packaging did not even hint of a comparison to Contac. I was beginning to understand the feeling of most of those in the sales department that "I wasn't the merchant, they were," and they had a lot to teach me.

Sure enough, the sales on the generic Contac product were very slow and I was beginning to wonder if we would ever sell it all. I was still confident a private-label product properly packaged and positioned on the shelf next to Contac would be a winner. I repackaged the product using the robin-egg blue color that I had originally submitted and had been forced to change. To avoid a confrontation, I did not change the item number in the list book of the original packaged and distributed product. When a store reordered the product, they would receive the new version of the package. The robin egg blue packaged product seemed to literally jump off the shelves and no one in the sales department ever said a word to me about the change.

In 1974 we opened 297 pharmacies, some in existing stores, and some in new Kmart stores. The stores were all opened between March and November. I believed that was a monumental feat due to several factors: the shortage of pharmacists (particularly any with management experience), time required for recruiting, training, store visits, meetings with the state boards of pharmacy to obtain licenses, and the time required for each district manager to be away from home. From the home office's perspective, it was very easy to order fixtures and merchandise for a new pharmacy. In addition to the above, there was a problem with supply since many wholesalers would not sell to Kmart because we were discounters.

Many wholesalers where a new Kmart opened refused to sell to Kmart because of the objections they received from the pharmacists in independent stores. Independent stores had been the wholesaler's bread and butter over the years and now the independents were threatening to stop buying from them if they sold to Kmart.

I did not understand the wholesaler's position because they all knew we were going to get merchandise somewhere. I did not blame the independents for doing everything they could to protect their business, but most independent pharmacists soon learned that all of their customers would not flock to Kmart. The one thing they quickly learned was they could not get by long-term charging some of the prices they had been charging.

In any event, I convinced Tennessee-Alabama Wholesale Drug, Kerr Wholesale and Lawrence Pharmaceuticals they could be profitable shipping to Kmarts in other states using UPS, FedEx or their own trucks since the dollar amount of each invoice would be large, the weight of the container small, and therefore the shipping expense would be affordable.

In 1974, I traveled a major portion of the time, including weekends, recruiting, stocking departments, dealing with state pharmacy boards, putting out fires in existing stores, and interviewing Kmart pharmacists who had been recommended for promotion.

In the fall of 1976, I was invited to join the E.R. Squibb Advisory Board. The meetings were held on the mezzanine floor of the Plaza Hotel in New York City. Occasionally we would visit the New Brunswick facilities. Those meetings provided as much information for those of us who were not in-house employees as it did for the Squibb executives. It was very helpful for me to be exposed to the viewpoint of those in the manufacturing and branded sector of the drug industry. Much of our input concerned new product approvals, packaging, distribution, advertising and product information.

In 1979, I was invited to join the Marion Laboratories advisory board. The meetings were held in Kansas City at the headquarters of Marion.

I was invited to join the Hoffman La Roche advisory board in 1980, but I only attended one meeting and that meeting was held in Pine Hurst, North Carolina. At that time, the Roche product, Valium, was scheduled to soon lose its patent exclusivity. I believe the primary reason for the invitation to those of us in the major chains was to get our feeling regarding their proposed physical change to the Valium tablets. It was certainly understandable that the company would do everything it possibly could to prevent a serious loss of sales on such a large-volume product line. Their proposal was to change the size, shape and color of the tablets. The new tablets would be heart shaped with an open space, or hole, in the center of the tablet.

Generics were rapidly becoming acceptable by the general public because of the price differences. As a rule, when a generic product becomes available, it will reduce the sales of the branded product by about 80 percent within 60 to 90 days, so you can imagine the effect a new generic would have on the bottom line of a branded manufacturer with such a high-volume product.

I thought they were wasting their time because there would be increased tablet breakage; some customers might think they didn't get all of the medication that had been prescribed due to the hole in the middle of the tablet; and most importantly, when the customer is finally convinced the generic product would produce the same or similar results, they would buy the generic product simply because of that price differential.

The passage of the Waxman Hatch Act, the ''Generic Bill,'' in 1984 dramatically changed the entire pharmaceutical industry. The branded manufacturers had patents that had granted them exclusivity for up to 17 years. That was changed to 20 years. Most companies continued to increase the price of their product on at least an annual basis. Many of those increases were as much as 18 percent on their entire product line. There are also significant differences in many of the prices of some of a manufacturer's products from one country to another. For example, the pricing in Canada of a bottle of Valium 5mg was $8 while the price in the United States was $38.

The first thing the new law did was reduce the time required for many small firms to enter the generic drug manufacturing business. Previously, most of the individuals who would have liked to enter the drug manufacturing business were prohibited because of the lack of capital and other resources needed to develop a new product and perform the exhaustive clinical studies prior to submission to the FDA for approval and then wait a considerable amount of time for the agency's approval.

The passage of the "Generic Bill" was intended to, and did, reduce the price on products that could be generically approved based upon patent expiration, comparative laboratory results, and successful completion of bio-studies comparing the generic to the branded product. The number of patients required to undergo bio-study blood level testing was reduced to as few as 26 subjects. Following the submission of all pertinent passing results, the generic products received faster approval compared to that of new chemical entities. The near-term effect was an increase in competition and a rapid price reduction as a generic product was approved.

While there was a welcomed reduction in prices, there were some unexpected quality compromises. Unfortunately, a small number of unsavory characters were the first to see the financial opportunities of this new industry. Although there were some products distributed of questionable quality, it was a short-term phenomenon. Part of the problem was the lack of experienced, trained FDA inspectors and the rapid entry into the business by small generic firms that placed undue inspection pressure on the FDA.

The branded manufacturers made a tremendous and short-term effective effort to create unfounded concerns with physicians and the public regarding the quality of generic medications. Doubts in the minds of the public at large as to quality had a profound effect on the use of generic drugs as the industry was getting started. With improved inspections, objectionable conditions corrected, required improvement practices, procedures and documentation by the FDA, coupled with the desire of the majority of the generic manufacturers to provide only the highest-quality products, I believe those who are knowledgeable and honest will agree the generic products produced today are equal in quality in every way compared to the branded products. There have certainly been ample recalls of contaminated, out of specification, or other problem products by both the branded and generic drug companies.

Many inside and outside of the pharmaceutical industry thought the branded companies would be severely and permanently crippled. Consideration had not been given to the R&D programs of the branded companies and the subsequent prices those companies would charge for their new products. No one anticipated the dramatic price increases the branded firms would take on their existing patent-protected products. Combinations of these factors may have reduced the price of healthcare in this country in some sectors but greatly increased the price in others.

Major pharmaceutical companies found they could raise prices on their exclusive products without a lot of clamoring from the customer, reduce the number of samples distributed, greatly reduce the number of salespeople, change their method of advertising, and continue to improve their announced quarterly earnings. Just one of the many things they do not tell the public is how much of their research is supported by the United States government through tax credits and grants.

Part of the problem, which I don't believe has been understood by members of Congress, is that the FDA is part of the problem with the escalation of the cost of prescription medication. The agency is extremely lethargic in their review of product submissions. Therefore requests for approval of new drugs, generic alternatives and minor consequential submissions like an attempt to change the supply of a raw material from one manufacturer to another takes months, even years. The annual fees are charged to the manufacturers for each product. Without the FDA's appropriate responsiveness, those fees are quite burdensome.

After Congress passed the Waxman-Hatch generic bill, the first state to pass a law permitting generic drug substitution was Michigan. Prior to the passage of that legislation, there was a little-known practice by the branded companies called "Man-In-The-Plant" rule. This practice was very simple. As long as an employee of the branded firm was in the plant where and when the product was being manufactured, the branded company could claim on their label the words "Manufactured by XYZ" as if they had manufactured the product in their own plant.

This "Man-In-The-Plant" rule really means the branded companies were also selling true generic products themselves. For example: Lederle received the first approval of tetracycline and marketed the product under the label and name Achromycin. After Lederle lost their patent, Squibb marketed a branded generic product under the label Sumycin and there were others.

As stated, part of the problem with quality was the shortage at the FDA of experienced personnel needed to inspect the onslaught of many new generic manufacturers. It literally took several years for the FDA to assemble the number of experienced personnel needed and then train them to police this new industry of generic manufacturing. As the FDA agents grew in experience, many problems with some of those new firms were discovered and some were closed because of failure to properly manufacture and test their products, falsification of data, and general failure to comply with the good manufacturing practices (GMP). As the years passed some inspectors expanded agency requirements simply based on personal opinion. For example, once I was written up for goose manure on the sidewalk. I said to the agent, "That is not part of the GMP's." He replied, "It is if I say it is."

As the quality of generic products improved, the public finally became convinced the quality of these less-expensive products was good and the branded companies with their lobbyists, claims of quality superiority, advertising and information detailed to physicians was incorrect. Little did the majority of the public know of the recalls branded firms had been required to make due to faulty product manufacturing and other quality problems.

In the generic drug industry's infancy, the majority of the drug wholesalers purchased the same generic products under many different labels and from many manufacturers strictly on price without regard to quality, size, shape or color. There could be ten approvals with ten different physical shapes or colors. Also, the pharmacist would purchase the product through their drug wholesaler without specifying the manufacturer and the next time they ordered that generic product they might receive a product made by a different manufacturer with a different size, shape and color. The price from one manufacturer to another often varied substantially. To improve customer confidence in generics, avoid confusion and prevent errors, something needed to be done to provide product consistency each time a prescription is refilled. When the physical characteristics change, the customers become skeptical and often question if they have received the correct product as prescribed by their physician as previously dispensed.

I was convinced Kmart Pharmacy needed its own private label products of generic prescription drugs to assure consistency in the quality, size, shape, color, purchase price and insurance coverage. Additionally, if there was a Kmart-labeled generic product, it would assist management to quickly scan a department and determine if the pharmacist is purchasing from approved sources. We had experienced several incidents where we did not know where the merchandise came from and why the cost-price marked on the bottles varied from store to store. Some pharmacists were simply purchasing from friends without regard to price.

Lou Adams, one of our pharmacy district managers who proved to have an outstanding understanding of private-label packaging and label design for health and beauty aid products, was promoted and brought into the home office from Kansas City. We set out to put together a private label program for Kmart where every product was required to meet certain standards. Very simply put, the requirement for each item as previously stated was it must be formulated to the established criteria and look like, act like, feel like, taste like, smell like, be like, and if it was a liquid it must also have the same viscosity. Many large-volume products were private labeled for Kmart adhering to that listed criteria. Those items dramatically increased the company's gross profit margins while continuing to build on the image of "Kmart the Savings Place." While Walgreen and others had private-label programs, their prices were substantially higher on their brand of products that were similar to the Kmart items.

After much thought, we decided to develop a Kmart generic line of prescription products. We began by visiting manufacturers to view their facilities, establish a good relationship, discuss quality, obtain a complete list of their products, prices, minimum orders and terms. We quickly learned prices from the generic manufacturers were highly negotiable.

We compared the current prices we were being charged by the wholesalers and distributors on each item. The prices charged by the distributors were much higher than those charged by the wholesalers, but the distributors maintained a much broader assortment of available generics since they carried the extremely slow-moving items and unusually stocked large package sizes. Common sense told us we could buy product from the manufacturers at a lower price than what we were paying the wholesalers and distributors.

Many things were required to be done to develop and bring a new full line of products to the marketplace. A name must be selected, corporation formed, trade mark registered, NDC number secured from the government, label designed, products selected, package sizes determined, purchase prices negotiated, sales prices established, case packs determined, price to be charged to the wholesaler and the price the wholesaler would invoice to the store and catalogs printed.

After much thought and discussion, we finally selected the name, Qualitest, a combination of the words quality and tested. Quotes on each product strength and package size were received which led to selection of manufacturers, although price alone was not the determining factor. It took quite some time and many decisions to put the entire product line together. Quality was by far the major consideration.

Since we were not knowledgeable as to the information needed and required on a label, we secured the services of a printer in Detroit who was supposedly knowledgeable of the FDA requirements, to write the specifications for each of the different types and sizes of labels including layout print size and color specifications. There are specific requirements for labels for different categories of products including tablets, liquids and scheduled drugs which at that time were known as narcotics.

One of our first learning curves was in regard to manufacturing lead times, some were as much as three months. Second, we did not realize the independents wanted some larger package sizes. We had to learn through trial and error the package size needed and the turnover rate of many products. It was also difficult to set the invoice price and discount for the drug wholesale distributors. At the beginning, we certainly failed to offer enough discount to incentivize the wholesalers and get them excited about the Qualitest line of products. An unanticipated resistance came from some of our generic drug manufacturers who were also selling their private labeled products to distributors.

Shortly after the first shipments by Tennessee-Alabama Wholesale of the Qualitest-labeled product to other drug wholesalers, we began to hear complaints about problems caused by Tennessee's failure to properly pack and shrinkwrap each pallet to ensure the products would be in an acceptable condition upon receipt by the wholesaler. When Tennessee failed to shrinkwrap a pallet, the boxes would spill all over the truck at the first turn, often damaging the boxes and product, and making it difficult to check the order once received. This failure to shrinkwrap unnecessarily increased the shortages and pilferage. This was especially true when scheduled or narcotic drugs were involved.

The first few years I was employed at Kmart, we were busy opening stores, obtaining drug wholesaler suppliers for stores in new geographic areas, recruiting and attempting to computerize our stores, either in-house or outsourced. During these hectic and busy times, I was focused not only on my job but also on completing the construction of a new residence. I began to consider during this time, my designated "outsider" position since I did not come up through the stock room as my peers had and the fact that my wife had been miserable in the cold weather and wanted to move back home, starting from our first day in Michigan. So I began to consider my options. In short, I was looking for a way to get back home to Huntsville. We had adjusted to the climate and school systems, and our children appeared to be happy. Our offices had been relocated only a short distance from our home, so we decided it would be best to stay with Kmart for the present. I certainly was not going to consider anything other than a move to the south and within driving distance of Birmingham and Huntsville, where our parents lived.

I was surprised one day to read in the Wall Street Journal that Walmart had agreed to purchase "Big K" Corporation, a discount retailer located in Nashville, Tennessee, for $16 million. I was just as surprised several weeks later to read that Walmart had withdrawn its offer. I decided to visit a few of the "Big K" stores to see if I could get a good feel for the firm's problems and turnaround potential. The firm was losing market share, reporting quarterly and annual losses and even losing money in stores with limited or no competition.

After I visited a number of stores and had done a lot of homework, I came to the conclusion that I could implement the necessary changes to make the "Big K" stores profitable. I set up a meeting with the owners, the Kuhn Brothers in Nashville. It was snowing very hard that morning of the scheduled meeting. As I was exiting the freeway on the circular interchange to the airport, I was involved in an accident. I missed my flight and tried to reschedule, but there wasn't another flight available until very late that day. I called and explained my plight and the meeting was regretfully cancelled. In later meetings, I thought we had reached an agreement. What I did not know was that Sam Walton had been advised of our pending deal and he matched our offer. The Kuhn's accepted. Naturally the banks favored Walmart, a known entity with an outstanding track record, over a new startup company. Walmart bought Big K for $8 million in stock and assumed the debt for those 117 stores, a real steal.

A very important benefit for Walmart was the fact the "Big K" store locations were spread over 17 states. Stores located in such a wide geographic area made it difficult for competitors like Kmart to mount a major price and advertising campaign against Walmart without seriously affecting their own reported results. Previously the Walmart stores were located in small towns with limited competition and the purchase of the "Big-K" stores opened up the metropolitan areas for Walmart.

I believe the most important difference in the long-term success of Walmart versus some of its competitors was Sam Walton's appreciation for and commitment to computerization. Other firms like Kmart failed to upgrade and make the high-tech commitments needed for fast inventory replenishment. It appeared to me that Kmart was headed in a seriously flawed direction. Top executive salaries were going up at a very rapid rate and that was creating a lot of talk among the buyers, assistant buyers and secretaries. Headquarters was bloated with new hires, and it appeared as though only a few people would or could make a decision. In fact, it seemed there had to be a meeting to decide when to have a meeting. Most decisions for executive personnel promotions seemed to be made from the buddy system without regard to qualifications.

I was tired, frustrated, increasingly negative and had become even more vociferous. My primary reservation about my decision to resign was Bill, Jr., our youngest child, who was a junior in high school. I had promised myself I would never move while one of my children was in high school. Upon graduation, Bill planned to attend Auburn University in Auburn, Alabama. The crowning blow for me came one day when an Executive VP speaking to the buyers and other executives made the statement that we were not going to let a small regional discounter dictate how we will run our business. That was it for me. I knew it was time to go.

In January 1986, I flew down to Nashville and talked to Bill Richards of Tennessee-Alabama Wholesale. I told Bill Richards that I would like to buy part of his and Kmart's interest in Qualitest. Bill agreed and told me to go ahead.

I now had to decide how best to present an acceptable proposal to the president and the chairman of the board of Kmart. Finally, I decided to write a paper on each of the entities for which I had responsibility. For each company under my responsibility, I wrote, "Here is where we were, here is where we are, and here are the options for the future. I make no recommendations." I presented each of the papers, one at a time, to Norm Milley, the president of Kmart. When Norm finished reading the Qualitest paper, I told him if Kmart decides to exercise option number four, I hoped they would consider me. My recommendation in item number four was to get a new partner for Qualitest. Norm flipped back to item number four, read it, and then said, "Why, you would have to leave the company." I asked, "What do you think I am in the process of doing." I really didn't think he was surprised due to his relationship with the one person who was aware of my desire to move back home and my intended proposal, Harry Hardisty.

Norm Milley and I talked for a while and then he asked if I could come see him the next day. I told him that I couldn't because I was going to be in Huntsville at a niece's wedding and looking for a house. We discussed the situation on and off for about a month before it was agreed that I would purchase some portion of Qualitest. Kmart wanted to increase its percentage of ownership and there was some discussion about what my compensation would be. We finally reached an agreement that Kmart would own 60%, Tennessee-Alabama Wholesale 32% and Propst 8%. The reason for the 8% limit on me was Sam Leftwich's concern that I may make more than the chairman of Kmart. Kmart would bear the expense of the Qualitest move from Nashville to Huntsville and my move from Michigan to Huntsville. Kmart also agreed it would purchase 90 percent of its generic products from Qualitest, and my salary would be increased 40%.

Mr. Milley and I traveled to Huntsville to talk about moving Qualitest from Nashville to Huntsville, visit stores, and find a suitable building.. The first night we were in town, we went to dinner at Boots Restaurant. Quite a number of people came over to our table to say hello, visit for a few minutes, and tell me how good it was to see me.

The next morning we went to Gibson's Restaurant for breakfast before we started visiting stores. As we entered Gibson's, a number of men were seated at the first table in the front of the restaurant. Each of the men stood up, said hello, and told me how good it was to see me. I introduced Norm to the group.

We went back to Gibson's for lunch and again there were quite a few people who came over to our table to say hello and just visit. Just before we finished eating, Charles Younger, the Huntsville city attorney, Tom Younger, a judge, and Macon Weaver, an attorney and the U.S. Marshal who with Katzenback, the United States Attorney General, had confronted Governor Wallace at the University of Alabama when Wallace made his "Stand In The School House Door," all came over and spoke to us. When we got back in the car Norm said, "Now I know why you want to move back to Huntsville."

Norm and I selected a new 50,000 square foot building located at the corner of Moores Mill Road and Jordan Road in northeast Huntsville. The landlord built offices and a small narcotic vault to DEA specifications.

I finally retired from Kmart on June 16, 1986. I stayed home for three weeks doing small things around the house and working on the new adventure while the landlord was completing the agreed-upon construction. We had a country kitchen with an island. On the third Thursday after I left Kmart, I was sitting at the island with the telephone cord pulled across the walkway, with my briefcase open and papers scattered all over the counter top. Eloise came in the back door, walked over to the sink, washed her hands, turned, cupped her hands, placed one hand on either side of her cheeks, placed her elbows on the counter, and asked, "Are you going to be home all day tomorrow, too?" I knew then it was time for me to go. I put the finishing touches on the house I had been working on for nine years, left Monday afternoon, and drove to Huntsville.

> "Bill simply said, 'Dad, I think it's time to go,' which were my sentiments exactly."
>
> William (Bill) Self Propst, Sr.

Excerpts From The Personal Memoirs of
William (Bill) Self Propst, Sr.
Regarding
Qualitest Pharmaceuticals, Vintage Inc. & Vintage Pharmaceuticals

We purchased the security and computer systems, had them installed and then hired a receptionist/secretary, an accountant, a warehouse manager and one other warehouse employee. We were in business.

When we received our first shipment of Ibuprofen 800mg from Par Pharmaceuticals, we were surprised to find Par had shipped 22 bottles more than they had invoiced. I asked Tim, the warehouse manager, what he thought I should do. Tim was a politician and he wanted to know what I would have done if the quantity received had been 22 bottles short? That was the answer I was looking for. I then asked the accountant three times what she thought I should do and her response all three times was "I know what everyone else does." We were then without an accountant and the hunt was on for an accountant that I could trust.

I secured the services of Arab Cartage, a local trucking company to transport the inventory from Nashville to Huntsville. Each morning for several days, I would meet the truck in Nashville, load the truck, place a security seal on the doors, follow the truck to Huntsville, unload, receive the merchandise into the warehouse and place the loaded pallets in the assigned spaces on the racks. To follow a locked truck loaded with drugs may seem to be overkill but when narcotics are involved, you cannot be too careful. It took quite a few trips to move all of the merchandise to Huntsville before we were ready to begin making shipments to the drug wholesalers.

I set about to do several things. First, it was a must for us to obtain a sufficient amount of inventory to routinely fill 97% of the items ordered. Second, we had to learn how to efficiently operate the facility. Third, I had to obtain the prices being charged by our competitors and make any needed price adjustments to be sure Qualitest was competitively priced. I worked nights and weekends.

ESTABLISHING NEW INDUSTRY STANDARDS

When I moved to Huntsville, it was an absolute requirement for me to quickly learn many things and to make adjustments in the product selection, package sizes, cost prices, make competitive changes to the different classes of trade, and establish returned-goods policies. It was very difficult to obtain competitors' catalogs and pricing information.

The first order we shipped was to Kerr Wholesale Drug in Novi, Michigan. Unfortunately, we only had enough of the products to fill 52 percent of the items ordered. No wonder the wholesalers were complaining, since Qualitest could only ship a little more than half of the products the customers ordered.

It quickly became apparent to me that a manufacturer may ship a product in case packs of 36 this order, and the next order they may ship that same product and size in case packs

ON JANUARY 23, 1987

of 48 or 60. Can you imagine how difficult that made it to accurately check in a product upon receipt, correctly pick the item for shipment, or the difficulty the customer had in checking in an order shipped by Qualitest? I am sure you can appreciate how difficult it is to palletize products in varying case pack sizes. To correct this problem, we repacked the item into what later became our standard case pack to assure accuracy and avoid charge backs. One haphazard em-employee in receiving or shipping can cost a company a lot of money.

I notified each wholesaler of the new Qualitest prices and those prices really shook the industry. For example: Bottles of 100 nitroglycerin 2.5mg capsules that supposedly had been competitively priced at $2.81 were now priced by Qualitest for $1.67 and the majority of the other products had been reduced as well.

At first I endured some pretty harsh comments from manufacturers and wholesalers about both the prices and the new case pack policy but it wasn't long before wholesalers and chains were insisting other manufacturers pack their products using the Qualitest stated policy. Although I got it right with the case-pack-policy and the pricing right-out-of-the-gate, at first I made the mistake of not increasing the wholesaler's discount.

Some of the manufacturers and competitors attempted to influence the independent and small chain stores across the nation against the purchase of the Qualitest-labeled product because of the Kmart ownership. Likewise, some wholesalers imposed restrictions on Qualitest that were not imposed on other firms.

One morning I received a call from Howard Kramer, a Kmart employee, advising me that in the future, Kmart would not accept merchandise with less than 12-months dating. This new policy, while burdensome, set a new industry standard. In the long term it was best for everyone, but especially for the wholesalers and retailers. We would have certainly appreciated the same policy being applied to Qualitest's competitors at the same time as it was imposed on Qualitest.

ONE DOOR CLOSES & ANOTHER OPENS

In 1989, it became obvious to me that being strictly a distributor would not be a long-term viable and successful option for Qualitest. I was firmly convinced for a company to remain in the generic drug business, it must be in the manufacturing business. I began to look at potential manufacturing candidates we might be able to purchase. Zenith Labs, a company with numerous ANDA approvals, filed for bankruptcy protection. My previous experience with Zenith was that the company was just simply mismanaged. I met with the CEO appointed by the court and we reached a tentative agreement for a total of $9 million, subject to Kmart's management approval.

I traveled to Detroit and met with Joe Antonini, the chairman of the board of Kmart. I explained the $9 million deal I had worked out with Zenith. He told me that Kmart was not interested in manufacturing. I literally could not believe his reaction since I had conveyed not just my opinion, but more importantly, the facts supporting my conclusion. After several attempts to convince him to change his mind, I told Antonini, "We either go into manufacturing or one of us has to go." He told me to get with Tom Murasky, one of his financial lieutenants, and work out a deal for Kmart to sell its Qualitest stock to me. Just so you understand, the deal I had struck with Zenith was a price of $9 million; another group paid $34 million.

I contacted Murasky and it did not take long for us to agree on a price and terms, but again it took forever to get the final contract executed. Although we had agreed on the price, during the extended time it took Kmart to complete the deal, Qualitest sales and profits had dramatically improved. At the closing, Kmart insisted on payment not only for the formerly agreed upon price but also the profits generated in the last four months.

The closing was done remotely, with me in Birmingham, Bill Richards in Nashville, and Anthony Palizzi in Troy at Kmart headquarters. A very important part of the agreement with Kmart was Qualitest would continue to be Kmart's primary supplier for a minimum of 90% of its generic drug purchases and those purchases would be through Kmart's wholesale suppliers. That part of the agreement was difficult to police and some antics, which we experienced before the sale, continued after it.

Qualitest - IN THE BEGINNING

Early one morning shortly after I had purchased 100 percent of the stock from Kmart and Tennessee-Alabama Wholesale, I began to receive telephone calls from some of Kmart's longtime drug wholesalers advising of their receipt of a certified letter from Kmart terminating their supply agreement, effective immediately, and that Kmart would no longer purchase any goods from them. There was absolutely no inventory adjustment period of time granted to the wholesalers for them to reduce their inventories. Tennessee-Alabama Wholesale became Kmart's primary supplier for all prescription products, branded and generic. The wholesalers did not understand the logic of Kmart's decision to not at least maintain a second source for items shorted from Tennessee-Alabama Wholesale. We all know that nothing runs perfectly, and each firm will be out of some items from time to time, if only for a short period. Although this move was not a major setback to Qualitest, it was a temporary one.

Due to my previous position at Kmart and the suspicion that Kmart still owned part of Qualitest, upon the receipt of that termination letter, some of the wholesalers made an immediate, but, as it turned out, only temporary, decision to discontinue purchasing the Qualitest line of products. I called on each of the wholesalers who were affected and persuaded all but one of them, Americsource, to continue purchasing the Qualitest product line. That hurried decision by the Americsource chairman, Mr. McNamara, was actually an attempt to punish me personally since I had previously taken some Kmart business away from one of his facilities in Iowa, due to its poor service and failure to maintain an acceptable level of inventory, after I had given him notice and ample time to make a correction. Several months later, Americsource put the Qualitest line of products back in inventory.

I was temporarily concerned with Tennessee-Alabama Wholesale having an exclusive supply agreement with Kmart due to Bill Richards' obvious hard feelings about my purchase of Qualitest. Thank goodness the person who really ran Tennessee-Alabama Wholesale was Mike Hohlfeld. Mike did not have a short memory. We maintained a great relationship then and over the years. Mike worked hard to maintain a good assortment, was very cooperative, and opened a facility near the airport in Huntsville, a short distance from the Qualitest building. This new facility was a significant upgrade compared to the building from which they had previously operated. This new facility was primarily used to supply the Kmart stores.

For financial stability, long-term growth and peace of mind, it was an absolute requirement for Qualitest to secure the business of additional wholesalers, chains, independent pharmacies, hospitals, and other firms and not depend on Kmart business. As I began to call on the broad market and especially independent pharmacies, I found many pharmacists wanted to purchase larger package sizes than what Kmart and most chains were currently stocking. After spending much time reviewing competitor's catalogs, comments and suggestions, we added many sizes that increased our sales and helped us considerably in obtaining new business. At the same time, we began telemarketing and shipping to independents on a direct basis. Salespeople were added who already had relationships with the wholesalers, chains, buying groups and hospitals. Special emphasis was placed on Walgreens, CVS, Rite-Aid, McKesson, Smith, Kroger, Kaiser and Walmart.

Qualitest continued to experience some resistance by small chains and a few independents due to some of our competitors' allegations of Kmart's possible ownership. We gradually overcame the stigma. We were really helped when Walgreens began to purchase product from Qualitest. On several occasions, I offered to let firms review my Kmart purchase agreement.

One of the major positive decisions we made was to increase the wholesaler's discount. That helped us tremendously. We also began to sponsor reduced-price promotions through the wholesalers. The wholesalers began to compliment Qualitest on its fill rate of items ordered and fast turnaround time since our policy was to ship the same day that an order was received, which reduced the wholesaler's inventory requirements. The standardized case packs of products made it easier for their warehouse personnel to check in the orders and place the items on the shelves. It also reduced errors by our warehouse personnel.

After wholesale orders were picked and stacked on the pallet, we would shrinkwrap each pallet thoroughly with plastic wrap and then spray paint the pallet. This plastic wrap reduced incidents of breakage and lost or missing items in shipment. By spray painting the plastic it should alert the receiving company if anyone had attempted to tamper with it. Being competitively priced, granting rebates, offering special promotions, rapid order turnaround and response time in solving problems, just made it easy for the wholesalers to do business with Qualitest. The longer we did business with the wholesalers and chains, the more comfortable and complimentary they became.

TELEMARKETING & NEXT-DAY DELIVERY

Spike Pannell managed our new telemarketing department that called independent drugstores on a regular basis with weekly specials. Each store's orders were shipped by UPS or FedEx for next-day delivery. This improved our business and acceptance by the pharmacists. The weekly specials gave us a lead-in and, if the pharmacist bought the specials, they would normally add other products to their order. Those additional purchases increased our sales, reduced expenses and saved the pharmacist a considerable amount of money.

GROWTH

In 1991, we built a new 68,000 square foot warehouse and office building on Jordan Road across from the Madison County Vocational School. The Chase Industrial Park adjoined our new property, and that permitted us to complete the construction, annex the property to the city, and hook up to the city's water and sewer systems without all of the hassle of some of the inspectors. Due to the rapid increase in the Qualitest business, we quickly outgrew the new facility.

Vintage – IN THE BEGINNING

In 1990, Bill, Jr. and I began to visit manufacturing facilities that were for sale. In the late fall of 1991, a salesman friend of ours, Larry Cowart, told us about Medicopharma, a small facility in Charlotte, North Carolina, that was owned by the Dutch firm Pharbita, a firm that was in the process of filing for bankruptcy protection. I contacted the person in New York who was in charge of disposing of several of the Pharbita facilities and made an appointment to visit the Charlotte, North Carolina and Pittsburg, Pennsylvania, manufacturing facilities. Eloise and I drove to Charlotte and visited the plant there. Later, I visited the plant in Pittsburg.

When the manager in the Medicopharma Charlotte facility was told a potential purchaser was coming to visit the plant, he naturally set about to make the facility as presentable as possible. One of the things he had the employees do was put a sealer on the floor. That would have been nice and much more effective had they taken the time to sweep the floor before applying the sealer.

Since I really didn't know anything about the specifics of drug manufacturing, Larry Cowart assured me there was a former employee of Medicopharma, Peter Greenwood, who was anxious to move back to Charlotte, who he thought would make an outstanding plant manager. I interviewed Peter and we reached an agreement that he would join us as the plant manager if we were successful in making a purchase.

While we were in the process of purchasing Medicopharma, a salesman from Memphis called on us and in general conversation, I asked what he would name a generic company if he bought one. Without hesitation he said "Vintage, since it denotes quality." That's how the company obtained it's name.

EFFICIENCY

When we bought the company, its annual sales were $3.6 million. When we sold the company, its annualized sales were $83 million, and we are told it was one of the most efficient plants in the country.

We finally reached an agreement with Pharma Medico to purchase the assets of the company and we closed the deal at about 4 a.m. on April 30, 1992. Part of the agreement required Medicopharma to terminate all of its employees to relieve us of potential liabilities since we were only buying the assets. The purchase of the business had also been contingent on our successful purchase of the land and building. Both deals were closed at the same time.

THE WORK WAS TOO HARD

After the purchase was completed, Medicopharma terminated all of the employees and the plant remained closed for three days. During that three-day period, Peter reviewed each of the approximately 90 employees and selected 30 that he felt were the most qualified to perform their duties at a high standard.

The third day after the purchase, Trey, Michael Reiney, Paul Higdon, Bill, Jr., and I arrived at the plant early in the morning. When the employees arrived, we gathered all of them in the breakroom for an introductory meeting. I introduced myself and each person in our group. I then told the group that none of them knew me and I was going to tell them our intended direction, but I didn't want them to believe anything I had to say until they saw us doing what I would tell them we were going to do. When it became apparent to them we were doing what I said we would do, I wanted them to get behind us and make Vintage a first-class generic pharmaceutical company.

I started off by telling them the plant would remain closed for the next few days for a badly needed cleaning of everything in the building. After being cleaned, some walls and ceilings were stained and still looked dirty so we painted them.

When we began the plant cleaning process, several employees quit. The third day at about 3 p.m., seven of us started cleaning the floor in the packaging room. It appeared to us that the floor in that room had not been cleaned for several weeks or even longer. About an hour after we started cleaning, I discovered that only Bill, John Schultz, Paul Higdon and I were still working on the floor. Three of the employees that were supposed to be helping us apparently thought the work was too hard and had gone home.

The four of us completed cleaning and waxing the floor and when we finished, the floor literally sparkled. The three employees who left without notice came back to work the next morning, but they were advised since they had left without notice, they were no longer employees of Vintage. In the first three days, we got down to 23 employees.

THE LEARNING CURVE BEGINS

When we bought the company, the narcotic safe was just a small metal safe kept in the scheduled cage and had very little capacity to house Schedule II drugs. The lab was also very small. I quickly realized I had my job cut out for me and it was going to take a lot of effort and time for me to learn the things I needed to know about manufacturing and FDA regulations. It quickly became apparent we had people in a number of critical positions who had an effect on manufacturing, packaging, quality assurance and regulatory affairs who were, in my opinion, either underqualified or not qualified at all.

I had been in the retail business and had absolutely no experience in the particulars of manufacturing, required documentation, required paper trail, lab processes or any of the FDA regulations and requirements. I was not familiar with the intricacies and fickleness of the FDA, nor the wavering opinions and interpretations by FDA investigators. For example: If an FDA guidance document conveniently supported an FDA inspector's viewpoint and opinion, I would hear, "There's an FDA guidance out that the company should have adopted." If the guidance supported the company's viewpoint, we would hear, "That's not a regulation; it's just a guidance that has not been adopted." There is a tremendous amount of enforcement discretion left to the FDA inspectors. Each time an FDA inspector inspected the plant, there seemed to be a different "Hot Button."

THE LABEL ROOM

I watched rolls of labels be issued to the packaging department and when the product had been packaged the line manager or packaging manager would "reconcile" the batch.

I did not know anything about the label room and how it worked, so I decided there is only one way to find out how it works and that is to go into the room, observe and ask questions. As I listened, I noticed that the tape on many of the cartons of labels received had never been opened since the tape sealing many of the boxes had not been cut. I went back to the office and thought about what I had seen and heard. In my mind I went over numerous things including the room size, layout, equipment, what I had seen and what I had been told about the operation. Something just didn't feel right, and I couldn't put my finger on what it was.

The count at the time the labels are issued by the label room to the packaging department is critical for proper reconciliation of the labels at the end of a batch run. If you start with a bad number, common sense tells you that you will end up with a bad number. I began to wonder how they had been reconciling each batch in the past. I discovered they were really not reconciling correctly. I met with the label room manager and asked him to double count each roll to verify the first count. That night I asked how the count was coming. He said he had completed the counting, of all the rolls. I had Paul Higdon check the progress and he determined almost nothing had been done. We just lost another employee.

We then established a written procedure for all requirements for the label room and the handling of labels including verification of the labels received to the labels ordered, counted, issued to packaging and the recounting and recording of information on partial rolls to be placed back in inventory.

DEALING WITH THE UNEXPECTED

One day I was walking from manufacturing down the hallway by the lab when the lab manager, Maia, walked out of the lab. I stopped and we talked for a few minutes. I didn't believe I had a complete understanding of what I was being told, so I asked her a simple question, "What would happen if the FDA came in to inspect the plant tomorrow?" Maia simply shrugged her shoulders and nonchalantly said, "They would probably close us." I couldn't believe what I had just heard. I just about had a stroke.

The lab was significantly understaffed for the volume of products we were producing. The number of chemists currently employed in the lab just couldn't keep up, even when working on Saturdays when the rest of the plant was closed. It was also a must for the lab to be expanded to accommodate the new chemists and equipment needed. I quickly came to the realization that the total plant had to be refurbished, and the sooner the better. I sat down and started drawing for a complete plant refurbishment.

I drew the basic plans which turned out to be the footprint of the soon-to-be refurbished building. My plans were interrupted early the morning of August 18, 1992, when I had a major heart attack. After the quintuple bypass surgery I could not concentrate nor did I have the patience to complete the finite details of the plans.

The first week home from the hospital, I contacted Elwyn Reed, an architect and friend, and gave him my rough floor-plan sketch and the job to complete the architectural drawings of the plant, secure the services of the engineers needed and put the plans out for bids from the local contractors in Charlotte.

I was not permitted to go back to work or travel until the weekend before Thanksgiving. That first trip to Charlotte, Bill and I went to the plant on Saturday morning and toured the plant with Peter Greenwood. To show you how little I knew, when we got to packaging, I asked Peter where the switch was to turn the line on. That's when I found out each piece of equipment had to be turned on separately.

YOU CAN'T SATISFY EVERYONE

During that November visit I reviewed the rates of pay of many of the hourly workers, and I couldn't believe how little most of the manufacturing and packaging employees were being paid per hour. Most were being paid between $4.50 and $6 per hour and that was before payroll taxes were deducted. That night, Paul and I were talking and I asked if he thought everyone would be able to afford a good Thanksgiving dinner considering the hourly rate of pay they were receiving. Paul didn't know either. The next day I sent Paul to buy a turkey for each person to be sure everyone would have a good Thanksgiving. Paul and I went back to Huntsville. When we returned on Monday, Rosemary, a lady in manufacturing, asked me, "Mr. Propst, why didn't we get a ham?" It just goes to show, you can't satisfy everyone, no matter how hard you try.

I decided I wanted to package a few bottles of the product on the line, since I did not know anything about package requirements. With only four of us working, we packaged 3,800 bottles of a thousand Apap tablets between 1 and 5 p.m. The most the regular shift of 11 employees on the line had packaged in eight hours was 2,700 bottles.

I didn't find out until Monday that the FDA rules require a QA person to be present when a product is being packaged. Peter did not tell me or we would not have packaged any product that day. It was not my intention to violate any of the rules of the FDA or company policies. From then on, I asked even more questions. In any event, something on the regular shift had to change.

Upon completion of the total plant renovation, there was much better use of all the space, better flow of product, much more lab space, larger locker rooms, larger breakroom, much more badly needed warehouse space and the facility was much easier to maintain.

We sold the only NDA we owned to Oclassen Pharmaceuticals for what I, a novice, thought was a good price, but later learned I had sold it far too cheaply. In the deal, we did receive enough money to pay for the refurbishment and we secured a long-term contract to continue manufacturing the Monodox at very favorable prices for Vintage. In the long run, the sale was good for Vintage by preventing it from being necessary to place debt on the facility.

I give most of the credit for the success of the facility to John Schultz. The first year John was an employee, he was in R & D and he formulated only a few new products. One day John and I went to the Chili Moose restaurant to eat lunch and I finally told him if he was happy making what he was currently making, he should just continue on his current path, but if he wanted to realize true financial success, he had to get off his duff and go to work. It was like lighting a fire under John and he began to formulate and develop one product after another. It wasn't long before we promoted him to the position of assistant plant manager, although he had never previously managed more than six people. John progressed rapidly and, in a very short time, we promoted him to the position of plant manager and moved Peter Greenwood back to R & D, the job he had held with Medicopharma before he had been moved by the company to Pittsburg.

FDA INSPECTIONS – A ROUGH START

The FDA normally inspects a plant every two years. Prior to our purchase of the plant, it had been two years since the last FDA inspection and it was two years after we purchased the plant that we were finally inspected. The inspector gave us a 483 with about eight observations that today I would classify as minor observations. We were inspected several times with most of the observations being on lab procedures, but nothing major. When we submitted our first hydrocodone ANDA we received a call from the FDA in Atlanta denying our application due to our lab results. I later learned a chemist in the lab in Atlanta had made an error when conducting the product analytic testing. Unfortunately Maia, our lab manager, who occasionally had problems communicating, did not handle the call very well and, in fact, was very argumentative. From that point on, the relationship of Vintage with the FDA seemed to decline.

In an effort to improve the quality of the products produced in our plant, lab reporting and FDA response, I hired Tom Wilson, a manufacturing consult. A short time later, we hired the former compliance officer in the Atlanta office of the FDA, Lamar Furr. He assisted us for some period of time, until I discovered the new FDA compliance officer had a grudge against Lamar.

We continued to build the business and began to submit ANDAs to the FDA for approval to manufacture a variety of products. Things seemed to move along fairly well with substantial increases in production and a number of ANDA approvals granted by the FDA.

QUALITEST TAKES SHAPE

In 1994, the Chairman of the Madison County Commission, Mike Gillespie, came to see me and wanted to buy some land I owned that the county needed to extend Shields Road from Jordan Road to Highway 72. We reached an agreement whereby the county received 105 acres and $1 million, and we took title to 272 acres of undeveloped land on Moores Mill Road. In the body of the agreement, Qualitest also made a commitment to, sometime in the future, build several buildings of 60,000 square feet or more, or a total of 360,000 square feet of manufacturing space.

In 1995, the first building to be completed on the newly purchased 272-acre parcel on the Moores Mill Road property was a 160,000 square foot liquid, cream and ointment facility. We had a lot of trouble finding lab personnel, and especially an experienced lab manager. At the recommendation of the former compliance officer of the FDA in Atlanta and our current consultant, Lamar Furr, we hired Jeannie Pratt as the lab manager and we opened Vintage's liquid facility. We were also unable to hire an experienced plant manager for this new facility. I ended up in charge of the plant, although I was not qualified. Occasionally, when John Schultz could get free, or we had a major problem that needed an experienced manager, John would come over for a few days and get us pointed in the proper direction.

WORKING THE NIGHT SHIFT

In the late fall of 1999, we began construction of a new 417,000 square foot hard dose, tablet and capsule manufacturing facility and a 379,000 square foot office and distribution center in Huntsville. The buildings were completed and the validation process began for the buildings, equipment and products in the fall of 2000.

The Qualitest business was growing at a very rapid pace and Vintage was not able to keep up operating just one shift, even with some extended hours on that shift. For the Qualitest business, it was an absolute requirement for Vintage to increase its shipments of products to Qualitest.

U.S. Air offered weekend non-stop round-trip flights to Charlotte from Huntsville for only $99. We could catch the flight Saturday morning at 6:30 a.m. and return Tuesday morning around 9 a.m. I started asking employees in Huntsville for 16 to 18 volunteers to go to Charlotte to work over the weekend. We would catch the flight Saturday morning around 6:30 a.m. and start work at the Charlotte plant around 10:30 Saturday morning. Usually I would bring in lunch.

Saturday night we would go out to a restaurant, not only to eat but also to take a break. After dinner, we would work until midnight and then go to the motel. Sunday morning we would start at 8 a.m., go to lunch around noon and go to dinner around 6 p.m. I would bring in a snack around midnight. We would work until 6 a.m. Monday morning and then go to the motel. Monday afternoon our group would start at 5 p.m., work until 6 a.m. Tuesday morning, go to the motel, take a shower, and go to the airport for the flight back to Huntsville.

From Saturday morning until Tuesday morning, the group would normally have worked 43 hours. As a rule, this small group from Huntsville would manufacture and package more product over the weekend than the larger number of regular Charlotte employees did during a normal workweek. I must admit that schedule was very hard on me, but I was not going to ask others to do something that I wouldn't do.

ASSIGNMENTS OF LEADERSHIP

It is very difficult to select one member of your family to be the chairman, especially since all of them have great attributes. It really doesn't matter which one you select, the others will question why they weren't selected. All three of the boys are very intelligent, understood the business and were very astute in their jobs. Those factors made it very hard for me to make the selection. I reviewed many things about each person's abilities, deficiencies, employee relations, personalities, temperament and overall knowledge of the business.

After I made my decision, I called Mike, Trey and Bill into the office and told them in the event of my absence or demise, Bill would be in charge. In the meantime I went outside of the company and hired Tom Young as the CEO. Tom was a very nice person, extremely intelligent, had a law degree,

NO TIME LIKE THE PRESENT

After I had quintuple bypass surgery, I was diagnosed with diabetes which, after a few years, seemed to get worse. Being in my mid-fifties, several of my friends, lawyers and other business associates advised me to tell Trey, Mike and Bill who would lead the company in the event I became unable to perform my duties. The people advising me thought if each person knew prior to an unscheduled health event, and there were concerns, hurt feelings or jealousies, the time to get them out in the open was while I was living. Their theory was that if there appeared to be any problems it would give me time to answer any questions from those who may be upset to help them get over it.

was a former Chief of Staff for Senator Shelby for 12 years, and was well-connected in Washington. Although Tom was young, lacked management experience, had not been exposed to manufacturing and packaging, and had no experience with the FDA, he progressed nicely with only a few bumps.

ISSUES WITHIN THE INDUSTRY

The industry was quickly changing due to consolidation in the retail, wholesale and manufacturing sector, rapid expansion of the chains, and loss of product exclusivity by the branded manufacturers. The entire industry was in a major change. Branded manufacturers, in a seemingly unified effort to maintain their position in the market, maintained targeted ridicule of generic products. Their message was that the only time a drug is bad is when a Contract Manufacturer manufactures, packages, labels and sells the Branded Manufacture's product under a generic label at a lower price.

If there were faster responses by the FDA on submissions it would create competition between suppliers and that would lower the price of a product. It would even prevent the loss of availability due to the inability of an original supplier to supply raw materials because of some accident, fire or other problems. In recent years, there have been unnecessary rule changes like the requirement to swab floor drains and analyze that sample. What are they looking for, a sterile floor drain? Walk down the halls at the FDA headquarters and observe the work ethic. It may help to reduce the cost of drugs if many of the unnecessary regulations were removed.

There were quite a few drugs on the market that were classified as Desi drugs. Desi drugs are drugs that were not approved nor disapproved under the 1962 FDA review and ruling. Those drugs had been manufactured and distributed for years with the full knowledge of the FDA and they saved this country millions of dollars. In 2007, the FDA notified the pharmaceutical industry to cease and desist manufacturing and marketing Desi drugs. Some companies had submitted what we call a paper NDA that did not require an exhaustive biostudy, just simple chemical assays, stability testing and submission to the FDA and an NDA was approved. Some of those Desi drugs approved by the FDA were even given exclusivity for three to five years. That cough and cold product that was previously being sold for $6 to $8 per hundred (six to eight cents per tablet) can now be bought over-the-counter under the name Mucinex, but the price was raised to approximately $1 per tablet.

Even worse, some firms who had been manufacturing a Desi product without FDA approval were permitted to continue to manufacture the product. Phenobarbital tablets is a good example. The price of the product was raised from $8 per 1,000 to $53 per 1,000. Later, other firms challenged the FDA by manufacturing that product and with one other manufacturer in the business, the price was reduced to $18 per 1,000.

In my opinion, consolidation has been a major problem not only for the pharmaceutical industry but also for other industries. As firms merge, there becomes less competitiveness and more reductions in employment. Look at the wholesale drug business. In 1985, there were over 300 drug wholesalers in the U.S. and today there are fewer than 50. As the big get bigger, they often demand lower acquisition prices than their competitors on the finished product they purchase, but quite often fail to pass along those savings to the retailers, ultimate consumers, insurance companies, Medicaid and Medicare. It is a fact that a manufacturer who has an exclusive product charges much more than when they have competition. Some of the big boy retailers not only demand higher invoice prices, but also require phantom billing and inordinate rebates to reach the net price of the product.

THE BEGINNING OF THE END

Eventually I began to think about selling Qualitest and Vintage, for several reasons. First, I had been the recipient of FDA officials' vendettas for reasons I still do not understand. Second, the majority of my net worth was tied up in these two companies, and I thought it might be time to take some money off the table. Third, the major chains like Walgreens, CVS and other like-sized companies were making demands that were over the line.

One day Mr. Leonard, a vice president of CVS, called Tom Young and invited Qualitest to a meeting at the CVS corporate offices in Rhode Island "to discuss how business will be done in the future!!!" When Tom and Trey told me about the invitation, I became skeptical and wondered what CVS was up to and I was pretty sure whatever it was, would probably not be in the best interest of Qualitest. After considerable thought, I told them to go to the meeting and I would stay home. If something was proposed that could be untenable, they could always tell CVS that it would be necessary for them to come back and discuss the item or items with me and then we would get back to CVS.

Tom and Trey told me when they arrived at CVS, they were escorted to a conference room where a number of CVS employees were already seated. Mr. Leonard, a CVS vice president, opened the meeting stating in the future CVS would tell Qualitest how business would be handled between the two companies. He then informed them that in the future CVS would only pay their invoices 64 days from the date the invoice was entered into the CVS computer. Second, freight would be received by appointment only. Third, it would not be necessary in the future for Qualitest to quote CVS a price for a product and size because CVS would tell Qualitest what they were going to pay for each product. Fourth, in the future, it would not be necessary for Qualitest to quote prices on its products to the wholesalers because CVS would do that for us. There were other items discussed that fit in that same dictatorial manner.

When Tom and Trey returned, they came into my office and informed Bill, Jr. and me of the dictates of the meeting. When they finished I said I'm glad I didn't go because I can't live with any of their demands. I was dumbfounded when they told me they had agreed to each of them. When they left, I looked at Bill and asked what he thought about what we had just heard. Bill simply said, "Dad, I think it's time to go," which were my sentiments exactly.

An acceptable agreement was reached with an English investment firm called Apax, which included an escrow agreement and a provision for Qualitest to keep its cash. On the very day that the greater portion of the money was transferred, I said goodbye and left the building.

"I told Bill I had learned something today, that he and I didn't know a damn thing about the real estate business."

William (Bill) Self Propst, Sr.

Excerpts From The Personal Memoirs of
William (Bill) Self Propst, Sr.
Regarding
Propst Properties

Within days of selling Qualitest and Vintage, we leased office space in the ServisFirst Bank building in downtown Huntsville, just a few blocks from our home on Adams Street. At the time we sold out, I had every intention of going back into the drug manufacturing business and had an agreement with Apax for them to market any product developed by any new company of mine during the three-year non-compete period. However, my plans changed.

Shortly before the sale of Qualitest, Bill was assisting Don Beck, a commercial real estate developer, coach a little league football team. I don't know how the subject of our interest in the real estate business came up, but it wasn't long before Don advised us of an opportunity to purchase a potential Walmart site in Huntsville that was owned by Colonial Properties, a real estate developer in Birmingham. When we expressed some interest, Don made and appointment for us to visit Colonial Properties in Birmingham and discuss the project.

The three of us - Don, Bill, Jr., and I - met with John Hughey, the Colonial Properties retail property executive in Birmingham, who was handling the proposed Walmart project. We knew how much Colonial had paid for the property before we arrived at the Colonial Properties office. The meeting was a very good, affable meeting. John showed us the project plans and then quoted us a price that was far more than Colonial had paid for the land and that would prevent the project from being a good investment. We talked for a short time and then I asked John if he would like to go to lunch. We went to Brio, a restaurant in one of the Colonial Properties shopping centers, and really enjoyed the fellowship.

Following lunch with John Hughey and Don Beck, Bill and I were traveling up I-65 on our way home when I told Bill I had learned something today, "You and I don't know a damn thing about the real estate business and, if we are going to get into that business, we have to get someone who is truly knowledgeable in that area." Bill asked where I thought we would find someone who would fit that bill and I simply replied, "Right here in Birmingham, that man we just left."

A few days later, I called John and told him Bill, Chris Byrom and I would be in Birmingham in a day or so and I made an appointment with John for us to meet at the new Target store in Fultondale. We talked for a few minutes and then I asked John if he would consider joining us as a partner. He quickly responded that he had absolutely no interest since he had been with Colonial Properties for 26 years and was very happy. John also told us of his recent serious abdominal surgery. We told him that if he changed his mind, we would certainly appreciate hearing from him. In the next couple of days, John called me and asked if he could come up to talk to us. That was really good news to us.

John came up the next morning and again we had a good meeting. At one point John asked how we would finance a real estate operation. I told him I was not trying to impress him, but I told him how much money we had in the bank that morning and asked if he thought that would be enough. John did not commit but went back home and discussed the proposition with Libba, his wife. In a few days Libba, and John came to Huntsville to visit and to see what type of feeling she had after meeting Bill and me.

A HIGHER POWER

It was the good Lord talking to me. It's that simple. I had no business being in Huntsville. Mr. Propst had no business getting in the real estate business. He didn't know me from Adam. The big decisions in my life didn't really come from me; I was guided by a higher power. I told Mr. Propst when I came up here I'm not sure why I'm here, but here I am. It's the only thing I can tell you because my mind said no, but my heart said yes.

- John Hughey

Apparently John made several calls and had discussions with some of his acquaintances in Huntsville about our character and financial stability. Evidently, he was satisfied with the responses he received and decided to join us. We bought John's Colonial Properties stock, signed a definitive agreement, and John joined us a month or so later. It was a tough move for John and Libba due to their having lived in the same house where their children had grown-up and leaving close, longtime friends.

John Hughey and I were talking one day shortly after he joined us. I told him we had gone into the real estate business at precisely the wrong time due to the economy in 2008 and 2009. That statement really bothered John and he wanted to know how long I thought it would take for the economy to turn around. I told him I thought it would take three to five years for the market to recover, but not to worry about it. I knew we would make it. It wasn't long before we were able to make some purchases and I believe John finally began to feel at ease.

We discussed naming the company and John insisted we name the company Propst Properties. It was and is my thinking if you are going to let a person run a company, they must be able to make the decisions and not be second-guessed. John is a person who studies a project backward and forward running the numbers and including all considerations, positive and negative, dotting every "I" and crossing every "T" numerous times before he makes a final decision. I listen, agree or disagree, and he makes the final decision. If I really disagreed, I don't believe he would pursue a deal.

There has only been one building that I really wanted to buy that John disagreed with and that was a high-rise building in downtown Atlanta. We didn't buy the building because John was skeptical due to the reduced rental rates per square foot in that market at that time, and the unusual $80 build-out concessions and the two years free rent being given by landlords. The building was only 26 percent occupied, and there was a very large number of vacant spaces available in the Atlanta market. Based upon the data we had at that time and our calculations, it would have taken a minimum of five years before we would begin to realize even a minimal gain.

John had not been with us long before he began to put together an outstanding group of people that will take this firm slowly but surely to be one of the major real estate companies in the country. First he hired Paul Glascock, a man John had worked with at Colonial Properties. Paul is a very good, honest, conservative, data-oriented real estate man with an impeccable record. He had developed a number of projects, the most notable of which was Turkey Creek in Knoxville, Tennessee, and that was an absolute home-run performance. John then hired Ben Hughey, his son, and put him in the field as the Propst Properties representative in our partnership with Signature Homes in Birmingham. Ben is a young recent graduate of Auburn University, very astute, detail-oriented, and easy to work with. After a year in the field, Ben was moved from Birmingham to the office in Huntsville.

Propst Properties is not limited to this small geographic area. It currently owns shopping centers, subdivisions, office buildings, commercial land and industrial properties in Alabama, Tennessee, Georgia and Florida.

Grandmother and Granddaddy Propst.

Bill Propst, center, with Hazel Green friends, 1948.

The Personal Narrative of
Paul Higdon
Former Purchasing Manager

Qualitest and Vintage Pharmaceuticals

I was born and raised in about as far east Alabama as you can go, kind of north of Fort Payne, up on Sand Mountain. It's a little place called Higdon, Alabama. Technically, it was named after my grandfather years ago. I had been in the pest control business for a while, but I decided it was time for me to get out of it. My brother worked for a man that owned the building that Mr. Propst leased when he first started in Huntsville, so I came down on a Saturday and spoke to Mr. Propst. I didn't fill out an application or anything. He wanted to know when I could start to work. I told him two weeks. I wouldn't come unless I worked out a notice. I did, and I wouldn't trade anything for it. I had no idea it would be like it is today.

I started working for Mr. Propst November 1, 1986. There were just six of us then. We grew from there. I think there were probably 700 or so employed when Mr. Propst sold the business. In April of '92, Mr. Propst purchased a manufacturing facility in Charlotte. By September of '92, he had plans to manufacture here in Huntsville, so I started commuting to Charlotte, North Carolina every week. I did that for three years, learning the facility and the manufacturing side.

I started working full time in Alabama again once he got ready to start his liquid facility. That was in '96. I believe it was the spring of 2000 when we got the other manufacturing building here in Huntsville up and going. By the fall of that year, he built a larger distribution center too. Everything just kind of built from there. We were producing probably 400 SKUs of products by that time. Of course, when we were just in distribution, we bought products from other companies. When Mr. Propst sold, we were mostly doing our own products. That's a lot of growth.

Just after he took over the Charlotte facility, he had a major heart attack. We were still in the first distribution plant at that time, at 1025 Jordan Road. [The second distribution plant was built on Moores Mill Road]. Shortly after his heart attack, he would come in to the warehouse and walk with oxygen on him.

Within a month, he was going to work with me to Charlotte again. He still had to take it easy though. We'd get to work early in the morning, work late, go grab a little dinner, come back and then we'd walk. Sometimes we might walk two hours. I learned to carry a notepad with me. I needed the notes for us to look at the next day when we got back to the plant.

He's as close to being a dad to me than anyone other than my father. I've never seen a guy with a bigger heart than he has. No matter what facility we were at, if he saw one of his employees needed help, he'd reach in that pocket and give them some money. "Maybe that'll help." If they were getting married, he always gave them a good present and usually write them a check. He did for my daughter. My daughter also worked with us for a good long while. She'd tell you the same thing. He's a fair man. An honest man.

Up until just recently, when John Schultz and I started Oxford Pharmaceuticals, if he had called me to come work for him, I would have mowed his grass to have gotten to work for him. I think anybody you talk to for any length of time that knew him well, would tell you the same thing. He has a heart of gold. You would never know that he's worth what he's worth by talking to him. You can't ever get anything over on him. He'll always say, "C'mon I'll let you buy my lunch." But you never get to. None of us do. Not that we haven't tried.

God called me years ago to be a minister. I felt like God wanted me to go into a certain community and build a church. I knew it was going to take a lot of money to do this. God gave us the land but we ended up financing the building at $94,500. After about a year and a half, Mr. Propst came up to me and asked me how we were coming on it. Were we getting it paid down? I told him we owed about $85,000. He told me he had the guy from the bank coming Thursday and he said, "I'm going to call you and I want you to come over here." When I went, he had Curtis Perry with him.

He said, "This is what I want you to do." And he told them what interest they were going to charge me. I tell people he's kind of like E.F. Hutton – you remember the old commercial from years ago – when he speaks, people listen. So he told them what he wanted and he said, "Furthermore, we're going to set this up and I'm also donating to him $1,000 a month until we get it paid." So, from that time to about three to three and a half years later, we had that $85,000 paid off. His generosity is what I'm trying to get across. I've never seen anybody like him.

He is also one of the smartest men I know. It's just unbelievable how smart he is. He can count faster than I can with a calculator. I would have to sit down with a pencil and paper or a calculator and add things up and he'd have them added up before I could even get started. It just blew my mind to know that he could do that. But the numbers are no problem with him.

After Christmas each year, the family would go to Colorado to ski, usually in January every year. Mr. Propst always took his briefcase with him. I can still remember it. It was kind of a hard briefcase, burgundy in color. One of his locks was always messed up. He'd have that thing packed full. He didn't fool with computers much during that time. He would have his spreadsheets and all his papers and everything. While the family went skiing, he was in the room looking at his paperwork. He's a workaholic. His hobby is work. That's all I've ever known him to be is that way. That's why he was able to build what he has... and so quickly.

It's my understanding that he gave the city of Huntsville almost 200 acres out there where Qualitest used to be. It might've been just a few acres above 200. He'd already sold the facility. He just went ahead and deeded it over to the city.

That is huge. Land in that area...commercial property...just perfect property. I remember bush hogging that land with Mr. Propst and Bill, Jr. so the construction guys could bring their equipment in there. There were hills and everything in it at that time. A lot of it had to be landscaped and leveled. He was proud of what he was doing. He wanted it to look good not only for the employees, but also the city of Huntsville. He took pride in Huntsville, Alabama. He wanted it to look good for people coming from out of town. The fence that runs along it is probably almost a mile long. It's made out of brick and iron. It probably cost well over a quarter of a million dollars. He had to put a fence there because of what it was, a drug manufacturing company, but he didn't want to just put up a chain link fence. He wanted something that looked good.

He drilled into everybody – if it's worth doing, it's worth doing right the first time. If you do it today and you do it the same way tomorrow – you'll get the same results every time. Another thing about Mr. Propst, he's going to do what he said he'll do. If he tells you that he'll do something, you don't have to have it on an iron clad contract; he's going to do what he said. His philosophy always was - if you'll lie to me, you'll steal from me. No doubt, you knew where he stood. If things didn't go right, he might scold you. That's just like when you're raising a child, you have to correct the child. But he never held anything against you. His way of letting you know that everything was OK, he'd come back by, maybe 15 minutes later, and say, "Let's go drink a Coke." That was his way. We'd go to the break room, sit down and we'd talk.

He watches his money, but he has always bought what's needed. He used to tell me over the years, "We'll buy what we need, not what it would be nice to have." That is another thing that helped me out as much as anything in life, to buy just what is needed.

If you worked for him for any length of time, you learned what he was about. He believed if you worked in the front office, you should dress professionally. That's the reason that I am like I am today. He taught us there's a certain amount of respect that goes with a man dressed professionally. A man looks professional if he dresses professionally. But, you also have to act professionally, too. Then you can earn respect. Respect is not just given out. You have to earn it. He taught that to thousands and thousands of people over the years.

A HEART OF GOLD

I can't stress enough that he has a heart of gold. Just a heart of gold. I have seen him have to leave the office because he'd get emotional about losing an employee who's moving on because of one life event or another. He was attached to his employees. He just hated to lose them. To me, that said a lot.

- Paul Higdon

He wouldn't hire temporary workers. His thought process was that when the workload went up, he'd give his loyal workers a chance at the extra hours. To hire a bunch of new people who he'd need to lay off later just didn't make sense to Mr. Propst. He never had a layoff. He knew people liked to work overtime for the extra money. He would work a thin crew so that people could get all the overtime that they wanted. Then he would pay them time and a half. It helped a lot of people. I was one of them. I was eager to work as much as I could.

I didn't know how to do purchasing when I first got promoted, so I had to learn it. I worked hard, learned it and I was able to save him quite a bit of money over the years. That just goes to show you, he would trust you if you proved yourself to know what you were doing. If you can draw in your mind what you think a perfect person would be to work with and be a friend, then you'd draw Mr. Propst.

He cared for the community, cared for the city, and that's going to be known a long time after he's gone. People who never met him will know him by that, by other people that have known him. His memory is in Huntsville. As long as I'm alive…I may die before he does…but as long as I'm alive, his memory is not going to die. And his legacy is not going to die.

DESCRIPTIVE REFLECTIONS

He's as great of a man as I've ever known. The only person I would put ahead of him would be my own father. Hard worker. Honest. Caring. One of us.

There was a time when we would play some basketball after work, just to let off a little steam. We'd play two-on-two, three-on-three, whatever we had. Bill, Jr. came out there a lot, too, and Mr. Propst. He was just one of us. You never got the idea that he thought he was better than anybody. He was down to earth. Just a humble person. I'm seeing him slow up a little bit nowadays. I just can't hardly stand it.

The Personal Narrative of
John Schultz
Former Plant Manager
Qualitest & Vintage Pharmaceuticals

I started working for Mr. Propst in April of 1992. He kind of got me in a package deal by hiring Peter Greenwood, who brought me on board with him. We started together, from almost the very beginning of Vintage Pharmaceuticals. I didn't even meet him or see him at all, any of my first day, until after 5:30 p.m. I went looking for him and found him in the packaging department. He was there with Paul Higdon, suit pants rolled up to his knees, stripping the floor, taking off all the wax. I said to myself, "Well, we're not going anywhere. We might as well just jump in." That's just how it always was. Everyone just pitched in and did what needed to be done.

For the first few weeks, it didn't matter what it was, Mr Propst was doing it. He'd be pulling a hand jack with pallets full of material, he'd be loading trucks, just doing whatever he needed to do to get things done. He never treated anybody any differently than the next person. That is how I know Mr. Propst. He's a humble, hard-working man.

I worked in product development for about a year and, within that year, I was promoted to assistant plant manager. Shortly after that, I was made the plant manager. I managed the plant in Charlotte from '93 through '97. In 1995, maybe early '96, he was designing and getting ready to build the liquid manufacturing plant here in Huntsville. Although I didn't do the design, he did, he relied on my experience and expertise to figure out everything, what kind of space was needed and how big the packaging lines needed to be. We spent a good bit of time talking about that.

We spent a lot of time together, obviously. When he made me the plant manager in Charlotte, I was just a kid. I was 33 or 34 years old. I'd never really managed more than five or six people in a line, and all of a sudden I had a whole plant. That's a lot of responsibility. It was a big learning curve.

In 1998, I moved out to Huntsville to manage the liquid plant. In the meantime, from late 1996 through 1997, I would come to Huntsville Sunday evening, stay with Mr. Propst and his family at his house on Sunday and Monday, then go back to Charlotte on Tuesday and work the Charlotte plant Wednesday through the weekend. After getting the liquid plant launched, I stayed at the Huntsville plant until he sold it in 2007. After the liquid plant, he designed and built the tablet plant, so of course, we spent some time together brainstorming and trying to figure things out... again, the room sizes, the flow, is this going to work, is that going to work, what type of equipment do we need, that type of stuff. Trying to work out the efficiency and placement of machines, human traffic around them, that kind of thing. That tableting plant ended up being the second-largest solid-dose facility in the country under one roof, capacity wise.

Mr. Propst started Vintage Pharmaceuticals so he could become better fitted on the distribution side because by doing so, he could control his costs better on the manufacturing side. He wouldn't be held to somebody else's schedule or price if he made his own. He knew the plant in Charlotte just wasn't going to be big enough because Qualitest was capable of doing much more than what the Charlotte plant was capable of producing. I don't think he wanted to spend time commuting back and forth to Charlotte as much as he was. I think at some point he wanted to just get in his car and drive to work. Plus, we didn't have any liquids. We were solid dose only at the time. He built the liquid plant first because he had a solid dose plant already in Charlotte, even though it wasn't big enough at the time. Once he got liquids going, he started planning a tablet plant in Huntsville too.

If you see the campus out there on Jordan Road, it's obvious he had growth in mind. He always talked about doing his own bottles and caps and making his own raw materials, so he could be better verticalized. He would then make his own active raw materials, his own bulk components and then you know, that would supply the manufacturing plants and the manufacturing plants would supply the distribution. So he could control his whole supply chain and costs from beginning to end. You skip all the mark ups from everybody else because when you buy the raw materials from somebody else, obviously you pay for the material and for all their overhead costs and whatever their premium is on it. Then we add that to the manufacturing part, and we have to buy the bottles and caps and components, you know? Even if you pay a nickel for a bottle, it's still a nickel a bottle and sometimes the nickels become important when you're in

THAT'S HOW HE WAS

Mr. Propst loved to hire people to give them a chance. One or two people that he hired to start the local plant, I think he took them from the shelter downtown. He said, "C'mon, you people want to work? I'll put you to work." And he got them started working on the building, just some general labor, so they could make some money. That's just how he was. If you worked for him and you were loyal to him, he was good to you. He was very good to you.

- John Schultz

A COMPASSIONATE MAN

One time we were sitting in the office up in Charlotte. I had a janitor that worked for me. We called him Speedy, although he wasn't really a fast worker. He comes in and says, "Mr. John, I need to cancel my healthcare insurance." There was an employee copay that he couldn't pay. He says, "I'm behind on my rent. If I don't catch up, I'm going to get evicted."

Mr. Propst was sitting there, working on something. He took his glasses off and said, "David, how much do you need?" The reply was, "Six hundred and some odd dollars." Mr. Propst reached into his briefcase, got a personal check out and wrote David a check.

- John Schultz

competition with somebody for a product. The more you can save, the better. Those bottles become a penny if you make them instead of buying them. Now you've got a huge advantage over everybody else.

I think we would have seen that. He had the space for it. He had the vision for it. He just ran out of time. I think if it was 1982 that he got started instead of 1992, we would have definitely seen all that.

Mr. Propst knew that you had to have space. That's why those plants are so big. He knew he would have the growth. He knew he would, in the beginning, have more space than we needed, but it wouldn't be long before we'd grow into it and then you don't have to think about trying to expand your plant. You'd have several years of growth there inside that plant. You simply don't build for the next three to five years, you build what you're going to need for the next 10 to 15 years. He always calculated that in to his process. He just had a way of looking at the industry and recognizing in advance the trends and practices that other companies, and his customers, had. There will always be peaks and valleys, especially in the pricing. That's typical. But he always seemed to have a good grasp on projections.

He was also wise and judicious where he undercut prices. You can really affect the market if you come in too low. You can ruin the market. He was canny enough to understand that. He knew how to go in and get his business without turning it upside down. But, if he had to turn it upside down to get the business, he didn't hesitate to do it. He was aggressive, but not in a negative way. He wasn't out to ruin everybody's life to get what he wanted. He wouldn't do that. He knew if he could get in the market without making a big change to the market, to the price for instance, then he would get his piece of the business. If everybody was in at $4 a bottle and maybe he had to come in at $3.75 just to get his little space, then he got his business. He got his business not just with price, but with delivery. Being able to deliver on time along with quality made a big difference. He wouldn't come in at $2.50 just so he could get all the business.

Par, the company that now owns the business Mr. Propst originally sold to Apax, is another generic group but they're a different kind of generic company than Vintage was. Propst was in the commodity generics, the things people take every day and the narcotic analgesics, because everybody needs a Percocet or Vicodin at some point. You keep your machines busy, you keep your people busy.

Par, on the other hand, is into niche products. They're the people that are the first to file; they sit around and look for products that are soon to come off patent. They see the drug has four years left on its patent so they go ahead and develop it and file it with the FDA. Their goal is to be the first ones to file with the FDA. When you're doing that, you also have to file a "paragraph 4" saying you won't market this product as long as it's not off patent. The FDA will tentatively approve the product, so that the day it goes off patent, you're the first with a generic to the market. You'll get 180 days of exclusivity before anybody else can be approved. In that 180 days, if the innovator sells them for $100 a bottle, a company like Par sells their generic at $70 a bottle. They'll get a lot of the sales. They'll capture the market in those 180 days. As other generic companies enter the market with the same product, the price comes down. Par, and other niche companies like them, come down on their prices too so they can keep up their volume. Depending on how many new companies get into it, they're still the main player. If the price trickles down to $20, they still keep the business at $20… that's Par's world, the world of a niche generic company. Qualitest, was the commodities company. It specialized in the old steady bread and butter items. There was always going to be a market for those, so that's what Mr. Propst sold.

> ### AN EXTRA $100
> There were times we'd be working a lot of overtime. The guys would be working hard. Even though they were getting paid time and a half, at the end of the day, Mr. Propst would reach in his pocket and give them each an extra $100 bill. That's how I remember Mr. Propst.
> - John Schultz

Mr. Propst always said one of the prettiest sights he's ever seen was bottles moving down the packaging line. Watching them get filled and capped and labeled and bundled and getting put in the box at the end of the line, just watching that whole operation go down was pretty to him. You'd find him sitting there watching, looking in the windows of the room with the tablet presses running. The table spins so fast that it just looks like a blur. You watch it knowing that there are 350,000 to 400,000 tablets an hour going into the buckets.

If you ever need anything, a piece of equipment or anything like that, all you had to do was tell him why. We were always behind, so he came up to me one time and said, "John, what do we need to catch up?"

"Mr. Propst, we really need to have two more tablet presses."

"How much are they?"

"They're a half million dollars apiece."

"Well, get them on the phone and get them down here."

In just a couple of days Mr. Propst bought two machines. That's just how he was. He knew what he needed, if it was a justifiable need. It wasn't like a big corporation. If you want to spend a million dollars, even in the biggest of corporations, the approval process would be four or five months, at least. Maybe it would even have to get shifted into the next year's budget. Mr. Propst could do it within a week. We had the best equipment, too. We didn't buy anything cheap. He spent money to make sure we had what we needed to make the best product that we could. It made it easy to work for him.

If Qualitest ran out of something, or he got a big order, he'd pick up the phone and say, "John, what do you have on the tablet press or what are you making in those tanks over there?" I'd ask him, "Why, what do you need?"

He might say, "I need 80,000 pints of Cheratussin and I need it next week." We'd stop what we were doing, if it was possible. If the tanks were full, we'd have to wait until they were empty. We would empty them as quickly as we could so we could get started. We'd make his Cheratussin for him, just as quickly as we could possibly get it to him. If you call some of these other generic companies and you tell them what you need, if they don't have it on their shelf waiting on you, it might be three or four months before you get it, before they can fit your order into their schedule.

That helps on the back end, on the distribution side, because now you know what your terms are, what your customers' buying habits are. Let's say McKesson is buying 50,000 bottles a month of a product. With a manufacturing company under the same ownership, you are set up so you can forecast for the majority of your customers... especially the big ones. Once the distribution center and the customer have their inventory, everything just rolls a lot smoother.

For approved drugs, you're always looking to copy what the innovator did. Every time I'd ask Mr. Propst a question about how he wanted the generic to look, he'd say, "You know, John, it needs to look like, taste like, act like, smell like..." He wanted it to look as close to the innovator's drug as it possibly could. This built consumer confidence, ya know? All of a sudden, the consumer was getting a pill that looked just like what they had been using. Nowadays, it is regulated. Generics have to match the innovator. Making the decision to have his generics look like its innovator was instrumental in making generics a real player in the pharmaceutical industry. That, and just by having previously made so many generics available through all the Kmart stores. Of course, that was accomplished by setting up Qualitest to supply a consistent generic with consistent brand labeling.

What was happening previously was the Kmart stores up in the northern part of the country were buying from generic manufacturer A. The Kmarts in the southeast were buying from generic manufacturer B, and in the northeast, they were buying from C. The same product would be different colors or different forms, one was a tablet, one was a capsule. They still had the same medicine in it, but people didn't know to trust it, until Qualitest came along.

That's what Mr. Propst was trying to do to give a patient confidence. When a patient got home and opened their medicine, they would would want it to be the same every time. He was instrumental in making sure there was consistency in what each of the products looked like. That trickled over into the other generic companies. They weren't doing it before Mr. Propst started. The government started to pick up on it too. Things evolved. Regulatory-wise, now you have to match the innovator, the name brand drug. If the name brand tablet has a bisect in it, yours has to have a bisect in it.

Here's an example of the process. We tried to develop, for instance, a sustained-release heart medicine, isosorbide mononitrate. Bill gave me the tablets to develop. First thing I have to do, because it's a sustained-release, is take them to the lab. I would give it to the chemist and tell them I need the solution profile. You have to try and match the profile over a period of time. Say it's a 12-hour tablet, they put it in a simulated gastric juice, or whatever the product requires. You check it at zero time point, which is right away, and 20 minutes. Then you check it at two hours, four hours, six hours, eight hours and 12 hours to see how much is released over that period of time. The product that I develop has to match the same release pattern. Not only does it have to match chemically in the lab, but you have to take it and do a biostudy.

Biostudies are expensive. Sometimes, for a sustained-release product, they are a half million to a million dollars. It depends on how many subjects you have to test. To test a product we took six tablets out of a bottle and their dissolution profile was so different between those six tablets that there was no way I could ever match it. I couldn't make it that bad, so to say. I obviously don't remember the exact results, but for instance, let's say the one tablet, at two hours, released 30%. The second tablet, at two hours, released at 80%. The third tablet, 40% and so on. The solution is equal and it goes into the same type of vessel. There are six separate vessels that it goes into and they take samples out of each vessel.

So we thought it was a fluke. We got another bottle thinking the first bottle was maybe a bad batch that they didn't know about yet. We get another bottle from a different company, and it was the same way. The technology back then, back in the early 90's, for sustained release was such that you couldn't duplicate the same results from pill to pill in the same bottle. We had to abandon it. I couldn't even have gotten it to pass in the lab much less a biostudy. Can you imagine spending the money to get it to a biostudy? It would never work.

They do what they call a double blind study. It's real simple. You have your product and you have the innovator product - what the FDA calls the reference drug. Depending on what the product is, the FDA tells you how many subjects you have to have in the study. Typically, it's between 24 and 48. Say it's a small study, that requires 24 subjects. What they do is bring everybody in to a clinic and give 12 of them your product. They give the other 12 the reference drug. The subjects don't know which ones they're taking.

They take blood draws depending on the half-life of the drug. So every two hours, four hours, eight hours, 12 hours, 18 hours, 24 hours, they might go out to 48 hours. Some of them are 60 hours. Some are even 72 hours. It just depends on what the half-life is of the drug.

Next, the patient has a washout period, two weeks or a month. When they go back in, they flip flop. Whomever had the reference drug the first time gets the other one and vice versa. The patient doesn't know what they are getting. Only the people conducting the study would know who got which drug.

Again, they analyze the amount of the drug in the patient's blood, at all those different sample points. You have to be statistically equivalent to what the reference drug is in order to get it to pass. So, when they say generics are as good as the name brand, well, they really are. They're the same thing because it would never pass otherwise. That's the only way you can get a product passed through the FDA. And every product requires an ANDA (Abbreviated New Drug Application) from the FDA. It's very regulated.

A HISTORY LESSON

In 2007, the FDA changed the generics industry. DESI drugs were drugs introduced before 1963. They didn't always have to have an approved application since there was a long history of their safety and efficacy. That allowed companies like Vintage to make them without an ANDA.

That's how we got into business in Charlotte so quickly. There were a lot of them - Guaifenesin and phenylpropanol, guaifenesin and pseudoephedrine, guaifenesin and dextromethorphan, and guaifenesin by itself - all in a sustained-release form, for which you could do your stability tests, your own validation. You could come to market with those in probably 120 days. You didn't have to go through the application process. But in 2007, the FDA just jumped in and said no more DESI drugs. You have to have an application for them. So everybody had to go out and do the application.

DESCRIPTIVE REFLECTIONS

I probably know more about him than the average person because of the amount of time I've spent with him. He's compassionate. He's smart. He's one of the smartest guys I've ever seen or ever met. He's driven. He is humble. As much as he has - and he likes nice things, who doesn't, he can afford them - he's not flashy with it. Really, for myself, I respect him as much as anybody, probably more than anybody but my dad.

He's used to always working. I think that's really what keeps him going. He just likes people, too. He likes to be around people. We've been meeting for breakfast at the Blue Plate on Saturday mornings at 7 o'clock for 15 years. I called him on the way up for this interview, but he didn't answer the phone at the office. While at Qualitest and Vintage, we never missed a meal. We might work 100-hour weeks sometimes, but he made sure we never missed a meal. Even now, that's important to him. Breakfast, lunch or dinner - he's hitting up somebody. You can't pay for anything when you're around him. He absolutely will not let you pay, even just to buy him a beer or something if you were out after work. He just won't ever let you do it. Even Bill, Jr. told me to stop trying. He said he's not going to change.

I've seen him in a lot of different environments. I've seen him in a business environment with other company leaders. I've seen him in the environment with employees, in a family environment, at Christmas parties. He's just very, very consistent. Genuine and sincere, he is. He's just a very, very generous man.

The Personal Narrative of
Chris Byrom
CFO, Propst Properties

I met Mr. Propst in December of 1997 when I went to work as the controller for the pharmaceutical company that he owned, here in Huntsville Alabama, Qualitest Pharmaceuticals. He was traveling when I interviewed with his youngest son, Bill, Jr., and the CFO, Gary Bledsoe, who turned out to be my boss once I was hired. I didn't meet Mr. Propst until two weeks after I was working for him. We met in the breakroom one morning during an unscheduled break time. I'd heard a lot about him from the employees, how tight of a ship he ran and how strict he was in his dealings, so he was really built up in my mind, but our first meeting was uneventful.

I walked into the breakroom about 8:30 one morning for a cup of coffee and he was standing there alone. He didn't know me and I didn't know him. I asked him if he was Mr. Propst and he said he was. I don't know if he knew who I was from Adam or why I was there. It was just a real easy introduction.

WHEN IT IS CHANGE YOU ARE LOOKING FOR, IT IS CHANGE YOU WILL FIND

I'd just moved from Houston where I had lived for 20 years. I'm originally from here, moved to Houston, married, had children, and moved back to Huntsville 20 years later. I was ready for a change. I found a newspaper ad in The Huntsville

Times, of all things, saying that somebody wanted to hire an accountant for a pharmaceutical company in Huntsville, Alabama. I was floored by that, because I couldn't imagine Huntsville having a big pharmaceutical company at the time.

As it turns out, I got the change I was wanting. It was a different environment than I'd ever worked in before. We had a staff of about 30 people at the time and I knew nothing about the pharmaceutical business. I was dropped into it all those years ago and now I've been with Mr. Propst and his family business for 20 years.

Very soon after I came on board, my boss came to me and said he was leaving the company in February. For my benefit, he recommended me to take his place in the accounting department after he left. When the first of March came around, I was the accounting manager, or whatever you call it. Mr. Propst wasn't much on titles.

Working for Mr. Propst was a different environment than what I was used to. There were pretty strict rules as far as dress code went. All the men wore, preferably, white shirts and ties. I'd never heard that a coat and tie was required, but a lot of people wore them anyway, just because Mr. Propst did, quite frankly.

It was an environment that was pretty strict on timing too. You had to be at work, at your desk, at 8 o'clock. There were bells or buzzers that went off throughout the day and, when it got to be about 9:30 in the morning, breaks started. There were a series of 15 minute breaks. I think there were three of them and you alternated which 15 minutes you wanted to go. We got an hour for lunch and a break in the afternoon. At 5 o'clock, typically, the majority of the people would leave, except for the people who had to work at night. Our offices were right next to the distribution center where they worked into the evening packing goods to be shipped.

Across the campus, there was a liquids manufacturing plant. It was Greek to me. It had just opened up and really wasn't full-force yet. It was just getting started. As time went on, multiple shifts were added. A second shift was added at all the manufacturing facilities. After it was sold to an investment company called Apax, it went to operating a third shift. They bought it and managed it for a few years and then Endo Pharmaceuticals purchased the company from Apax. It was then called Par Pharmaceuticals.

Some of the Propst children stayed onboard afterward and did very well. They were big players, but when Par came along, I think things changed.

Mr. Propst sold on October 31, 2007, and within two or three months he was in the real estate business. My recollection is that we had about 580 people in all three locations when we sold, but he didn't skip a beat. He went right from that to this.

MOVING RIGHT ALONG

I came over here and helped them do things that just needed to be done, like pay a few bills, that kind of stuff, whatever they needed me to do, but I didn't formerly start until right after the first of the year. I was working solely for Bill and Mr. Propst. I'm not sure of the timing of it, but real early on they met a fella named John Hughey who became and still is president of Propst Properties. He comes with high regard. He's very energetic, very intelligent, knows the business extremely well. I was with them when we went to a meeting with an attorney in Birmingham one day. Mr. Propst had previously met John and called him to see if he would meet with us. We met on the north side of Birmingham at one of John's Target shopping centers that he had developed - a very nice center. I remember John looking at me; he didn't know who in the world I was. We were introduced, but I was just sitting there. Mr. Propst was talking, asking if he'd be interested in coming to work for them. John was caught by surprise, I think. Initially he didn't think it was a viable opportunity for him to move to Huntsville, but he went home and talked to his wife about it and, I think, the next day he said, "Maybe we should talk a little bit more." The rest is history at this point. John came to work for us and brought a coworker of his, his longstanding partner, Paul Glascock. He's the vice president, if you will, of the business.

While at Qualitest and Vintage, I was just primarily responsible for the accounting and reporting, you know, keeping up with the numbers and how the company is monetarily gaining or losing. I had very little involvement in the operations of the plants. I tried to understand what they were doing so I could do my job, but I wasn't involved much in the decision-making process at all. That was primarily Mr. Propst.

Transitioning over here to Propst Properties went great. We started with just myself, Bill and Mr. Propst, and then a couple of months later, came Paul and John doing their thing, buying properties. I just assist them in whatever their endeavors are and report it. Mr. Propst tells me what he basically wants to do, and I just facilitate what he wants. He'll do some investments though that he doesn't even mention to me.

HOW TO SELL A MAJOR PHARMACEUTICAL COMPANY

The sale was an extremely hard time for me. It was the second largest deal in which I was a player. I wasn't necessarily a big player, but I was involved on a day-to-day basis and, a lot of times, on a night-to-night basis. There were a lot of long hours involved....It was just us three, Bill, Mr. Propst and me, plus the investment bankers that we had hired to help us find contacts and, of course, instruct me as to what I needed to do to help them sell the company.

The way you do it is you hire an investment banking firm, or sometimes two will work together. There are people in the industry who work for major banks. They're all very industry driven. For instance, the guys we worked with were from Bear Stearns. They are a financial company headquartered in New York. These guys are in tune, they know people in the industry, they know what they are doing. So you interview a number of investment banking groups. You decide which one, based on what they tell you and what you've learned from the industry about who is viable in selling this kind of an entity. You choose one or two, and they instruct you on what you need to do. You put together this huge booklet of information that covers every aspect of the company from sales and marketing to manufacturing to development. They set up and make your contacts for you and tell you what information to put together and they market that information to prospective buyers. So that's what happened. I would say it took us over a period of two years, maybe three. Things would run hot and then cold, and then one day it sold.

DESCRIPTIVE REFLECTIONS

I could say a lot of different things about Mr. Propst. I could say he's got a kind heart. I'd say that's obvious, what with all the giving he's done for the community, and continues to do. But what gets swept under the rug is that he kept a lot of people employed. He gave people an opportunity they might not have had if he hadn't been around.

Another way I think of him…one short story…right after we began to know each other, he was telling me about some of the opportunities he'd already had to sell his company. He could have sold the company, even that early on, for almost a billion dollars. But he didn't. Instead, he kept building his buildings and working hard. I'm thinking, how do you do that? Moral to that story is that I don't even remotely think like he thinks. Nowhere near it.

It just goes to show you, you have people who go above and beyond…a very elite group of people that can lead and acquire things and just to grow their impact on people and their communities. A crude way of describing it, he's got more guts than most people ever dreamed about having.

On a personal note, I think he's a thoughtful person. I think he is obviously courageous and intense. And at this point, I consider him a good and very close friend.

The Personal Narrative of
John Hughey
President & CEO
Propst Properties

I had an old friend tell me a long time ago that in business the dollars are all the same. It's the people that make the difference. The money is all green; everything else is all the same. It's the people that make the difference in business. I'll never forget that. It told me volumes about him, and it was also why I chose to work for the Propsts.

I've been in the shopping center business my entire career. There was a broker here in town that was trying to help Mr. Propst and Bill, Jr. buy some real estate, so they came down to Birmingham to meet with me. I was working on a Wal-Mart [deal] which hadn't even gotten started yet. We spent two or three hours together and just talked about it. They went home saying, "We'll get back to you." They called me back a couple of weeks later and said, "I don't think it's for us; thank you very much." They were just really nice people. I just figured that was the end of it.

A couple of months later, they called me back and said, "We're in town, do you remember us? We'd like to come by and meet you." I said, "Sure. I know y'all are from Huntsville. I've got to go to the north side of Birmingham this afternoon. Why don't you meet me at the Fultondale Target? It just opened. I'll meet you in the coffee shop there."

I walked in and it was Bill, Jr., Mr. Propst and Chris Byrom. Mr. Propst said, "Hey John, how are you doing?"

"Great. It's good to see y'all again."

"We'd like you to think about starting a company with us and moving home to Huntsville."

"Well, that's complicated because my home is here now and I'm not interested, but I'll help you find somebody."

"You've got our number if you change your mind."

I went home and told my wife I was really flattered by these people, but I'm not going to pursue it. I got up the next morning and, I don't know why, but I called Bill, Jr. and said, "I'd like to come sit down with you and your dad." I got up here [to Huntsville] and I said, "I'm not sure why I'm here, but I am."

We talked for a couple of hours. I finally had to ask, "Well, it sounds great, everything we talked about, but how are we going to finance it." I know real estate costs tens of millions. I hadn't done any research on Mr. Propst prior to coming because I wasn't looking for an opportunity. Mr. Propst just smiled at me and told me the story about him selling his [pharmaceutical] company. When I got home that night, I told my wife, "I think there's something to these people, and I think I want to pursue it."

She said, "I'm not selling my house." She didn't want to come up here. She was very negative about the whole situation because she loved Birmingham and our house so much. I said, "Well, come up there with me and meet Bill Jr. and Mr. Propst. I'm going to do this. If you want to stay, we'll have two homes or whatever and work that out."

She came up here [to Huntsville] and we spent an hour or so with the Propsts. After the meeting, just as we stepped out the door - I can remember it clearly - I was standing on the curb and I looked at her and asked, "What do you think?"

"I really like them," she laughed. She had seen the same things in them that I had seen.

You never know... I knew I could do the job but you still worry about the people side of it. It's been fantastic for me because the Propsts are the kind of people you want to be associated with. So, not only do I work for them, but I consider them to be very, very good friends. I'd say Mr. Propst is now one of my best friends on this earth.

The timeline was a quick one. I met them in August or September of 2007. We met again that December. I came to work here, I think it was the third of February, 2008. I loved where I was. I was just attracted to the Propsts and the way they thought about business. I'd been in a big public company, running it for a long time. I'd done about everything you could do in the real estate business. The thought of starting something new, and being part of that, was exciting to me.

Bill and his dad had a mindset about business unlike any other I'd seen. Mr. Propst had worked in a public environment like I had, so he knew the stuff you had to do with Wall Street, dealing with your investors and things like that. Your decision processes are a little different in that environment. Of course, he had also started a new business that he and his family members had grown from scratch and built into a huge business for which they made all the decisions themselves. There weren't any outside forces [with that business], other than the regulatory groups, that influenced what they did. They took risks and built a tremendous business. That combination appealed to me.

I think what Mr. Propst did in his Kmart days, opening close to 1,300 Kmart pharmacies, is remarkable. He knows more about retail than any of us know. He has a better sense of what's going on [in the market] than most people do and he hasn't been in the retail business in 30 years. He's very intelligent and very thoughtful about things. He can see the big picture. He understands what the little guy is dealing with, too, because he's been broke, too. He's done it all. He lived when they had outhouses at his home.

I can remember we were buying a multimillion dollar piece of property in Saraland, Alabama. It was a $10 million piece of land. He didn't know me very well at the time. I said, "I'd like you to come down and see the property before we close on it." He replied, "I don't have any need to do that. That's why I have you. Besides, if something goes wrong I have to have somebody to blame." He laughed and I did too.

But, what he was telling me was 'I have confidence in you to do it. Go out and make the decision and I know you're going to try and do your best to make it work.' That's the way he is about everything. Not many people have that much confidence in other people, especially when they're spending your money. It means a lot to me and it's quite a responsibility. Not only is it Mr. Propst's money, it's Bill's and Emily's and Trey's and Mike's and all the grandchildren. It means a lot to me that I help them make money. I think we've had some success doing that. Luckily, we haven't lost any money yet. I try to treat it as if it were my own money.

When I first came to work here, I knew I'd be able to run the business side of it, but at that time, my time spent with Bill and Mr. Propst was probably no more than five hours. I had met a lot of people who worked for him at Qualitest though, and I had found them all to be quality people. I soon learned the Propsts were too.

Coming on board meant leaving a company I had been with for 27 years in which I was not only emotionally invested but also financially invested. I had a bunch of stock they owed me and I was concerned that they wouldn't give it to me. Mr. Propst said, "If they don't pay you, then I will." Guess what? They didn't pay me and he did. It was a lot of money. Just shows you the kind of quality folks that they are, Bill, Jr. and Mr. Propst.

I'd been here about a week or two and one day I asked to go see the Qualitest and Vintage campus. Of course, it was owned at that time by Apax. We drive down the driveway to the guard shack and I was thinking they'll let him right in. Not only did they let him in, two security guards came out and wanted to hug his neck. They loved him and that told me everything I needed to know. Here's the owner, the president of the company, and the guys in the guard shack loved him. I saw that interaction and I went, "Wow, I made the right call." Even to this day, we'll be out having lunch and people that worked for him 10 years ago come up and hug his neck. I see that all the time. It just warms my heart. It's everywhere you go. Remember, he had several hundred employees. and I can't tell you the number of times I've seen people come up and want to thank him. A lot of past employees don't want anything to do with former employers. You can tell he treated them well, just like he does now.

This may seem small, but it's so big it's not even funny. Mr. Propst brings breakfast into our office - every single day. He's here by 7 o'clock with breakfast for everybody, so he's getting up, going out and buying breakfast and bringing it into the office, all by 7 o'clock. That just tells you the kind of service leader that he is. He just gives to other people. Every day. He's been doing that for nine years. We ought to be cooking him a Spanish omelet every morning, but he'd have none of that.

I used to be skinny. I think that's my fault - I just blame him [laughs]. We either have Little Rosie's or Gibson's or Hardees or Bojangles. He's thinking of all of us, all the time. When we all go to lunch, he wants to know where we want to go. Again, for him, it's always about what others want to do. Not many people are that way all the time.

Our business has been very profitable since the start of our company. We're very conservative in the things we're doing. We're not trying to grow for growth's sake. We're trying to be profitable in the business ventures that we have, and we have been. We were buying things early in the business cycle. We've been selling things lately because prices are high, which, for somebody like me, is hard because I like to have things going on all the time. It's funny, Mr. Propst is one of the few people that saw the recession coming. I had just come on board. He came in my office one day, February of '08, and said, "John, just put your feet up on the desk and wait for the phone to ring."

"What do you mean?"

"It's going to be bad and it's going to be bad for the next three to five years."

He walked out of my office and I was thinking, have I made a mistake? Because I came from a real energetic, let's-go-get-it-done kind of place, and he's saying, "Just put your feet on the desk and just wait."

Slowly, but surely, the world started falling apart like he had had a sense about. As it did, I remembered his words, "the phone will start ringing."

Everybody knew me in the business, but they didn't know anything about Propst or what kind of capital we had behind us. In our business, you have to have capital or nobody cares. You have to be able to get it done. So, we got the word out.

There was an article written about Mr. Propst that told about his character and the way he thinks, but also a little bit of a hint about what he sold his business for. With that article, people knew Mr. Propst had capital, and of course he was right, the phone started ringing. The jets started flying into Huntsville. People that had known him for a long time, but had really never called on us, were now coming to see Mr. Propst.

On our end, we couldn't tell things were falling apart because the world was still keeping its head above water, but the banks were starting to squeeze the real estate companies, not letting them have any loans. So, they were coming to see us. They knew we had capital.

Every meeting was very similar. Mr. Propst said, "Just wait." And we did. He had vision that not many other people have. Luckily, we didn't have a lot invested at the time. We just waited until the pricing was right and we got in the game.

We bought some land in Huntsville. Then we bought Flex Office Steel down in Tampa, Florida, about an $18 million asset. We bought and sold some land down in Saraland. We bought a 100-acre site and sold 60 percent of it to Infirmary Health Systems to build a hospital. We were going to build a Target there, and the market crashed. The hospital wanted to buy it, so we were thankful for that. We bought a shopping center that I'd developed at Colonial that was probably the prime asset that Colonial had left. That took a little time because I don't think they wanted to sell it to us. We bought it and it was a great success story for us. We bought a little shopping center in an online auction. We paid about $3.8 million for it and sold it for $7.5 million. Those are the kinds of things we've been trying to do.

We've gotten into the residential home business and that's become a very profitable part of our business. I think it will become a bigger and bigger part of our business. We've been selling assets. We'll be back in the buying mode again when the time is right. We own this building we're sitting in and we've been offered a really big profit on it, but we decided to keep it. We love this building.

The retail business has changed. I don't know who is safe out there in terms of retailers. You have Macy's closing 100 stores. Sears-Kmart won't be here in two to three years, in my opinion. Payless is closing 1,000 stores. They say Gander Mountain is about to file bankruptcy. Everybody in the retail industry is having issues. We just sit back and see how things wash out. When they do, we'll get back in.

Meanwhile, we are going to try and develop some grocery-anchored deals. We've got 1,400 to 1,500 residential lots and we're building houses on them. We're in Nashville doing a development there. We've got 500 lots we're doing with Signature Homes in Birmingham. It's all residential construction. We're just going to be very thoughtful about what we do. We don't want to grow just to grow. We want to grow and make money doing it. Pricing is at an all time high right now, so we're just backing up a little bit. Showing a little discipline, which is hard to do sometimes.

Places like Amazon and other online retailers have set the pace. In fact, now they [the other big box stores] are all trying to figure out how to do it [e-commerce] themselves. I've read recently, Target did such a good job with their e-commerce, they think they've hurt their own same-store sales from their big boxes. Everybody is taking a bite of the online market. But it's still only about 10% of the retail trade. It's not a big part of retail, but it's growing every day and every percent that goes online is coming out of all these other stores. So, they've got a shrinking business versus Amazon that has a growing business. What it's going to do long term, I don't know, but we've got to figure it out. Great retail sites are still going to be strong. I think the outlying retail is going to struggle.

Business is changing every day. I think we have a great future because we have great people. We've got some really talented, smart people here. There are four of us that have a tremendous amount of experience doing all kinds of retail stuff. Then Ben Hughey is one of the young people who is looking at the world differently. He's a sharp young man who happens to be my son.

I think I'm going to let the market dictate what we do with the business. I'm not going to dictate it. The market is so much more powerful than we are. You can't outpace the market. We've done things I never dreamed we'd do. We bought and sold mortgages. We've been in the flex office business. We're in the residential construction business. I didn't have any experience with any of that, but we've been successful in all those ventures. We try to hire smart people that share our values and morals and hopefully we'll have some success doing that.

I think we closed 200 homes last year in Nashville. It's become a big part of our business. Well, we're more of an investor there than building the homes. We're partnering with some quality people. Dwight Salmon and Jonathan Belcher own Signature Homes. They're high-quality people. When you think about it, they've built thousands of homes for people. I knew Dwight when I lived in Birmingham; we lived five or six houses apart from each other. I had no idea what his business was all about until we started talking about getting in the residential business.

We've built a few homes here. This market is a little tougher. The kind of homes that Signature builds are architecturally very pleasing and cost a little bit more than I think Huntsville is geared to pay, unless you're downtown or whatever, for new-home construction. We've had a lot of success in Nashville and Birmingham.

It's funny, before I met Bill Propst, I said I was going to retire by the time I was 54, and luckily, I had the means to do that. I had done about everything I could do in that big organization [at Colonial Properties]. My kids were just about through college. But, the day I walked in here to start a new company, I was energized like I hadn't been before - because there wasn't anybody to fix the computer, fix coffee, type a letter. I mean, it was just us. We didn't have a business name. We had a desk to sit at. We started it from scratch. We've made a significant amount of money in a fairly short period of time based on what we've invested. I hope the Propsts are happy with what we've done. I hope they continue to allow us to grow the business.

You know the thing I would say that is probably as meaningful as anything, is the wealth that Mr. Propst has doesn't define him. Really, that's just something he has. He told me one time that having a lot of wealth can be a curse. I happened to work for two families that were extremely wealthy, the Lowder family and the Propst family.

Everybody that knocks on your door, are they coming to see me or do they have a motive to see me? Are they coming to see me because they want something from me? How do you let them in your life and how do you go from here to there to get to know people? People wear his phone out trying to get in to see him, a lot of times, just because they want something from him. Like I said, he never leaves an old friend to make a new one. He's done some incredible things for people in this town that you'd be blown away by. Lending them money, helping them out, without asking for anything in return, just because they needed help.

If you go anywhere with him, he always wants to pick up the check. You have to get there ahead of time to have half a chance to cut him off, give them your credit card or whatever, or go get the check while he's got his back turned.

Bill, Jr. told me one day, "John, quit wasting your time.

Dad's going to pay for it." One day Mr. Propst said to me, "I don't know why so-and-so minds me picking up the check." I said, "Because he's your friend, and your friend doesn't want to use you for that."

He said, "Well, if I thought he did, I wouldn't do it. John, I've been blessed beyond belief and I like to share that with people." And he does.

Another thing that is pretty remarkable to me... I've seen Mr. Propst give the city of Huntsville tens of millions of dollars. They asked him for a million for something; he gave them five. He gave them a $10 million piece of property, too.

You know when Bill, Jr. was going through trouble trying to build his house, it was just remarkable. Bill Propst didn't say, "Hey, I've done all this for the city, I've done this and that." He didn't do that. He said we'll go through the same process everybody else does.

He just loves Huntsville and wants to see Huntsville do good things. He met with Jim Hudson at HudsonAlpha; they had asked him to do some things. He asked me what I thought, not that I mattered, but I said, "I'll tell you what I think. I think of all the things I've seen, you probably have the biggest opportunity to make an impact for the world in that deal than anything else I've seen." He said, "I agree with you." He wants to make a difference. That's the thing about Mr. Propst, he wants to make a difference in your life. Not in your day... in your life.

You've read about the escalating prices and all that in the pharmaceuticals industry. He thinks it's wrong. He said, "I'd never do that. It's not right to do it." Yeah, you can make money and he made a lot of money while in the business but as he says, "I was successful because I was trying to bring a product that was not too expensive to a generic level, to help people to be able to afford it, where I could make money and they could buy it cheaper, and everybody wins." But he says, "Even generic companies today, if it'll cost a dollar or 50 cents to make it, they think it's ok to charge $200 for it. That's what's wrong." You have to respect that about him. I do.

He would have been successful at anything he did. Even Bear Bryant couldn't have competed with him if he'd been a football coach because he's that kind of man. He believes in people, has a lot of faith in people. He gives them an assignment, lets them run with it, doesn't micromanage it. I wish he was 60; I'd encourage him to run for president. That's the kind of folks you need in leadership. He's a blessing to Huntsville, and he's a blessing to the state. He's also a blessing to the United States in the things he does. I've seen him give money to political issues and he says, "I don't want anything in return; I just want them to do the right thing." I've never seen him ask anything that you or I wouldn't ask. But, let me be clear, he doesn't use his money or influence to get things done.

DESCRIPTIVE REFLECTIONS

He's not a religious person. When I say that, I mean he doesn't tell you how faithful he is, he just shows you. He's a very faithful person. Things that don't go the way he wants them to, he says, "Everything happens for the best." Meaning, we don't control it, the good Lord is making the calls on these things, so don't worry about it. He's a remarkable person in that regard.

He's kind. He's thoughtful. He's proactive. He takes action when other people watch. Instead of saying, "If I can do something for you let me know," he just does it. He doesn't care if he upsets the apple cart if he knows it's the right thing to do. He sets a great example. If we all lived our lives like he did, this place would be a lot better place.

You'll never walk behind him through a door. He won't budge until you walk in front of him. You go somewhere with him in his car or whatever else, you're going to be in the front seat. I've seen him take the back seat in his own airplane. He puts everybody in front of him. It's just heartwarming. Like I said, it's a great example for all of us to see. He's taught his sons the same way and his grandsons, too. I've seen him do it too with Bill, Jr.'s son, William. I'm sure he does it with his other grandsons. He believes in teaching them to do it right. He's done a great job of that.

If somebody is sick, he sends them something. I'll never forget when my wife and I were moving to Huntsville and he showed up with food for us for lunch at our house. He didn't even tell me he was coming. He just showed up.

One of the most disappointing business days I ever had - we got turned down on a deal we wanted, and he came in and gave me a bonus check.

I tore it up and I said, "No thank you." I went to lunch and I came back and there was a check sitting at my desk on my chair. I voided it and put it back on his desk. I said, "I didn't do anything to earn this."

He said, "I really, really appreciate you being here. You're doing a great job for us."

I said, "But I can't accept this."

He came back in before the end of the day and said, "Now, you can either take this check or I'm going to give it to your wife and she can go blow it on whatever she wants."

He does those kinds of things. He knew I was disappointed. It wasn't anything that he did; it was my loss. I didn't get the deal done. It's just the kind of man that he is. He knows how to inspire people. I'd run through a wall for him. I'd do anything for him. Anything legal or moral, of course. He wouldn't ask me to do anything otherwise.

Sometimes you have to listen to what he says because he'll give you just a little bit and you have to really think about what he just said to you.

He's one of the most down-to-earth, grounded people. I would tell you what really defines him is the people around him. You don't meet anybody that doesn't love him. If you don't love him, you don't know him.

Bill Propst at the lake with father, Paul.

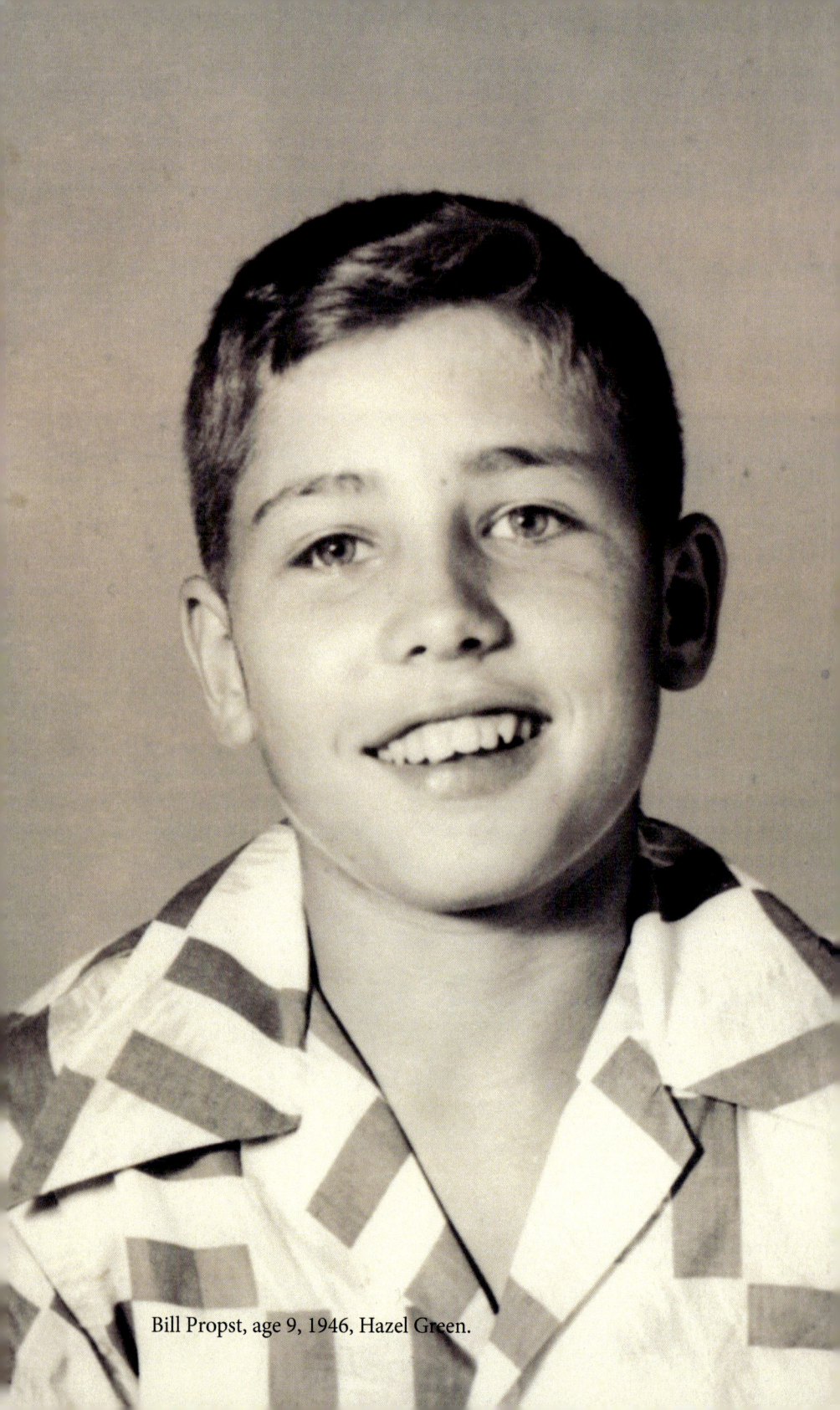

Bill Propst, age 9, 1946, Hazel Green.

ICONIC & UNFORGETTABLE

Community Involvement

William (Bill) Self Propst, Sr.

"We like to give to the needy, not the greedy."

Mr. William (Bill) Self Propst, Sr.

Excerpts from Interviews with

William (Bill) Self Propst, Sr.

Regarding

The Community He Calls Home

In 1945 or '46, we moved to Hazel Green, Alabama. Daddy was a Methodist minister. I could tell you every house [along the] 14 miles between Hazel Green and downtown Huntsville. All you saw were cotton fields and the occasional corn field. Most of them were cotton fields. Huntsville was a real small town. Drake Avenue was a dirt road called Donegan Lane.

We watched it grow. There's a lot of things that the city fathers didn't anticipate far enough out. Rideout Road should have come all the way around the mountain to the river. Of course, you can't do everything at once. You've got to do what your resources allow.

Normally, we get things done when we have vision. You hear people say things can't be done. But we've got good vision here, with our current administration. We've brought in some people who are aggressive. We'll make headway. We've

LOOKING AHEAD

He is not worried about his lifespan; he is worried about the next one. He's worried about my kids' and his kids' children and grandchildren.

- Mary Lynne Wright

still got to get where we can take care of our streets, etc. At this point, we've got a lot of potholes. They're putting money other places. I'm not being critical…I would like to see some potholes gone, but that's a temporary thing. [Mayor] Battle has done a good job since he's been in office. We haven't had any scandals or anything. With [Mayor] Loretta [Spencer], we didn't have any. She was there for a long time. I don't think there were any scandals with Mayor Joe Davis either.

I know Huntsville is active in soliciting manufacturing, I think we need a lot of other things that aren't related to Redstone and rockets and so forth. One of these days, the government may cut back on money for this area. If the entire country is having cutbacks, I think we should cutback too. I don't want them to take it away. That's not what I'm saying at all. I'm just saying that politicians have to be responsible.

[Senator] Shelby has done an outstanding job of keeping this place running, but I think we can do more. We are prudent now, but if you've got 35,000 people working on the Arsenal, you better have a whole lot of plants to support it.

MONEY

So many people are hung up on money. But money can make you miserable. People drive me crazy calling me. I had one lady call me and say that her granddaughter wanted to go to college and she understood that I paid tuition for kids. She wanted to know if I'd pay tuition for her granddaughter. I'd never seen her or heard of her prior to that conversation. Just totally out of the blue, out of the wild blue. Now, we like to give to things. We like to give to the needy, not the greedy.

We gave money to HudsonAlpha yesterday for a new research center. Well, it was announced yesterday. They couldn't get going until we agreed to [help]. And I had to call the governor and say, "Here's what we're going to do; how much will you put up?" Then, he came through with the money, the rest of the money that was needed. But they weren't going to get it off the ground until then. I hope I'm not wrong about HudsonAlpha's mission. I think they will come up with some good answers for health in this country and the entire world.

It wasn't done for the recognition. Jim [Hudson] asked me what I wanted to name it, and I said I wanted to name it after Paul Propst. That's my stepdaddy. Not many folks would name something after their stepdaddy, I'll tell you that, but Paul Propst was one of the few people I've ever seen that really practiced what he preached. He was a heck of a nice fella, good to us, you know. He didn't have to take us [my brother and me] in, but he did.

Mother and Daddy never lived in Huntsville, per se. Well, they did the last few years of their life, but daddy was confined at that point. He didn't get out of bed for the last eight and half years of his life. Arthritis. I'm talking about his feet didn't hit the floor. Nobody around here really knew Paul Propst. Daddy died at '96. But now his name is on that center out there [at HudsonAlpha], and it's going to do good for the world.

So, some people ask me, why did you give money to HudsonAlpha? I'll tell you why. HudsonAlpha, from what I understand, is making some tremendous strides with cancer. If there's anything that we need to cure, it's cancer. Cancer and diabetes. I don't know if they're working on diabetes, but I know they're working on cancer. They've made a lot of headway. They're in stage three with a product or two and

I thought if there's any way I can help, then fine. It really wasn't done for any other reason.

Eloise, my wife, has had cancer. I had rickets as a boy and now have diabetes. My daddy had arthritis. There have been other illnesses and such in our lives. It has had an effect on how I feel, charitably wise. Eloise and I give to different things, a variety of things.

Take the Botanical Garden [for example]. Butch [Mrs. Damson] about drove me crazy to give some money to the Botanical Garden. Well, you know, I kept thinking about it and looking at it. The reason I did it is you'd be amazed how many people drive from Birmingham, Nashville, etc., just to go through our botanical garden. It's a big plus for the city. You have to think about everybody and everything.

We just need to bring people to town. When people come to town, they don't just look at things and drive through. They might buy gas or get a Coke. They do this or they do that. We get taxes from it. They stop at a restaurant. There are any number of things they may do. To me, it's a boon for the city. Just like the Space and Rocket Center. When Gene McLain and the Chamber were working on that, I thought, I couldn't envision what they were talking about, but Gene could see it. He could see years and years out. He was one of the founders of the Space and Rocket Center. He really worked for the financing [of it] and so forth. He had the vision that people would come to see it. And they do. I couldn't have envisioned all of that. I wouldn't have known where to start... to get a part of a rocket, and so forth. For me, helping the garden is important to the city like what Gene did for the Space and Rocket Center.

Gene was a highly intelligent person. He was born south of Anniston. His father was a sharecropper who died when Gene was six. His mother remarried and married another sharecropper. Gene had two pairs of overalls, one he wore and one they washed. He was smart enough to get a scholarship to Auburn. He ended up going to Oxford on scholarship. In other words, he was a bright person, he had a good personality and he had vision. And he had stamina to go with all of that.

When Gene got on his feet and got wealthy, he was still the same old Gene. He never changed. He would go down to the Little Farm restaurant across from the hospital where the gas station is now and eat breakfast in the morning. It was a dumpy little old place. He'd go there and talk to the fellas from all walks of life. He was a tremendous fella. You don't run up on many like him.

I got to know Gene back in the early or mid '60s. He was the attorney of a friend of mine. I was doing a deal [with this friend], and he said, "Let me get the attorney." He got Gene. We met and from there on, we were good friends.

When I first sold out, we gave money to Randolph School and different schools. Since then, we've helped Samford University. We put in a new lab down there, a pharmacy lab, named after my brother, also a pharmacist. And then I gave the primary finances for the building that's named after me.

Oh, and that community college, Calhoun Community College. They couldn't build that building on their new campus until we helped with it. We gave enough to get them started. We didn't build it. They just needed help getting started.

We also did the arena [at the Von Braun Center]. For the arena, they asked what I wanted to see in it. I said I wanted some more ladies restrooms. They said, "Why? Why would you think of that?" My reply, "I'm tired of women coming into the men's restroom. Let's have enough restrooms."

Like I said, money can make you miserable. I like to give

to what I like to give. I asked a number of people to find me some real needy families. Let's say their daddy got hurt and they've got two or three kids, primarily on the west side of town, and they've really come under hard times. Thanksgiving and Christmas is coming. I asked around, "I need 15 or 16 families and let me take care of them. I want to make sure the kids have a good Christmas, some decent clothes for the winter. Make sure they have enough food for Thanksgiving." I asked for two or three years and couldn't get anybody to tell me anything. I knew they were out there, so I was getting really disappointed.

When I was finally pointed to the Boys Club, I went down to Wal-Mart and talked to the store manager. I told him we're going to send some folks down here and they can buy from these categories and that's it. I didn't want them buying fishing rods and so forth, if you know what I mean.

THIS IS AN EASY PLACE TO SELL

You know when I went out to recruit, I had a hard time getting chemists and formulators interested in coming to Huntsville. To give you an example, I was talking to a fella who was a good cream and ointment formulator in New York City and I said, "Why don't you just come down here and look?" He said, "Well, what's the closest city, the closest airport?"

"What about Huntsville?"

"OK. What size plane?"

"What are you going to leave New York on?"

And so he came. When he debarks, you know, he sees that we have a nice airport. He comes out [of the airport], sees the roads were paved and that I was in a nice car. We drove around town and went out to look at the plants and so forth. I drove him around and the most impressive thing that he saw was downtown Huntsville and the Von Braun Center. The long and short of it, he moved to Huntsville and retired here.

You know, all you have to do is bring people here. This is an easy place to sell. After they've lived here for six to eight months, they're not going anywhere. It's reasonably priced, cost of living is fine, it's a nice place, the people are nice, you can get anywhere in 10 or 15, 20 minutes...

THIS IS HOME

We gave the city property on Moore's Mill Road. The city can develop it and so forth. I didn't think I had the time to do it. We've done a few things for the city but I don't keep up with what we've done.

This is home. My son [Bill, Jr.] had problems with [his house]. He bought a house that had belonged to a doctor who died many years ago. Part of the basement was crumbling, [and the] foundation was questionable. It had mold, fleas and you name it. I don't believe you can ever get rid of mold. That house wasn't worth the time, trouble or investment. Bill took architects up there to look at it. The contractors and architects said there wasn't any way [to save it] so Bill, Jr petitioned the city to let him tear it down. They wouldn't give him the permit at first, but eventually they did. It was in all of the newspapers. This one fellow wouldn't give him the permit, after the historical society had approved it. That was on a Tuesday. Friday, he finally gave it to him, at a quarter to five.

When Bill got back to the office, he was telling me about it. I told him to call S.O. McDonald and have him over there the next morning. He said, "Why?"

> "Son, if you don't get it down, you're going to have trouble."

The next morning, when I got over there, S.O. had his backhoe front end loader at the back of the house. I told him, "S.O. that's not where you want to do it. What they care about is the front of the house. Pull that thing back around here." And he did.

It wasn't long before most of it was gone. People stopped and threatened him with lawsuits and so forth, saying that he shouldn't tear it down, that it was a historical house. I put the steel and handrails on that house back in 1956 or 1957. To me, there wasn't anything historical about it. But it was, according to a few people, I guess. They were set to take it to court on Monday and get a restraining order, but it was gone on Saturday. He did end up going to court though... to get his plans approved. The house he built in its place is large and may be too big for the neighborhood, but I guarantee you it has helped the neighborhood.

Someone asked me if I was mad at the city. "Are you not going to do anything for the city in the future?" I simply said, "We had a disagreement, but this is home. I'm still going to do everything I can for Huntsville, because it's home." You don't walk away and tear down your house just for the heck of it, you know. I'm not mad at anybody. I thought some of the stuff that went on was a little excessive, but outside of that, they're entitled to their opinion too. But some of them that did most of the objecting didn't even live in this area. They live way over on the other side of town. I wondered what they had to do with it.

A THANKSGIVING GIVING

I'm sitting in the office in the plant in Charlotte looking at the payroll the Monday before Thanksgiving. I'd had that heart attack and this was the first week I could travel. I'm looking at the payroll and most of the people were making $4.50 to

$6 an hour. I couldn't find anybody making any more than that. So, I asked Paul [Higdon], "Do you think everybody here is going to have enough to eat for Thanksgiving?" If you've got a car payment, apartment rent or whatever, and you make $4.50 an hour, you've got troubles. He said, "I don't know, Mr. Propst."

I said, "Well, go buy a turkey for everybody here." Paul got them and passed them out. If I gave up there [in Charlotte, at Vintage], I'd have to give one here [in Huntsville, at Qualitest], you know? So, I called down to Huntsville [to Qualitest] and told them to get a turkey for each employee.

We went back [to Vintage] the following Monday and a female named, Rosemary, came up [to me] and said, "Mr. Propst, how come we didn't get a ham?" I'll never forget her name because of that.

That's when we started giving hams. This year, I gave about 85 turkeys at Thanksgiving and 85 hams at Christmas, not to employees, just people and friends. I'm not trying to impress them. I just want them to know that somebody thought about them. Most of them can buy anything they want, any time... neighbors and so forth, just friends. Of course, I still buy them for some of the folks that live up on the mountain and Scottsboro... people that had worked for me.

PRAISES FOR BUTCH DAMSON

In this town, people ought to be thankful for Butch Damson. Huntsville wouldn't be what it is today without her. [chuckling] She's quite a character. To show you how she is, she has a station wagon that is 19 years old. She could have any kind of car she would like. They keep trying to give her a new car. But she keeps saying, "No, I like the one I've got." She's not trying to impress anybody, but when she decides there's a project that is worthy of her time, she'll stick with you until you help her. I've been friends with the Damsons a long time, [since 1952, when I met Jerry at Columbia Military Academy.]

I'll tell you a little story about Butch Damson. Butch kept talking to me about Burritt Museum. They needed some help so they could get the their new building started. She kept after me and I finally gave her the amount of money she asked for. I hadn't been up there to see it until the child of a friend of ours got married at Burritt. A few days after the wedding, I called Butch. I said, "Butch, you know you bugged me to death for money for the Burritt museum, and I contributed. I was up there this week and what do I see just as I'm coming into the complex? I see a statue of little red riding hood!" [Laughing] It's a statue of Butch. We have a good time. I was just bugging her. You have to be able to laugh at yourself…

I leave a lot to laugh at.

The Personal Narrative of

Steve Maples

Chief Executive Officer & Executive Director Von Braun Center

I'm a native of Huntsville. I grew up here and went to Lee High School. I attended an area tech school where I was trained in air conditioning and refrigeration.

When I was hired on here at the center, I worked part time. That was the summer that we first opened, in 1975. I worked with air conditioning and refrigeration as well as keeping the mechanical rooms clean. I hired on full time two years later in 1977. During this period, I attended Calhoun Community College and Athens State University, graduating with a Bachelor's Degree in Business Administration.

I have been the Executive Director of the VBC since 2007. I was new in this position when we first started looking at an expansion and renovation of the arena and concert hall.

WHAT THE CENTER MEANS TO THE COMMUNITY

The city owns this facility, and I work for a seven-member Board of Control. Most of the board members are Huntsvillians with families going back generations. Our annual operating budget is approximately $13 million. Internally, we generate about 85% of the total revenue.

Then there's the lodging tax. It is the biggest contributing portion of our revenue. Part of our job as a facility is to to put "heads in beds," so to speak. That's why we go after conferences and conventions. The more of that we do, the more return we have. It's been great. We've been growing every year. Last year [2016] was our very best year in the history of the Von Braun Center, with 800,000 visitors attending events and a total economic impact of approximately $75 million.

THAT'S THE KIND OF PEOPLE THEY ARE

The Propst Arena was renovated at the same time as the Mark C. Smith Concert Hall and because of that effort, I've gotten to know the Propst family pretty well. Actually Bill, Jr. and I became really good friends. He had an interest in the concert business and promoting shows, so he asked me to teach him that side of the business. I spent a year trying to help him learn that, and he started a new company, Big Spring Entertainment. He started off in Huntsville, and now he's expanded to other parts of Alabama and into Tennessee and Mississippi. He has hired some people and he's really getting the company going.

I've traveled with him to a few shows. It has been quite an experience because they have their own jets. The morning we flew down to Dothan, the weather was really bad and we got caught in a storm. We ended up landing somewhere down in Florida, 100 miles away. We had to get a car and drive over.

They're all interesting people. They're good people. Mr. Propst, he's a character. He likes to tell jokes and he's good at it. He's funny and has a real sense of humor! I tell Bill, Jr. his dad intimidates me though. [laughing] He's always in a suit and tie and thinks I should be too. I feel like I should put on a tie just to sit here and talk about him. [laughing] I'll tell you something else, too. He makes me feel like I just want to do a better job even when he's not around.

Mr. Propst does so many good things. I know things he does that I probably shouldn't talk about because he doesn't want a lot of credit. But I can tell you he does a lot of good things. He makes a lot of nice contributions and gives a lot. I know he buys a lot of bicycles for Christmas every year. And, speaking of Christmas, Bill, Jr. called me this past Christmas and said he needed to see me. He asked me to stop by his house because he had something for me. So, I stopped by and he had like 50 hams in the back of his car! His dad also had 50, or thereabouts. They just spend the day delivering them to all of their friends. That's the kind of people they are. We go to lunch with Bill, Sr. sometimes. You can just forget about paying for lunch, because he won't let you. They're just good people.

THE LIFE AND BLOOD OF THE CENTER'S FUTURE

All that takes us back to the Propsts and Linda Smith, who made the concert hall renovation possible, along with our board, in whom I have a lot of faith. The VBC board and city officials all worked closely together as a team to accomplish our projects on schedule and under budget. Because of the renovations we all did back in 2007, we've had the kind of success and growth needed so that we are now able to make our expansion plans. It takes a quality board to help pull everything together.

FORGET THE TIE

Like I said earlier, I've been here 40 years. I started here when I was in high school and I've never left. That's due largely because of the quality people we've always had on the board and the support of the city. It's a great place to work. Obviously, I've worked my way to the last top job which I've had for probably 10 years now.

Don't tell Bill Sr., but if I could dress like I want to, I'd wear my blue jeans to work every day. Forget the tie. [laughs]

The Personal Narrative of
Paula Steigerwald
President & Chief Executive Officer
Huntsville Botanical Garden

I refer to Bill Propst as Mr. Bill because, for the longest, I only knew him from a distance - for what he's done and contributed in the community. Even his involvement at the Garden for a long time was kind of from a distance. He didn't want a lot of attention. That makes me a little bit uncomfortable at times, because I think quite often about what I would like to do for Bill and Eloise [to show my appreciation].

My relationship with the Propsts came through Butch Damson. Butch is my interpreter [chuckling] because she's pretty straight to it. It was Butch who talked to Mr. Bill about the Garden's welcome center. She made sure that he was aware of what we were doing while we were doing it.

Mr. Bill monitored and watched this [construction project] as it took shape, encouraging us to do the right things and not cut corners. I do think that he is proud of being a part of it. He knows that he helped raise the bar. Of course, we are very proud that Eloise would allow us to put her name on the building. When you think about who the Propsts are in this community, it's a proud moment when they'll allow you to directly associate with them. It is one thing to just contribute to something, but to allow your name to be used is another.

He trusts [and expects] our stewardship but he also appreciates quality and making sure that things are done well. If you're going to represent Huntsville and bring tourists from all over the country, all over the world [even], you have to put the right face forward. He gets it that we're putting a good face on Huntsville. I think everyone involved has been proud that we are doing just that.

OUR CONTRIBUTORS

Mr. Propst's donation was large enough for the naming opportunity which was very dear to me, very personal. There are about 500 contributors that made this center possible. The original contributors, Linda Smith and Butch Damson, encouraged us to the point that I thought, okay, I guess we're really going to do this because now I've got supporters. We had our master plan updated and that's what did it... I guess I shouldn't have showed it [to them] if I didn't want to build it. (laughing)

Several years ago, Mr. Bill responded to another appeal, a private appeal to our members. It was the year after the tornadoes. Because so many people had given to the Red Cross, as another nonprofit, we didn't feel like it was the right time to [publicly] promote ourselves. But as we were ending our fiscal year, we were also having difficulties so we made an appeal to our members. The Propsts made the largest response. I felt quite honored by that too.

Of course, the Damsons [Jerry and Butch], the Propsts [Bill and Eloise], and the Smiths [Mark and Linda] – they do more than write a check. They make you think about your stewardship as a nonprofit. They are some pretty savvy business folks that will challenge you. They're doing it to help you grow the organization, beyond financially.

CHANGING THE TRAJECTORY: ONE STEP AT A TIME

We kind of adhere to the Dave Ramsey school of financing, so we did things in stages. We did the parking lot first.

We used it as an example of how you can build parking lots that are sustainable. There are rain gardens, LED lighting, eco pavers and things of that nature. That was all about laying the groundwork. Next, it was time to build the welcome center. The big question was, "What do you want it to be?" The word from our board was that it needs to be iconic. We broke ground January 20th of 2016 and opened March 10th of 2017. It was an aggressive effort by all.

The first meeting with Mr. Propst was probably spring of last year [2016]. We were already committed [to the project]. The lot was already cleared. Of course, he had made his commitment to us in February. But the first time I was really able to tell him the rest of the story was early spring, probably March. Butch and Jerry brought him out. Butch helps edit a lot of the things that come his way. Knowing the kind of [generous] folks they are, through Butch and Jerry, I can only imagine that they need a filter.

Butch is definitely very influential but she also understands that all she can do is tell the story. The Garden had grown incrementally and had gotten to this threshold that we were going to be one of those nonprofits that was going to struggle to maintain if we didn't think bigger. So, creating rental revenue was the primary opportunity to ensure a successful future for the Garden.

OUR COMMUNITY IS OUR FUTURE

I loved what Mayor Battle said the other day. "You've always talked about this being the community's Garden. Now this is the community's house. This house is open to the public. It's the community's house. Anything else would be like a country club to which everybody isn't invited, but you made it a house so that it's warm and inviting."

Like he did, in saying that, people like to give me credit. But to that, I always say, "I just get out of the way." This garden is run by a dedicated staff, its volunteers and by the community, and we have a very talented and generous community. Why would I want to control that or get in the way of that?

The Personal Narrative of
Jim Hudson
Co-founder of HudsonAlpha Institute for Biotechnology

Bill made a generous contribution for our next building. I've known Bill for less than a year. Obviously, we knew of each other. My accountant of many years, Ronnie Hamilton, is close to Bill. They used to take morning walks together.

For the last seven or eight years, Ronnie would say, "Jim, you really need to talk to Bill. You would enjoy Bill." When we finally met, he came here to HudsonAlpha, walked in and sat right there. I started telling him about HudsonAlpha and everything we were doing. He interrupted me and went straight to it, saying, "What can I do for you?"

"Well we're building a building and I need $10 million."

"I can help you with that."

He continued, "I will give you half now and put half in my will." It was really that quick. Bam, once he got that out of the way, we just started talking. With some people you just have good chemistry, and that's what we had, really good chemistry. After that meeting, I started stopping by Bill's office in the mornings and having coffee and biscuits with him. We started comparing life stories, all sorts of stories. There were just so many things we had in common. We're just two old guys loving to share stories. I really enjoy my time spent with Bill and admire what he's done with his life. After he told me, "I can help you with that," he said, "I've been watching you for years, and before I go, I just want to do something for you." [with a gentle laugh] I guess I should have asked for more. But I knew what I needed for that building, and that's all I asked for.

I do wish we had managed to connect sooner because I think we would have enjoyed visiting and walking together. I still go by about once a week to see him at breakfast time.

Bill must get up at 3:30 or 4 in the morning, I don't know what time exactly, but I know he always goes by Gibson's, picks up ham biscuits to take to the office by 7 or 7:30 a.m. Every time I go, there's this bag of biscuits he's brought in that you can see through because of the grease. I like the friendship so I still visit. Bill is just a great guy. We connect; we have good chemistry. He's just a really good guy.

I've enjoyed talking to him about the generics business. He has expressed pride and a real satisfaction from designing his plants. One comment that he made to me was, "I've always wanted to design an injectables plant." It's preloaded syringes with drugs. That's something I'd like to see on the campus so we talk about that, what would be involved, how many square feet. He obviously knows that stuff inside and out, and he gets great satisfaction from designing and thinking of the work flow that would go into making an efficient pharmaceutical manufacturing facility. That's close to me because I would like to have something like that on the HudsonAlpha campus. We have 155 acres, room for 13 more buildings and I want one of them to be a pharmaceutical manufacturing facility. So, I've been talking to him a lot about that kind of thing. Just kind of getting some knowledge. He lights up when he gets to talking about that.

Bill figured out how to build a plant and manufacture generics more efficiently than anybody else and make a reasonable profit. So it makes him mad that nowadays, everybody gets the lowest possible cost and then marks it up as much as they possibly can. The costs haven't gone up; people are just extracting more out of the healthcare system than he feels is fair. I admire him for that.

Bill's gift allowed us to go forward with our fourth building, which is a very big step for us. What that building is going to represent is our genomic medicine program, a brand new thing for HudsonAlpha. But Bill's gift is more than a bricks and mortar thing. It's a center within the new building, the Paul Propst Center for Genomic Medicine, named after Bill's father.

HudsonAlpha formed with three legs: nonprofit research, economic development and an educational outreach arm. Those three things were the foundation of HudsonAlpha getting started. In the future Lonnie [McMillan] and I wanted to bring our discoveries into the clinic. We thought that would be 10 or 20 years down the road. Through Bill's contribution, and an earlier one from Linda Smith, we now have both a clinic and a research arm to expand clinical genomic medicine. Linda gave us the money for the actual clinic; it is treating people now. Bill's money is building the center that will make the research discoveries necessary to expand the genomic medicine program.

A big part of genomic medicine is the computer part, the bio-informatics, as we call it. It's a real word when you Google it, believe it or not. I used to wonder if we made it up, but I guess we did and Webster adopted it. Probably 40 percent of everything we do is in the computer, 'in silico' as people like to say. We don't have the room for that in this building. That whole operation will be moving into the new building, allowing us to expand our bioinformatics role in genomic medicine. We're going to be expanding our education outreach over there, too. Because the genomic medicine program is one of our largest-growing areas, the center will outgrow that building and will eventually be in even more buildings.

We're on 155 acres, with three buildings on the campus now. The fourth building is the one that's going to be the Paul Propst Center for Genomic Medicine. I believe the easiest way to be the big fish in a small pond is to pick a niche and dominate the niche. Genomics is a small pond.

HudsonAlpha is a genomics-based facility. We're probably third or fourth largest in the world in that area. It depends on how you want to measure though. The Chinese have some massive facilities. We might not be quite that high in regard to facilities, but if you look in the publications and the research coming out, we're definitely near the top. It is a small world. There are only a few thousand people in genomics worldwide. We have some of the smartest. Rick Myers was the chairman of genetics at Stanford. Howard Jacob's team was the first to ever sequence somebody and save their life. We recruited him and 15 members of his team here. All our people are really top notch.

The Smith Family Clinic is the first and only clinic devoted exclusively to genomic medicine. It's a little bitty place, but it's the only place in the world that that's all they do. And now, with Bill's support, we will expand our genomics medicine program such that we will impact the health of every person, first locally, then in the state, then in the nation, as the program grows.

Smith Family Clinic is devoted to people who have an undiagnosed disease. Bill's contribution expands that research, as well as application, into all forms of genomic-based medicine. There are a lot of ways to talk about that. There's cancer genomics, there's pharmacogenomics, which is how you react to a drug or don't. Then there's obviously the genetic disease part, which is in the rare disease space. That's what Smith Family Clinic is focused on. But, in a complex disease space like diabetes and heart disease and things like that, that will all be what falls under the Paul Propst Center for Genomic Medicine.

So, in short, Bill's contribution is allowing us to increase our impact on the world and create wonderful jobs for Huntsville at high annual salary rates. By the time Bill's building opens up, we should be over a thousand jobs. I'd like to see it at 3,000 before I'm out of here. That will fill up the campus, then we'll be overflowing into other space and really and truly establish biotech in north Alabama.

DESCRIPTIVE REFLECTIONS

He's direct and he's honest. Obviously, like the story I told of him going directly to the point, there's no beating around the bush. He has a real sense of fairness about him, like how the world should be a little fairer than it is. I think about all the stories he told about how the health system is just corrupt and the way it is overcharging and denying access to medicine for the people who can't afford their medicine, just because of the pricing structures of things. That really upsets him, so there's a sense in him, a desire, for the system to be fair for everybody. And, obviously in his space, he was a visionary, especially in the sense that he saw the opportunity to go into Kmart.

ALUMNI NEWS

Propst Glad He Stayed in Pharmacy

William S. Propst, Sr., earned college credits in the early [5]0s, then worked for six years before entering Samford [ph]armacy school in 1958. But [the] transition back into college [wa]s a bit rocky.

"In the beginning, every [da]y for two weeks, I told Dr. [Si]gurd) Bryan that I was [goi]ng to quit," Propst remem[be]red during Homecoming [we]ekend. "When you're out [tha]t long, you don't concen[tra]te like you once did."

With persistent encourage[me]nt from religion professor [Bry]an, however, Propst stayed. [On]e day it just all fell [tog]ether," he recalled.

Samford's 1996 Alumnus of [the] Year planned to attend [me]dical school, and chose the [pha]rmacy undergraduate [pro]gram only because he [wan]ted a profession to pursue [par]t-time while studying [me]dicine. After earning his [deg]ree, he decided to work [par]t-time in pharmacy for a [yea]r.

He's glad he did. Not only [did] he like the field, he hit [upo]n a plan that made him [one] of the nation's most suc[cess]ful pharmacists.

Propst initiated the [con]cept of leased pharmacy [ope]rations in Kmart stores [nati]onwide, and served as [pres]ident of Kmart pharmacies [for 1]7 years.

[T]he 1961 graduate is [fou]nder and president of [Qua]litest Products, Inc., and [own]er of Vintage pharmaceu[tica]l manufacturing facilities in Charlotte, N.C., and Huntsville, his hometown. His companies make liquid, ointment, creme and other medicinal products, and he holds a major interest in a plastics plant in Chattanooga.

Propst's companies are developing new products such as a vial with a cap that can be adapted to be childproof or not, and other items.

It didn't take Propst long to discover that he enjoyed pharmacy. He worked at a Walgreen store in Huntsville, and his managerial talents helped make it the number one store in the nation.

"I could meet people and be helpful," Propst recalled. "I enjoyed the hustle and bustle of the business. Also, I thought I could make a good living."

In 1964, he opened the first of five Propst stores he would own in Huntsville.

Four years later, he sold Kmart on the concept of leased pharmacy operations, admitting that it took "some slick talking."

Beginning with an experimental store in Florence, he quickly exceeded Kmart expectations, and moved into other states. The program was so successful that, when Propst took early retirement in 1985, Kmart pharmacies numbered 1,258 and could be found in most states.

"Bill Propst is a remarkable man," noted Samford President Thomas E. Corts in presenting the Alumnus of the Year award. "The son of a minister, he has built a career and a business on sound Christian principles. He is a great illustration of a person willing and eager to work, to follow high standards, and to meet with success."

Propst "demonstrates the kind of initiative that proves that 'the American dream' is alive and well and living in Alabama," added Dr. Corts.

William S. Propst, Sr., '61 of Huntsville initiated the concept of pharmacies in Kmart stores, and ultimately saw 1,258 of the discount stores in operation.

Bill Propst, Sr. featured in Samford University's Alumni News.

EUGENE MILTON M^cLAIN

November 30, 1996

Bell,

Congratulations for doing good and for the Honor that goes with it. Enclose article about you. We are proud of your success and contributions!

Gene & Jerri

LAUDERDALE STREET
MOORESVILLE, ALABAMA 35649

(205) 881-5176
(205) 350-5636

Top: Bill Propst, Sr. and wife, Eloise.
Bottom: Personal Note Card from Gene and Jerri McLain.

Samford University School of Pharmacy

*Dean Joseph O Dean, Jr and faculty of the
Samford University School of Pharmacy
cordially invite you
to the dedication of the
Michael Andrea Propst Pharmaceutics Laboratory
Ingalls Hall, Room 210
Samford University
on November 6, 1992
Tour of the lab 11·00 a.m. followed
by luncheon in the Rotunda Club*

*RSVP
870-2820*

Top: Invitation to the Dedication of Michael Andrea Propst Pharmaceutics Laboratory
Bottom: Propst Family Home in Arab, Ala.

Bill Propst, age 11, 1948.

The Personal Narrative of
William (Bill) Self Propst, Sr.
What's On The Horizon

It never was enough, the amount of money that I was making when I was with Kmart. I wasn't making a resounding salary, I made a good living. Some people just want more. I wanted to be able to take my kids to Florida when I wanted, to have a nice car and a nice house and go to dinner if we wanted to go. I've just always wanted to do more, to do big things. So I did. What I've learned though is that it's harder to give away at the end of life what you spent your life earning.

THE PROPST FOUNDATION

You have to distribute 5% of a [foundation's] total [assets] each year, and so we try to find the needy but not the greedy. We help John Croyle with the Boys Ranch. We give to a lot of different things.

I let the kids do a lot of it. Well, we all meet and agree, the five of us. Of course, I could overrule them but there wouldn't be any sense in having it if I'm going to overrule them, unless the vote is two-to-two, you know. I'm going to double the size of it [the foundation] when they sign my death certificate. It's pretty doggone meaningful now, what we give away, but it will really be meaningful then.

W.F. Sanders was in here yesterday asking about the Constitution Hall. I told him, "I'm going to send some painters over there to scrape that thing and paint it." I thought, [laughing] I better get permission.

I'm not one to get directly involved in anyone's business. The only thing I feel like I can help anybody with nowadays is with a little financing. However, I would like to create a new business, maybe for my grandchildren to take over. I keep looking, but I haven't settled on anything just yet.

We almost bought a company a few weeks ago down in Birmingham that can take a sample of your DNA and tell you if this drug will work for you or if it won't work for you. But they were charging like $400. I said no way in this world will Blue Cross pay for that. You know, you've got to get down to where it's $25 or $30 or $50.

Jim Hudson is doing a heck of a job at Hudson Alpha. I hope what we did for them goes forward to curing cancer and other things. What they're doing won't be for just this area; it will be for the world. That's what I like to give to, things that serve the masses.

The main thing I'm trying to do now is get Propst Properties on their feet where they don't have to depend on me. I'm about 60% there. In another year and a half, or two years maybe, I'll be there. From that point on, they won't need me. (laughing) Thank goodness.

WHAT'S IN THE WILL

I have directions in my will for everything and everyone, not just for the foundation. Everything is earmarked. You couldn't do it any other way, I don't think. I'm going to take care of Eloise first. After that, when she's gone, everything will be distributed.

Jerry Damson
P.O. Box 2086
Huntsville, Alabama 35804

March 10, 1993

Mr. William S. Propst
517 Adams Ave. SE
Huntsville, AL   35801

Dear Bill,

    Although this is not to thank you for your business, I hope you know I truly appreciate it.

    I read in last night's paper that you donated one hundred thousand dollars to Samford in memory of your brother. I sincerely commend you for your generosity. I know many people who have made a lot of money and think they can take it with them. I want you to know I am very proud to have known you as a person and friend for over forty years. You are in a class by yourself.

    With much admiration...

                                Most sincerely,

                                  Jerry

Letter from Jerry Damson to Bill Propst, Sr.

Bill Propst, #87, Brilliant Junior High School Football Team.

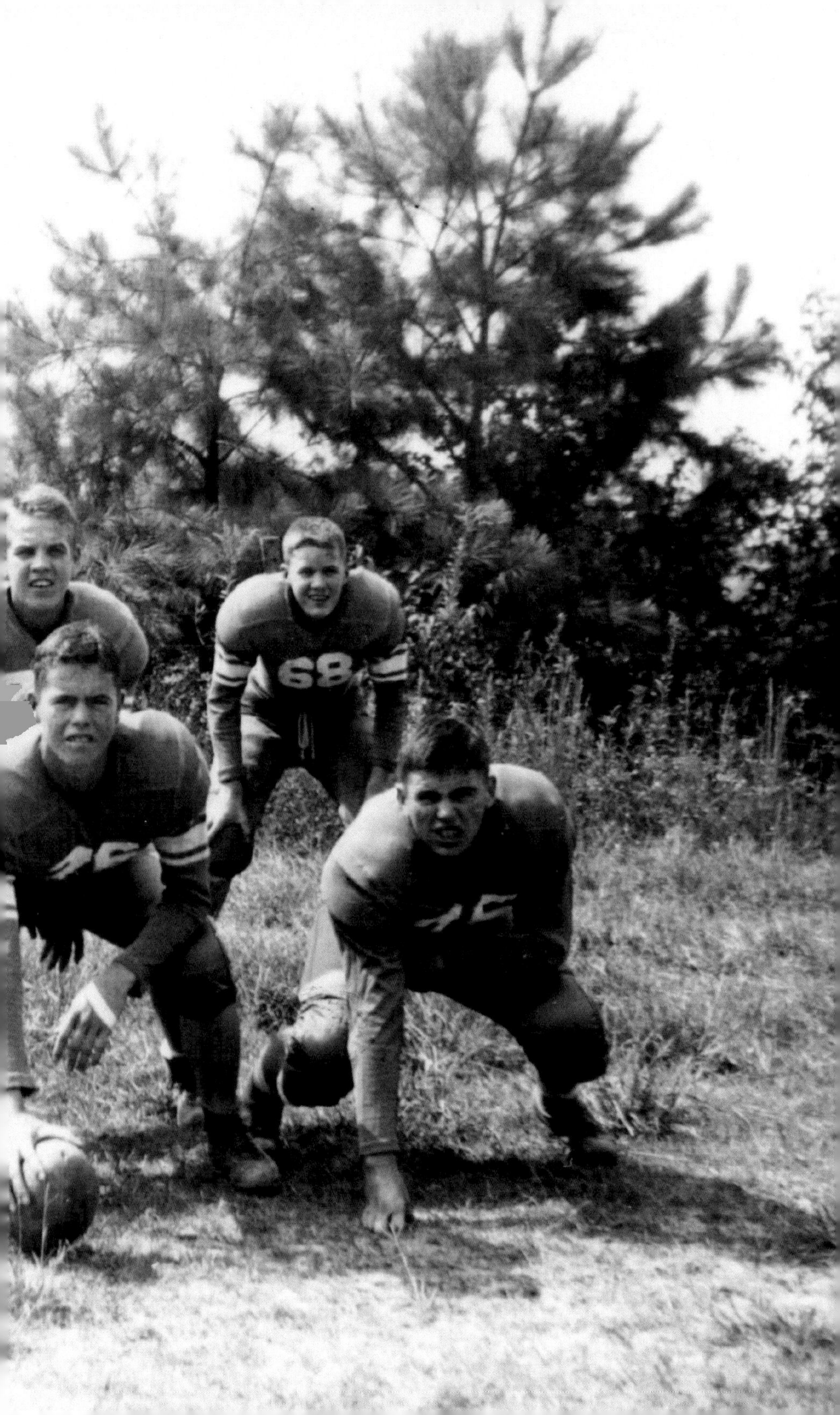
68

Bill Propst, far right, Coffee High School Homecoming.
Times Daily Staff Photo.

William (Bill) Self Propst, Sr.

A Legacy Letter

The legacy I want to leave behind is that who I am and what I've done is a reflection of how I lived when I was a boy growing up on my grandparent's farm. Papa and Mama's farm was a working farm, meaning we relied on it for our food and income. On it, was their farmhouse, and when it got hot or cold, we didn't go to a thermostat on the wall to warm it up or cool it down. Our heat source was the kitchen's wood burning stove, a small wood stove in the heater room and two fireplaces. When it was hot, we opened windows and doors, and then spent the day fanning the flies away. Instead of indoor bathrooms, we had an outhouse, and we had oil lamps instead of electric lights. Life was simple, but we had each other, so we were happy.

Before long there won't be anyone left who remembers living like that, and I really think that's a shame. Getting up every day and getting directly to the work-at-hand was what everybody did. All our friends were doing the same thing. We didn't know any other way. Life required work, so we worked. Eloise and I wanted that for our kids, too. That's why we moved out to the country when we lived in Michigan, so the kids would grow-up accustomed to doing chores and having responsibilities.

From my stories in this book, I want people to understand it takes a real enjoyment for hard work to bridge the gap from the kind of life I had as a kid to this one that Eloise and I have today. Where we are now, we've been able to give

Huntsville a little help as it has grown because as a family we spent our lives doing our best to work together and press forward in the same direction.

The point I'm making is that it didn't take somebody special born into special circumstances to do what I've done with my life. I figured out what needed to be done and did it. What did the businesses need so that they could grow? That's what I did. What did the family need? That's what I did. I had setbacks along the way, some I might could have prevented and some I probably couldn't have. Regardless, I used them, and kept pressing forward. I believe in being honest and fair, so I hired people I thought I could trust. That made a difference in the businesses because your work family has to be able to work as a team, too.

I've said it plenty of times that everyone knows this about me, "It is a beautiful thing to watch a packaging line run." You can see the fruits of your labor in motion right there in front of you.

The thing I am most proud of isn't the businesses. What matters to me are the people in my life. Spending time with my family and friends is my greatest pleasure in life. I think that also goes back to how I was raised. We kept things simple back then; we didn't need a lot to be happy and enjoy ourselves. That's what life is like now for Eloise and I. We are happy just eating dinner with the kids, grandkids and a few friends. That time together is what matters.

I want my life story to help people in today's world to see what is important in life. In years to come, when people see the Propst name on a building, I don't want them thinking about the money I made. I want them to think of the life I lived.

A Phone Interview With
President Andrew Westmoreland
Samford University

As you can guess, universities like ours are heavily reliant on private support. We don't receive any direct government support. Most of the primary progress that we are able to make comes from the support of people like the Propst family. It is difficult to find people who will have the willingness and the resources to help us with building. We can't pay for all of that [the building expenses] out of tuition income. If we can find folks who can assist with dedicated spaces within buildings or, in the case of Propst Hall, the whole thing, my goodness that makes a tremendous difference to us and our ability to recruit students and to recruit faculty who want to serve in places that are on the move. All of those things are crucial to places like Samford.

The school needed the building so desperately that they proceeded with the construction of it without the benefit of being able to fund it in advance. Once I arrived, it still had significant indebtedness. I began talking with Mr. Propst soon after I arrived, but I think there were others that had already mentioned it to him before I did. Now, Mr. Propst is one of the most careful people that I've ever known. He takes every question very seriously and he acts according to his own timing. I learned quickly in working with him that it was important to plant the idea, but to give him adequate time on those sorts of things. I really respect that in him. He is both one of the most careful people I know and perhaps the most generous. It's nice to see those two qualities fused together in one heart and mind. I never leave an extended session with him without feeling, well I mean the phrase is overused, but without feeling blessed. He's a remarkable man.

Back to the building, as I said, I came in 2006, and I think that building had been completed for two years already. It was up and running, but it needed to be underwritten. Consequently, we were able to use Mr. Propst's support to pay off some indebtedness and also create a very significant maintenance endowment for the building. We were also able to do some other things in terms of endowment for the sciences that were crucial for those disciplines.

You know there's a little vignette about that gift. He had been telling me that it was coming and that he was going to give it as $5 million the first time and then $1 million per year over the next five years. He exceeded that time table, by the way, and paid off the pledge.

So the story is, he called me, shortly before Christmas of my second year at Samford, 2007. He said that John Hughey would be delivering the check. I said, "Well, Bill, I can drive up there; that's no problem." You know, for $5 million, I can drive to Huntsville.

He said, "No, it's fine, John is headed down there. Now, you guys need to coordinate where you're going to meet."

I had never met John. So John called me and said we would meet on the parking lot of Edgar's at The Colonnade, at whatever time, on Christmas Eve. I didn't know what John looked like. I didn't know anything about the Colonnade. I got to the parking lot, and it turns out we were the only two guys in the parking lot. I looked at him and he smiled. Then he gave me the $5 million check.

I said, "This is a Christmas I'm going to remember."

That was the intrigue of receiving the gift. I'm sure there are probably dozens of people who have said the same thing. I've never known anybody like him, just have never known anybody like him.

The endowment funds are in perpetuity. We're careful about not spending that down. We want to keep it so that if the building needs a new roof, or whatever it needs, the money is going to be there. We're practicing pretty careful stewardship of it so that, forever, there will be a maintenance endowment for the building.

All told, including the students within the college of sciences, which would include some graduate programs, our science student body is about 42 percent or 43 percent of our student enrollment. It's a significant percentage. We've seen some nice increases in our enrollment numbers of science students since building Propst Hall. It has been a great addition to the campus. Anytime you can present prospective students with the kind of facilities that we have here, that makes quite an impression on them.

We keep our enrollment in the pharmacy programs at about 125 per class. So, by definition, that enrollment has not expanded because of the building, because we're focused on a certain number of students and providing a quality education.

You know, even if he had done nothing else, that [gift] would constitute him as one of the best donors that we've ever had. I probably see him about once a quarter, and I try to talk with him about program expansions or various ideas that I'm considering. He always gives wise counsel. He's a great listener and when he speaks, it's from an overflow of wisdom that I'll never have. So he's helpful in that way. He also knows a lot about people, a lot of the members of our faculty and staff and they think very highly of him. He's just consistently been a great alum in every way that you would want them to be.

The president of a college kind of develops a special relationship with key donors. You know, you spend time with them, you listen, you really get to know them. That has certainly been the case with Bill. If I had to list off the top of my head five people in my entire life that have had the greatest influence on me, Bill would certainly be on that list. They don't call it the wisdom of the ages for nothing. My own father died years ago, more than 20 years ago. Since he passed, I haven't had that kind of person in my life that you can just sit with and listen to them. With Mr. Propst, I've been real close to that. I wouldn't say he has necessarily been a father figure to me, that would be a little silly, but he has been pretty darn close to it.

After a session with Mr. Propst, when you have asked him questions and he asks you questions back, you leave those sessions with the understanding that he wants you to succeed. That is not fake. That is just Bill.

DESCRIPTIVE REFLECTIONS

Bill is a careful man.

One thing about Bill, he tells the truth in everything that he says and he expects everybody speaking to him to tell the truth. He's very discerning when people aren't telling the truth. I think that is how you would get yourself in trouble with Bill Propst. You better tell him the truth, the whole truth and nothing but the truth. Wouldn't it be great if the whole world lived by that code of conduct?

Jim Folsom, Jr. and Bill Propst, Sr.

Bill Propst.

The Personal Narrative of
Loretta Spencer
Former Mayor of The City of Huntsville

One day in May of 2008, I took Bill to lunch and asked him if he would consider helping the Civic Center [the Von Braun Center]. By that time, I'd already worked with Linda Smith on the Concert Hall. I told him, "I would need $5 million for naming opportunities for the arena, or $1 million for doing the North Hall." He thought about it before getting back to me. "I think I'll do the North Hall," he said. I was thrilled. It was tired and needed it.

That August, he and Eloise were at a fundraiser for a cancer benefit. He approached me with, "Loretta, I changed my mind. I want to do the arena."

"Do you mind if I ask you why?"

"The arena is for everyone."

It makes me have tears even now. He caught me totally off guard. I needed the North Hall fixed, but the arena was really the diversity part of the building. It would hold big things. I think the sign on the building was bigger than he thought it would be. Of course, that was up to the architects though. We used the same architects I used for the Mark C. Smith Concert Hall. Bill really didn't do things for show. Eloise is humble that way, too. I thanked her that day and her simple and humble reply speaks to her attitude: "Well, we're proud to have been able to do it."

THE ICONIC & UNFORGETTABLE

And that's just how it happened. It was a great deal of financial difference; but, it so suited him to be thinking of the impact on others. He is so unassuming and so…just himself. He's a beautiful person to know because the heart shows.

I had also talked to Bill about Calhoun [Community College]. We rode out there together to look because it was really hurting for identity. He ended up doing for Calhoun, too. His help made it a better-functioning facility than it was before.

I was really glad that he put his daddy's name on the newest HudsonAlpha building, too. I never really asked him about the signage for the arena. I went out-of-office so the Civic Center [Von Braun Center] and the architect, Paul Matheny, dealt directly with him. I don't know if the size of the signage was unsuspected... I just know they had approval of the plans when I left office, so I know he was well-aware it was a naming opportunity. He's proud of his family, but putting his family name on something that is such a positive thing for the community is not about him or his family name. It is about his heart for the community.

Top Right: Aerial View of Coffee High School: Florence, Ala.
Bottom Right: Propst Family Home in Florence, Ala.

Coffee High School, Florence, Ala.

Aerial View of Coffee High

Home Florence   *Florence*

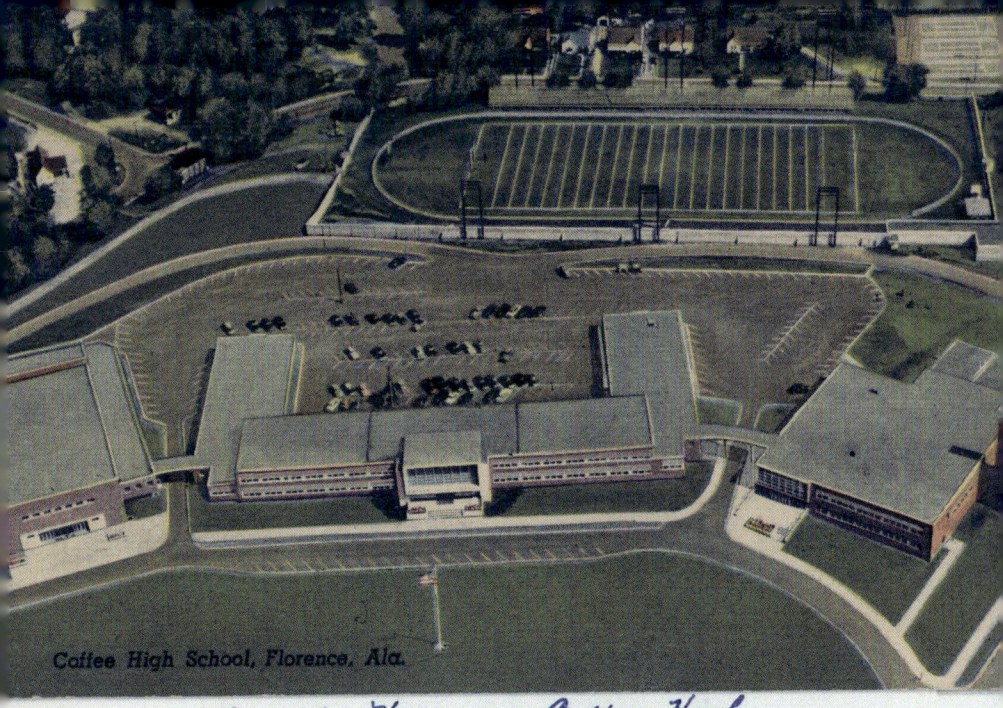

Propst Family Portrait, March 2017, in Bill & Eloise's Home Library.

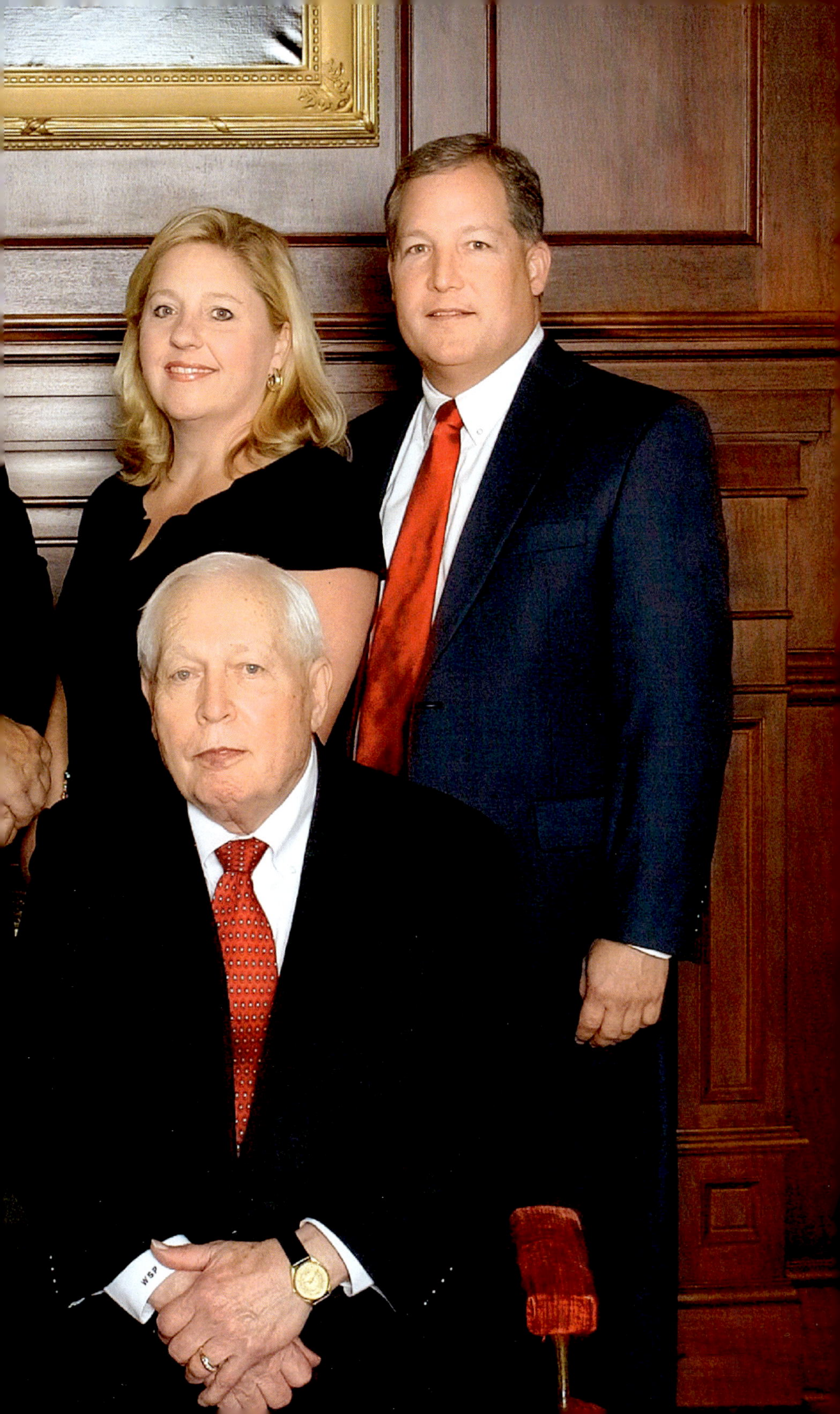

Bill Propst diving off a boathouse.

THE AFTERWORD

William (Bill) Self Propst, Sr.

DESCRIPTIVE REFLECTIONS

I can tell you what I'm not and that is political. If I'd have been more political at Kmart I could have done more. But I wasn't. In fact, I got a bad start right out of the gate when the president asked me what could be done to improve Kmart.

It was about three months after I joined Kmart, and I was sitting at the round table in the cafeteria early one morning. I had just finished eating breakfast and about to leave to go to my office when Mr. Wardlow sat down. He looked at me and said, "Now, Bill, you are new to the company. What do you think we could do to improve a Kmart?" I asked if he was talking about the drug department and he said "No. Since you come from outside of the company, I'm sure you have an opinion about something that could be done to improve a Kmart." I told him I didn't think I had been with Kmart long enough to be qualified to answer that question.

I knew he was up to something, but I didn't know what, so I did my best to avoid a trap. Finally, he said, "I know that you have shopped in the menswear department. What do you think we could do to improve that department?" I hesitated for a moment and then told him if I had anything to say about menswear it would be that we might need to improve the quality of some items. He quickly wanted an example. I told him, in my opinion, we needed to improve the quality of the Kmart T-shirts.

He quickly raised his voice where many at other tables could hear him and loudly said, "Fruit. Fruit. Fruit. All you damn southerners think about is fruit."

I then asked, "What is fruit?"

He told me in a very loud voice, "Fruit of The Loom!"

The rest of the table was very quiet, and I am sure they were wondering how I would respond. I sat there for a moment and then said, "There is a label in the back of a T-shirt that has the letters K.M.A.R.T. on it. Is that fruit?"

He said, "No, that's the Kmart brand."

"Well, by God, that's what I'm talking about because that is what I am wearing that has shrunk up to here," I said, pointing to the middle of my stomach and the bottom of the Kmart T-shirt I was wearing. I then got up, placed my tray on the belt and left. As I walked down the hall to my office, I could still hear him raving.

That is why I say I know I'm not political.

I think people know me as a little, fat, half Italian, a lucky person, financially, caring and, I don't know what you call it...sharing maybe, or generous. I like to pick up the check for my friends when I see them out at restaurants. And, some people say I'm hard headed. (laughing) If others are honest, they'll say that too.

EPILOGUE

Dawn Renae Carson

THE FULFILLMENT OF A LEGACY

For me, getting to know a man whose inner drive and passion for productivity has not waned at the age of 81 invited personal reflection and had me asking some serious questions of myself. Will I have the same kind of drive at 81? Do I have what it takes to push through adversities as great as Mr. Propst's? Or better yet, do I have what it takes to triumph over my adversities as he has? Am I willing to keep working day after day even if my bank account were to tell me I could retire and live a luxurious life? Do I look for excuses? Or, like Mr. Propst, do I stay so busy finding and working on my opportunities that I refuse to accept obstacles as excuses?

Is pushing hard through adversity the full breadth and depth of Mr. Propst's legacy? Are we to be inspired to push hard and never stop? If so, that would be a fine legacy, and it is one I'd be pleased to leave behind. However, I think the myriad of Mr. Propst's life stories tells of a legacy far more meaningful.

Because of Mr. Propst's great success, many of you may have read this book because you wanted to know how he became successful and wealthy. "What is that one thing that made him so lucky," you might have questioned. Before I knew him, my question was also a simple one: "How did this man go from owning the drug store in Five Points to having his name on such a large public venue as the Von Braun Center's arena?" That curiosity, as superficial as it initially was, deepened the more I spent time with Mr. Propst and read his memoirs. I quickly learned to look beyond his accomplishments, and even his benevolence. I learned to look at the man himself, and when I did, it wasn't a lucky man that I found.

Mr. Propst's real legacy presented itself time and again while conducting the interviews that created this book's collection of narratives. Regardless of who was being interviewed and how they knew him, their affection for Mr. Propst was revealed. From one interview to the next, I encountered spontaneous, authentic and sincere expressions of the interviewee's affection for Mr. Propst.

The volume of love that Mr. Propst's community has for him made an impactful and lasting impression because the way I see it, love is not something that is created by luck. Nor is it purchased. Financial benevolence yields gratitude not sincere outpourings of affection. So even if you set out to read this book only because you know Mr. Propst to be a successful and wealthy man, it is my hope that as you close its back cover you know and care more about his heart and his drive than his wealth. His legacy isn't about his success and the wealth created by that success. It isn't even about his generous donations. We can no more look to those things as defining his legacy than we can look at luck as the source of his success, at least not as we typically think of what it means to be lucky.

Mr. Propst's life, lived as it has been, is the fulfillment of a legacy that began on the cold winter morning of February 15, 1937, when young William was lucky enough to be born into a drafty and primitive farmhouse in rural Alabama under the care of a loving family whose members were role models as much as they were firm disciplinarians. The guidance he received as a result of the circumstances of his youth created the compass that guided young William throughout life.

As you think back on this book and the man whose life it narrates, certain stories will stand out to you. From these you'll form your own takeaways and develop your own impression of William (Bill) Self Propst, Sr. You might call him one of many things - smart, frugal, wise, cunning, energetic, quick-witted, humble, compassionate, resourceful, loving, kind or a visionary. You might even go into more detail and describe him as a moral and humble man of good character with a hefty dose of confidence and gumption. You might even call him lucky. Characterize him as you will, just don't forget what made the man - the circumstances that created his character and his heart.

Mr. Propst's great success is impressive and he certainly deserves our respect. His great philanthropy is even more impressive and unquestionably deserves our gratitude. But if our focus lingers there, we'll miss his true legacy - the man himself and the moral compass that shaped his heart and kept his path pointed due north.

Think back to the narratives in this book that tell the stories of a young boy in leg braces trying to keep up with his older brother. Think of the compassion he was shown by that older brother. Think of the six-month-old baby abandoned by his father, but left in the care of three parental guardians who were strongly-convicted of their morals and their responsibilities. Think of the many character-shaping, practical life lessons inherent to living on a rural farm in the late 1930s and early 1940s. Think of these things as you think of how "lucky" Mr. Propst was.

In any man or woman, it is their heart that creates their spirit and is the thing that forms our lasting impression of them. As we single out Mr. Propst's epic life, let's not overlook why he has shared it with us in this book. He has shared himself to inspire us to choose our own paths, to not be defined by others or our circumstances, to have dreams and to work, really work, to achieve them. Likewise, he has shared his family with us, not only to pay his respects to them but to purposefully continue their inspiring legacies. He knows his humble beginnings, the time spent with his mother, grandparents and brother, on the Self family farm was a special gift. With this book, he puts that gift firmly in your hands.

My lasting impression of Mr. Propst: he is a man who learned early in life to value his relationships and that it was up to him to create his own luck.

DESCRIPTIVE REFLECTIONS

I know Mr. Propst to be humble, discerning, sincere, kind and strong of mind, spirit and character. He's honest, loyal, disciplined, direct, humorous, measured and quick-witted. He's a loving father and a proud husband. He's a man who values the fellowship of living and working with others. He's a giant of a man whose great success is less defining of him than is the size of his heart for his fellow man. He's the type of man who it is a gift to know, a gift that will last my lifetime as I aspire to be like him by giving my life my very best efforts.

ACKNOWLEDGEMENTS

Most thankfully, the publishing of this book was not a solo affair. Instead, and to my great pleasure, it was a collaborative effort with many talented and kind individuals.

I am thankful to Adriane Van Kirk of Fave Creative for capturing the vision of The Iconic & Unforgettable Memorial Project in the design of the book's cover; Ron Pollard of Ron Pollard Photography for his professionalism in providing the family portrait and the fun photo session that produced mine; Erica Parker of ReForm Studio for applying her designer's eye to the book's layout and graphics; Ann Vann of Ann Vann Art for her clever illustration and timeline of the notable events in Mr. Bill Propst, Sr.'s life; Ginny Langbehn for lightly editing the narratives of this book to maintain the authenticity of the narrator's spoken words; the many contributors - Mr. Propst's family and friends - for openly sharing their stories of, and hearts for, Mr. Bill Propst, Sr.; local author and descendant of Huntsville, Alabama's original settlers, Ray Jones, for his guidance and support; my many mentors (business leaders, family members and friends) for giving of their time and their hearts to invest in me over the years; Mr. Bill Propst, Sr. for so much, but for brevity I'll leave it with this: for sharing his life story with the community as part of the inaugural group of vanguard business leaders within The Iconic & Unforgettable Memorial Project; Mark Carson, my husband and daily sounding board, for his unwavering support and counsel; and my Heavenly Father for His sovereign hand over The Iconic & Unforgettable Memorial Project.

PHOTO CREDITS

ENDPAPERS
 First Home: ca. 1943. Walker Chapel. *This Is Your Life*, family scrapbook presented by Margaret Self, page 20. 1960. Family archives. Huntsville, Ala. 2018.

 Michael 9, William 5: 1942. This Is Your Life, family scrapbook presented by Margaret Self, page 21. 1960. Family archives. Huntsville, Ala. 2018.

IN-TEXT IMAGE
VIII *Dawn Renae Carson*, Personal historian portrait: *May 2017.* Ron Pollard Photography Studio, Huntsville, Ala. Ron Pollard of Ron Pollard Photography. Huntsville, Ala. 2018.

FRONT MATTER
II *William Self Propst, Sr.*, Print of pastel portrait: ca. 1995. Kenyon Studios. Andrew Manry Kenyon. Family archives. Huntsville, Ala. 2018.
XIV - XV *Bill Propst, Sr. Timeline*, pen-and-ink illustration: 2017. Ann Vann of Ann Vann Art, Huntsville, Ala. 2018.

TITLE PAGE AND PART-TITLE PAGES
XXI *First Birthday*, William Self Trippi, framed black-and-white photograph: April 1938. Margaret Self. Family archives. Huntsville, Ala. 2018.
XXII *William Self Trippi*: 1942. *This Is Your Life*, family scrapbook presented by Margaret Self, page 20. 1960. Family archives. Huntsville, Ala. 2018.
23 *Michael 9, William 5: 1942. This Is Your Life*, family scrapbook presented by Margaret Self, page 21. 1960. Family archives. Huntsville, Ala. 2018.
24 *William S. Propst*, hand-colored photograph on canvas board: 1954. Columbia, Tenn. Columbia Military Academy. Family archives. Huntsville, Ala. 2018.
53 *First Job and Office Building*: 1955. *This Is Your Life*, family scrapbook presented by Margaret Self, page 58. 1960. Family archives. Huntsville, Ala. 2018.

54	*Eloise McDonald Propst*, framed black-and-white photograph: 1955. Senior portrait. Family archives. Huntsville, Ala. 2018.
65	*This Is Your Life*, family scrapbook presented by Margaret Self, page 11. 1960. Family archives. Huntsville, Ala. 2018.
66	*Football Days: Brilliant Junior High School*. Brilliant, Ala. *This Is Your Life*, family scrapbook presented by Margaret Self, page 41. 1960. Family archives. Huntsville, Ala. 2018.
71	*Mother, George Harold & William*: Brilliant, Ala. *This Is Your Life*, family scrapbook presented by Margaret Self, page 41. 1960. Family archives. Huntsville, Ala. 2018.
72	*Mother, Thru The Years*, Margaret Propst age 35: 1950. *This Is Your Life*, family scrapbook presented by Margaret Self, page 37. 1960. Family archives. Huntsville, Ala. 2018.
97	*Daddy, Thru The Years*, Paul Propst: *This Is Your Life*, family scrapbook presented by Margaret Self, page 30. 1960. Family archives. Huntsville, Ala. 2018.
98	*William 7, with Bob Maxwell and Ensley Com. House Boys*: 1945. Ensley, Ala. *This Is Your Life*, family scrapbook presented by Margaret Self, page 30. 1960. Family archives. Huntsville, Ala. 2018.
109	*Papa Self:* 1949. *This Is Your Life*, family scrapbook presented by Margaret Self, page 24. 1960. Family archives. Huntsville, Ala. 2018.
110	*Two Months with Grandmother Self*: 1937. Walker Chapel. *This Is Your Life*, family scrapbook presented by Margaret Self, page 11. 1960. Family archives. Huntsville, Ala. 2018.
111	*William* 5, *Michael* 9, *Mother* 27: 1942. *This Is Your Life*, family scrapbook presented by Margaret Self, page 13. 1960. Family archives. Huntsville, Ala. 2018.
112	*8 Yrs, Lake Junaluska, NC:* 1945. Lake Junaluska, N.C. *This Is Your Life*, family scrapbook presented by Margaret Self, page 14. 1960. Family archives. Huntsville, Ala. 2018.
213	*Grandmother and Granddaddy Propst: This Is Your Life*, family scrapbook presented by Margaret Self, page 31. 1960. Family archives. Huntsville, Ala. 2018.
214	*Hazel Green Friends:* 1948. Hazel Green, Ala. *This Is Your Life*, family scrapbook presented by Margaret Self, page 13. 1960. Family archives. Huntsville, Ala. 2018.
253	*William, Paul and Michael: This Is Your Life*, family scrapbook presented by Margaret Self, page 58. 1960. Family archives. Huntsville, Ala. 2018.

254 *Nine Years*: 1946. Hazel Green. *This Is Your Life*, family scrapbook presented by Margaret Self, page 17. 1960. Family archives. Huntsville, Ala. 2018.

281 *Samford Alumni News, page 9*. Samford University, Birmingham, Ala. Family Archives. Huntsville, Ala. 2018.

282 *Samford Alumni News, photo page*: Samford University, Birmingham, Ala. Family Archives. Huntsville, Ala. 2018.

282 *Personal Note Card from Gene and Jerri McLain*: November 30, 1996. Huntsville, Ala. Family archives. Huntsville, Ala. 2018.

283 *Dedication of Michael Andrea Propst Pharmaceutics Laboratory Invitation*: 1992. Birmingham, Ala. Family archives. Huntsville, Ala. 2018.

283 *Arab Home*: Arab, Ala. *This Is Your Life*, family scrapbook presented by Margaret Self, page 49. 1960. Family archives. Huntsville, Ala. 2018.

284 *Age 11:* 1948. *This Is Your Life*, family scrapbook presented by Margaret Self, page 43. 1960. Family archives. Huntsville, Ala. 2018.

287 *Personal admiration letter from Jerry Damson:* March 10, 1993. Huntsville, Ala. Family archives. Huntsville, Ala. 2018.

288 - 289 *Football Days*: Brilliant Junior High School. Brilliant, Ala. *This Is Your Life*, family scrapbook presented by Margaret Self, page 41. 1960. Family archives. Huntsville, Ala. 2018.

290 *Coffee High School Homecoming:* Times Daily Staff Photo. *This Is Your Life*, family scrapbook presented by Margaret Self, page 57. 1960. Family archives. Huntsville, Ala. 2018.

297 *To Bill With Best Wishes, Jim Folsom*, Jim Folsom, Jr. and Bill Propst, Sr.: Family archives. Huntsville, Ala. 2018

298 *Olan Mills*, Black-and-white photograph. 777716: Family archives. Huntsville, Ala. 2018.

301 *Aerial View of Coffee High School*: Florence, Ala. *This Is Your Life*, family scrapbook presented by Margaret Self, page 51. 1960. Family archives. Huntsville, Ala. 2018.

301 *Home in Florence, Ala.:* Florence, Ala. *This Is Your Life*, family scrapbook presented by Margaret Self, page 51. 1960. Family archives. Huntsville, Ala. 2018.

302 - 303 *Family portrait*: March 2017. Ron Pollard Photography Studio, Huntsville, Ala. Ron Pollard of Ron Pollard Photography. Huntsville, Ala. 2018.

304 *William!!*, mirror image: *This Is Your Life*, family scrapbook presented by Margaret Self, page 58. 1960. Family archives. Huntsville, Ala. 2018.